MW01640363

The Bold Survivors!

VINTAGE

by Joan Dufault

The Pilgrim Press New York · Philadelphia

Cover design by Beehive

Book design and layout by Bill Davenport Studio

The excerpt in the Frank Waters interview is from an article entitled "Lessons from the Indian Soul" by James Petersen and is reprinted from *Psychology Today Magazine,* copyright © 1973 Ziff-Davis Publishing Company. Used by permission.

Library of Congress Cataloging in Publication Data
Main entry under title:

Vintage, thirty-eight life stories.

1. Aged—Biography—Addresses, essays, lectures. 2. Aged—Pictorial works. I. Dufault, Joan, 1925–
HQ1060.5.V55 301.43'5'0922 78–17574
ISBN 0–8298–0356–4

THE PILGRIM PRESS, 287 PARK AVENUE SOUTH, NEW YORK, NEW YORK 10010

To my Father and Mother
Who died too soon one way or another

William Scott Pyle

Mita Waller Pyle

Contents

Acknowledgments

I WANT TO thank, first of all, my four children—Tadea Gottlieb, Scott, Mark, and Ethan Dufault—who have, throughout the long years, listened patiently to all my hopes and thoughts that finally culminated in this book.

A deep gratitude goes to Arnold A. Rogow, my friend, who first thought I could and should do the book, and then by his never-ending support and enthusiasm kept me at it.

Perhaps most of all I need to thank Annette Phillips, without whose cheerful, expert help at the typewriter it would never have materialized.

I owe gratitude to the staff of the *Journal of Current Social Issues* for first seeing the value of these interviews and pictures, and to all the many people, friends and strangers, who helped me find the interviews, especially Kirsten H. Bech, Camille de Bellet-Sauge, Ginette Billard, Sir John Butterfield, M.D., Dr. Lucy Campeanu, Jonathan Chapman, Lea Chesner, Florence Cohen, Asborg Eeg, Yael Gordon, Dr. Michael Hall, Enid Hilton, Dr. Rolf Jorge, W.J. Kakebeeke, Dr. Anton Káldor. Also: John Manchester, Jacqueline Meppiel, Reidun Ruethemann, Wilma Tanzler, Dr. Pauline Waller, Franz Weissenböck, Betsy and Malcolm Wood. Many of these served as translators as well. Finally: The American Friends Service Committee, the Ministry of Foreign Affairs of Hungary and of Rumania, and the Ministry of Social Affairs in Denmark and in The Netherlands.

I owe my deepest gratitude to those who generously shared their lives with me.

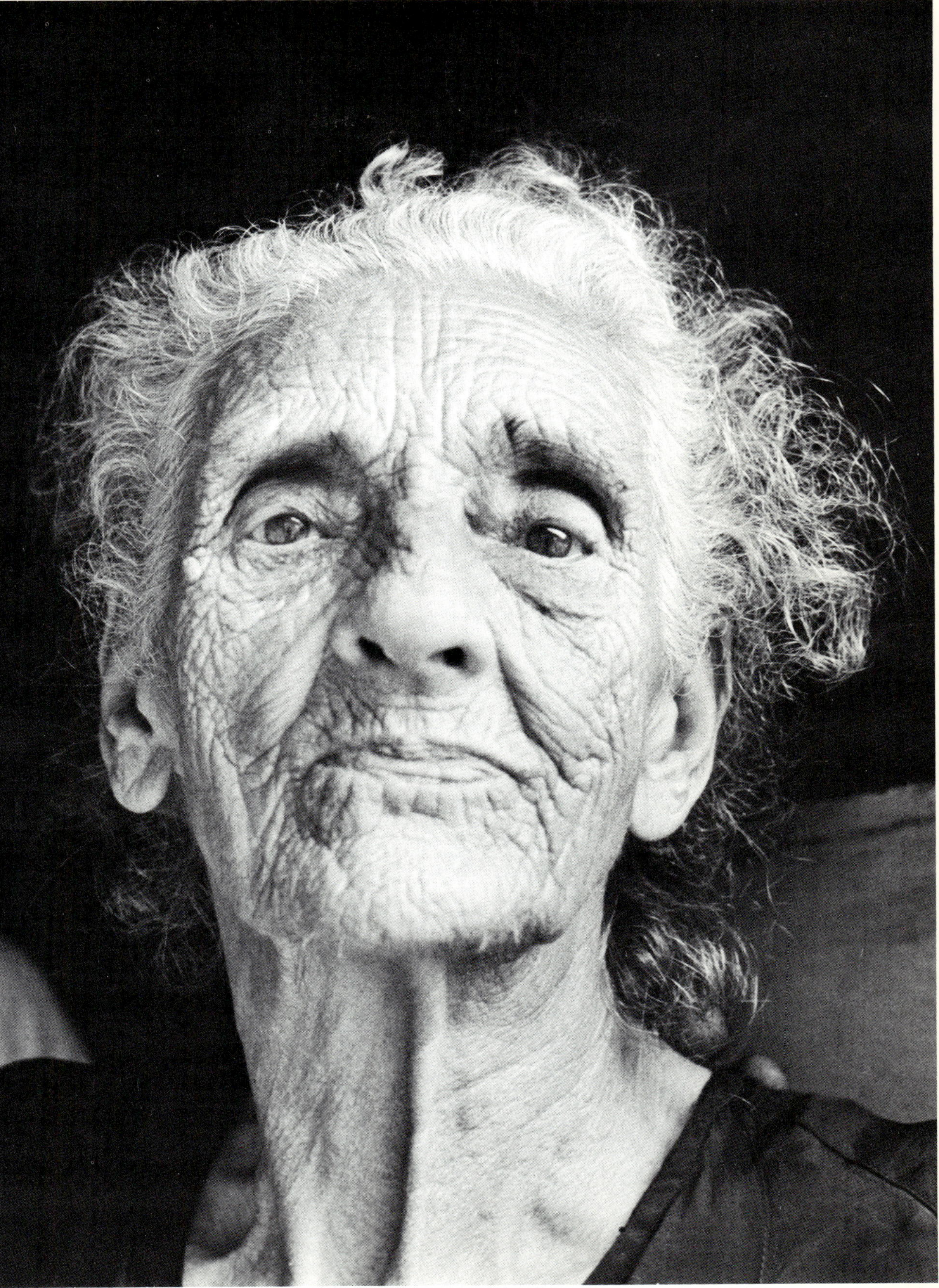

Introduction

WHEN I STARTED photographing older people twelve years ago I had no idea of doing a book on aging; I was simply doing some documentary work for various agencies. But as a result of that work, certain faces remain in my memory, faces that still engage me with their power and meaning.

A day in Brownsville, Texas stands out. I was visiting an old Mexican American farmworker. He was dressed in his nightshirt, thin and frail-looking, suffering from a serious heart ailment, alone on his bed in his waterless shack, relying for food entirely on the kindness-of-heart of a neighbor woman. The gratitude and warmth that he showed in response to concern and sympathy was quite overwhelming; even now, when I look at the picture of him sitting on his bed, a hat and calendar pegged to the wall and an old alarm clock to keep him company, I am just as affected as I was that day. I felt then that I knew the old man and that he recognized me, that on some deep level we were responding to a sense of kinship which brought tears to our eyes. I wonder why it is so necessary for us as human beings to see one another's joy and pain if our lives are to have dignity and meaning.

The portrait of Mrs. Hatfield (page 7), taken in a small "holler" in Appalachia, was included—although I don't have an interview with her—because I have lived with her on my living room wall ever since I came back from Appalachia, in 1969. She hangs over the piano, next to my father's last portrait of my mother. All I know is her name and that she was ninety-seven years old. I met her and also her dignified, kindly-faced miner son through the Williamson, West Virginia Office of Economic Opportunity. I visited the house she lived in and saw the way she lived in it but I did not hear her life story, and since then I have often wondered what it was that gave her that eagle's look. Why does a face tell us so much, suggesting that the individual has mastered the life process? Some faces have the look of conquerors.

Being the daughter of a portrait painter must have influenced my fascination with faces and the mysteries of the life they hint at, but the transition from simply photographing old people to doing a book on their lives found its impetus in my own life.

As a small child I thought of my mother as Sybil-like. She looked like a Sybil: unusual, tall, and remarkable somehow—my good Dutch burgher mother. An only child, I was separated from my parents at the age of eight, brought up by a nurse, and later sent with her to Switzerland for my schooling. I rarely saw my parents more than a week or so a year between the ages of eight and twelve. My father died when I was twelve, and a year later World War II, as well as the legacy of my father's financial difficulties, forced my mother and me to emigrate to America, my father's birthplace. When I was fourteen severe arteriosclerosis began to affect my mother's mental faculties.

As my gifted, sometimes fey, and yet beloved mother suffered for fourteen long years, until her death in 1954, the gradual starving-off process of the brain cells, which finally rendered her speechless and childlike, I did a red charcoal drawing of her on gray paper that still haunts me; she had the hollow face of a Lear as he must have looked as he stood raving on the moors. In that face lay the seed for the book, I am sure, as it ripened so many years later into a consideration of life stories and their meaning, imprinted on the faces of the elderly.

The book has certainly forced me to think about aging but also to confront the abrupt, unfulfilled ending of my father's life (of a sudden peritonitis following an appendectomy) at the height of his powers as a painter. Perhaps with this exploration of aging I am saluting the ripening old age which neither of my parents was able to experience.

Only recently my mother's favorite nephew and godson (for whom my mother was a spiritual mentor), older than I and whom I hadn't seen for many years, told me something my mother once said to him: "There is a thin thread which runs through our life, like the little red band in a cellophane wrapper, and it behooves us never to lose sight of that thread, for it represents the trajectory of our individual destiny."

I hope the sense of recognition that I experienced on hearing my mother's words about the delineating thread of destiny, of the particularity of each life, is contained in the interviews collected here. Each time I listened to someone's life story, I uncovered a small key to the puzzle of my mother's life. Although wise at the beginning and middle of her life, she had to forego that maturing process of wisdom which I found evidence of in interview after interview.

A heuristic awareness of where my own life may lead me developed as I heard echoes of my experience in the stories of others. Wrestling with the form and substance of this book has helped me to formulate a clearer, much more positive and challenging image of my own old age, as it stretches toward me on the other side of fifty.

The idea for this book of interviews developed quite organically out of a body of photographic work on old age that I had amassed over a period of years. The earlier pictures came from a geographical cross section of the United States and from many different sources. Some were taken simply for myself, sometimes on travels (for instance, the trip to Appalachia). Other pictures were the result of agency work.

In the spring of 1972 there was an exhibition of my work. Upon seeing the exhibition a friend suggested the material would lend itself to a book. I had just read and had been deeply affected by Simone de Beauvoir's *Coming of Age.* So I was delighted when my friend Arnold A. Rogow was able to arrange a meeting with de Beauvoir through her agent, Ellen Wright. It was de Beauvoir who gave me the form of the book by telling me, "The pictures are good, but you need the story—each person's story—to do anything with them." And so the interviews started.

First, there were just a few lines of conversation, a short descriptive paragraph, and the pictures. But after a time the interviewing process became all-absorbing, and I was almost tempted to leave the camera behind.

The interviews started in 1972, during a year spent in Israel, took me across a good portion of Europe, both eastern and western. (The final interviews were done in the United States.) I spoke to Muslim Arabs in Gaza, to Christian Arabs on the West Bank, to kibbutzniks near Tel Aviv, and to Jewish residents of Jerusalem. I traveled to Austria, Denmark, England, and France; to Holland, Hungary, Norway, Romania, and Switzerland. The stories certainly are no worldwide cross section, but they do reflect a variety of cultures and life-styles.

When I reread the interviews in order to select and edit them, the meaning of the book really began to take shape for me. True survivors among the aged, it seems, can be distinguished by a developed sense of selfhood, a sense of having the reins of their life firmly in hand. Then I began to ask myself, Why these people? Is there any particular meaning to be derived from this gallery of portraits?

I found the answer to lie in the diversity of countries, life-styles, work profiles and in the religious, economic, and educational backgrounds represented. The point that comes through clearly is that each life weighs equally, has the same importance. One person may have a sense of humor, another a philosophical bent; one perhaps acted with heroism, another stoically endured ill health. But in the end there is no way to say after reading these life stories that one is more valuable than another. To me they all say something of importance.

The reason for choosing a particular interview was often pragmatic: length of interview or a clear tape. Sometimes I had to leave out an interview because a good picture was not available. I had found my subjects by using as contacts friends, colleagues, officials of governmental and social agencies in the various countries, and even strangers who crossed my path. The people had been randomly chosen; the basic criterion was only that they be in possession of their faculties. I had no formal credentials—just a belief in my basic intelligence, empathy, and sensitivity, a reliable tape recorder, and a knowledge of a few foreign languages.

Although I had a questionnaire ready, I used no real system in gathering the material, except that I hoped, despite my reliance on chance (or perhaps because of it), I would find a microcosmic cross section of the elderly, covering a wide enough spectrum of countries and economic conditions so that, as an aggregate, it would be seen as a significant sampling.

It is obvious that often there were reverberations from my own experience which lent intensity to my consideration of another's life. In the introductory paragraphs to the interviews I intended to explore some of these connections, as I recalled the settings and the interviews. As Helene Moglen says in the introduction to her biography of Charlotte Brontë, *The Self Conceived:* "I have pursued my own shadow through the beckoning recesses of another's mind, hoping to discover its substance at the journey's end."*

Endless curiosity about how people live, how they put their lives together, propelled me. There is an undoubted voyeuristic element in photography which is one of the most intriguing aspects of the art; the camera gives us the ability to enter into the space, the daily surroundings of another individual. Only by daring to look honestly and with true respect into the eyes of another can we hope to reach the threshold of that ultimate chamber, the soul.

Because old people have so often been left alone, either through fate or neglect, I found they may gladden when they encounter someone with a genuine, noncategorizing interest in exactly what they want to say. And so they willingly share their lives with the interviewer. Yet I also remember, in Desert Springs, that humorous old American Legionnaire army nurse, Nancy Farrell, telling me without embarrassment when I asked a rather personal question, "You know you shouldn't ask that!" Her response was not rare, for this is a generation speaking that has not learned, as so many in the "therapy generation" have, "to let it all hang out"; but many people surprised me by their candor.

When I began the interviews there were occasions on which I found myself naively caught up in some mythologies of the self as they were presented to me. Later I grew more cautious, until finally I became aware that, although an occasional story might be exaggerated, these myths serve an important purpose: They help to organize the sense of personhood and often give cohesion and meaning both to the life that lies ahead and to the past. A few of the stories were poignantly like songs children sing on their way to bed, passing through a dimly lit hall.

Of course, differences in economic conditions and states of health profoundly affect how a person deals with the loneliness and pain that often accompany old age. I also saw that the inner resources an individual brings to the situation are just as important; so are the supportive, respectful attitudes of significant others. What impressed me especially in Europe, where I visited a great many facilities for the elderly—nursing homes, day hospitals, state-supported residences—was the empathetic caring, which cuts across bureaucratic red tape. I would like to describe some specific examples—which impressed and delighted me.

In Denmark, in one of the most beautiful new state homes, the enlightened director allowed an old man to bring his wine-making equipment so that, as she said, "On the long winter nights there would be a little wine to warm the heart and help the digestion." (How much better, I thought, than the tranquilizers used so constantly in nursing homes in the States.) In Norway a

*New York: W.W. Norton, 1976.

ninety-year-old fisherman was allowed to keep his skiff anchored below the cliff on which the "home" was built, by the edge of a fjord. In an aside the director reasoned: "What harm if an old fisherman whose first love is the sea should perhaps be caught in a storm? I suspect that is the way he would like to go." Knowing the boat was there changed the man's attitude toward going to the home.

Persons in these homes may bring their own furniture, paintings, rugs, bric-a-brac, and they are supplied with mechanized wheelchairs so that they can get about by themselves, get down the hall and out to the street (and, in Denmark, to their own lockers stocked with beer supplied by the homes).

In Holland, my mother's country, there have been *Hofjes*—excellent, cheap residences for the elderly—since well before the seventeenth century, when Frans Hals painted their lace-collared boards of governors. In Budapest I visited a couple admitted jointly to hospital to aid in the recovery and to assuage the loneliness, although only one was acutely ill: a logical conclusion where hospital beds are not too costly. In Southampton I was shown one of England's pioneer day hospitals, Moorgreen, which are much more economical to operate than regular hospitals and evidently, for appropriate cases, conducive to a faster, more organic, and less traumatic recovery. On the Israeli kibbutz where I spent some time, there is a workshop especially geared to the older worker, and *everyone* on the kibbutz works in various capacities unless he or she is seriously disabled.

Yes, on my travels I was privileged to see a great many alternative solutions to the problems of aging. In such climates I believe it is undoubtedly somewhat easier to grow old, and so, old age isn't made a taboo. In Denmark, in the residential homes I visited, the inhabitants were *encouraged* to go to friends' funerals, which were seen as celebrations of the life lived, and death was discussed with frankness.

Perhaps my most important discovery was that it is still the sense of selfhood in old age as well as youth that continues to prompt one in the setting of significant tasks and that gives the impetus to further growth. The tasks can be the most diverse, as is apparent in the interviews: the weeding of a garden or the writing of a poem; reading medieval source material is as rewarding as the daily riding of a bicycle or the retraining of one's muscles to learn to walk and even to talk again after a stroke.

Many familiar insights on aging were, of course, reinforced as I listened to the interviews: that when we become old our bodies make more demands on us and we can no longer take them for granted; that our peers may desert us, often dying before us; that our children, to a greater or lesser degree, will turn from us to their own affairs; that, in any case, dependency on one's children can be degrading; that for most of us our place in society will probably be usurped by younger people whose views of things will often be in conflict with ours; that we will feel our personal power diminishing, as well as our strength and tirelessness, and even our attention span. But I also learned with delight that the satisfaction derived by a task that one does well remains the same; that pleasure in companionship, if anything, increases, perhaps because people are more aware of the preciousness of close companionship as they become more threatened by its possible loss. It was clear that the familiar joy inherent in telling a good story or weaving a basket or throwing a pot hadn't paled; delight in a flirtation or in the sweet/sad pangs brought on by unrequited love were still present. In other words, *we* don't change much at all, *life* doesn't; only in the eyes of "others" are we suddenly seen as diminished when we reach old age.

Recently, we have all become aware of how much contemporary Western society, while also assuming responsibility for the aged, has felt empowered to disenfranchise them, to set them apart. Poet May Sarton says, "I mind being stuffed into a pigeon hole . . . as though I had ceased to exist as a growing person."* Alas, all this pigeonholing is usually justified in the name of better care and is done as the result of sociological studies, psychological analyses, or medical research. Behind this degrading categorizing, no doubt, is the fear of growing old. By describing the old as "other," people hope to separate themselves from their experience. For instance, in America we have allowed the growth of a nursing home industry, with a return of 15 to 20 percent on the invested dollar, that exploits the helplessness of the aged population. This would not have been permitted to happen if the nonold had not managed to separate themselves psychologically from the old.

What the men and the women in the interviews are telling us is that *they* know best what is needed for their own lives and that they are still the same people they have always been, just a little older. At least seventy-two years old now (and most either eighty or ninety), they see their long life as continuity, through which runs a meaning—a meaning that can be symbolized by that thin thread of destiny I spoke of earlier. From their great vantage point the old are, I feel, closer to understanding the significance that underlies our lives.

*"More Light," *The New York Times,* January 30, 1978.

Now if they ask me questions I don't want to answer, I just pretend I don't hear them.

Nancy Farrell

Desert Springs, California

Born 1898

Nancy Farrell lived in a unit of a small jerry-built residential motel in Desert Springs. Dust-laden desert winds whipped across the walk that led to her quarters. I found her sitting on her bed in a room painted institutional green. Next to her stood a canister of oxygen, and in the corner next to an old wicker chair was her walker. A radio was placed on the bedside table, and a few Polaroid shots were stuck in the mirror above her bureau. A religious calendar had been tacked over the bed. The blinds were drawn and other than the small bedside lamp only a forty-watt bulb, hung from the ceiling, lit the room. She strained her face toward me, as the blind sometimes do, seeming to assess me by some sixth sense of perception.

I HAD A very unhappy childhood, but there is no need to talk about it as it can't be changed now anyway. My mother died and my father remarried twice. I didn't get along with my stepmother. My father was a builder of railroad stations and worked on hospital construction in the South. He was a very good mechanic. In those days it took four years to become a master bricklayer or a carpenter or one of the boys who ran the trains. He told me, "Always join the union, because in time the unions are going to run things. They are going to be something really big. Any union that is organized is better than a whole lot of people speaking separately. You are recognized when you are organized." We were Democrats all our lives.

I graduated from high school down South, and that is where I also got my nurses' training. I will tell you something no one else can tell you. I am a very talented woman, have been all my life, but not many people know it. D'you know why I am a talented woman? I will tell you. My father used to go fishing and he didn't have no son, so he said to me one day, "You clean this fish." So I cleaned it and he said, "In time you are going to be one of the best fish cleaners in the country." From that time on I worked hard to earn the title, but I never was called up on it.

Down on the Florida Keys there are many, many snakes and some Seminole Indians. One day a knock came at my door and there were two Indian women standing there; they were looking for the smell of cucumbers, because if you smell cucumbers you know you have a mother snake in the bushes. So they gathered up their skirts with safety pins, and with long sticks they caught the snake. They took it home and cut the head off and slit it open and hung it up. From then on I knew how to make snake oil and how to clean fish, but I never made a cent out of any of them. Then the nicest thing and the proudest thing I know to do is to make good whiskey. You get a great big pumpkin and lay it on its side. You pull out the seeds and things, and then you put in a layer of sugar, a layer of corn, more sugar, pound it down, take a quart of oil, put the plug back in, and let it start to ferment. Then you put it in an iron pot. It is called Poki De Nuck, and after drinking it when you walk a block you fall down. I learned to make it down on the Keys—my grandfather had a home there. I have seen alligators over fifteen feet long down there. They used to scare me to death.

My grandmother, with whom I went to stay as a child, was a gracious woman and very nice, but how she ever had a family I'll never know; she was so prissy, it must have been a miracle. When I was about eleven years old and had started to menstruate I tried to hide it from everyone, and my grandmother caught me washing out my pants. She phoned her friend Mrs. Mitchell and told her to tell me about "those things." Even after I started working in nursing and had delivered many children she would tell me not to talk about people in that delicate condition. I had a very modest background.

I tried to learn the violin once when I was young. My grandfather sent me every Friday afternoon for lessons for fifty cents, but I had to give it up as I was terrible. Then I decided I was going to be beautiful. I had learnt to read and was very impressed with "creamy complexions." I tried a trick I'd read about using iodine, but it did not work. In fact, I ended up, as you can imagine, with terrible stains all over my face.

Then I met John, who later became my husband. He was a lovely person, very well educated. But he was Irish, and my people being English they didn't like the Irish. He came from Boston. His father, upon immigrating, dropped the "O" in O'Farrell to help him get a job. In those days nobody would hire the Irish in Boston. I had come from the South where they hated New Englanders, and when I first took John down to meet my people he was not received very cordially. "Marrying a Catholic and what's more a Yankee?" they said. But we lived through that, and in the end they loved him. I married when I was twenty-three.

I have been to many schools and many night classes. And I learned Spanish, which never amounted to a hill of beans. But I have been around the world. I was abroad during the First World War and served as a nurse in France in 1918. I worked hard as hell, like everyone else, and had a grand old time. One time General Pershing came to the schoolhouse where the hospital was located and asked for coffee. It was raining cats and dogs, and there were lots of badly burned-up boys lying around, but all he said was, "This is the damnedest coffee I have ever had!" The next time I saw him I was coming back from Cuba, and at the same time my boat was landing the *SS Devlin* came in, too. The first one off was General Pershing. In his arms he had several copies of *Good Housekeeping* magazine, the last thing you would expect; he was reading a continued story. I met him twice since and I love him. When he got sick and was paralyzed I wrote to him and told him how much I admired him, and two days before he died he wrote to me, dictated it from his bed. I have carried it around all these years and have been asked to show it at Legion conventions. About a month ago I gave it to Joe Kelly, who was also a general. During the Second World War I was all over the States. I went wherever I was sent; they were so short of nurses. My husband served in that war, too.

I went back into government service in 1936. Then the war came in December 1941, and about the following fall all the nurses were recalled and assigned. I loved my work. For a time I was sent up North. I worked from four in the afternoon until midnight in New York City and lived on Welfare Island. Oh, I loved nursing, and living there in a big residence gave me something to do in the evenings. I met some of the nicest girls in the wide world, though I have met some stinkers, too, but we all do as we go along in life, right?

Do you know that the English nurses were terrible to the American ones during the war? They had been in the field three years when we got there and had had to work like the devil, so we were Johnny-come-latelies. We were definitely not welcomed by them. Upstarts, that's what they thought we were. I guess we were a bit rougher, less well spoken, but we were good nurses.

Do you know something: The girls who work as checkers in the grocery store are some of the highest paid women in America today. And they are able to save to get married during the five years others are studying to be nurses.

I did not want to come to Desert Hot Springs as I was really contented in Los Angeles, where we'd lived for many years. I belonged to many societies—senior citizens, Masons, all different kinds of societies. I liked Los Angeles, the stores, the company. But my husband had health problems with his lungs, and we were told to move to a drier climate.

My husband once told me that I am a joiner, but I think it is not always good to join everything. This story I am about to tell you actually happened to me while I was in New York: A woman said to me, "Isn't it too bad what's happening in China?" (The starving population, she meant.) She said, "Everybody is going to buy them rice." So I said, "Put me down; I will buy some rice, too." About a week later I got a beautiful letter thanking me and appointing me to a committee. Then a week after that a friend comes up to me and shows me a brochure saying I had joined the Communist party! Evidentally the food shipment was being organized by them. That's what you get for joining too many things.

I belong to the American Legion. I was once made to answer a charge of chauvinism. It seems it meant showing discrimination against Blacks. I had sent a Black woman out of a room where we were arranging food because her baby had wet the doughnuts which had been set on a tray on the floor. I told her she'd have to take the baby out of the cafeteria. Well, she went off to complain to the authorities, but of course the whole thing had nothing to do with discrimination.

John once said that being married to a woman who gets into so much trouble in fifty years is like being married to a woman who gets into no trouble for two hundred years. I even got a ticket for jaywalking in San Francisco and also joined a Bank of Widows organization, which turned out to be illegal.

I receive financial help from the Bob Hope Fund; they send me household help three times a week, three hours each time. I have been sent all sorts of people, alas, most of them worse than the one before. The interesting ones always turn out to be the worst housekeepers I'm sad to say. One of them ended up in prison for not paying for a breakfast she had ordered at the Riviera Hotel. She had been given a job in their kitchen and thought they would take the breakfast out of her salary when she started work. That's hardly the right kind of thing to be sent to prison for, don't you think? Another of my houseworkers drank all my wine. I had two full bottles in the icebox and had not realized that they had been drained empty after her afternoon of working. Yes, I have had all kinds of experiences with my helpers, though I can't really complain as they have never cost me anything. Still, it was irritating.

Early in January this year a woman (from public assistance, I'm sure) came to see me and said, "I know of a beautiful home you can go to." But I am tired of people arranging for me to go into a home. You know, in the olden days when a woman became widowed and she could not do anything else, she set herself up as a practical nurse and got a job in some home. They usually knew less about nursing than my dog. As long as I am capable of making some judgment I am not having my friends put me into a home.

I have a government pension, but I think that is personal and I don't want to talk about it. I never ask questions like that and I don't think anyone should. Dorothy, my present helper, is the only one who writes checks for me. She signs my checks and I put my signature under it. She only goes to the bank when I need money. I used to write beautifully, but I got so I couldn't write good since my eyes went; also, I shake too much.

The latest good turn of events was a man came to see me and said, "If you will pick out a housekeeper that you like, we will be happy to pay spot cash of one hundred fifty dollars a month for her." I had heard of Frances, a nice woman from the neighborhood, and asked her to come work for me. She is a wonderful woman, kind and helpful. The only trouble is that she is very busy with other people, too, but she is great.

I have had quite a few bad falls lately. I don't know what brings them on except I feel myself going before I fall. That's all I can tell you. I was having attacks—I suppose small heart episodes—where I wouldn't be able to breathe.

A terribly frightening feeling. When my friend Wanda's mother died recently, Wanda gave me the walker she had had. That helps prevent the falls at least. Also, I have the oxygen now.

I've found when God takes things from you, you are often compensated with others. One morning after John, my husband, had died this young priest we knew called Father Bowdry came to visit me. (I had had no idea up till then of becoming a Catholic, although I had been religious as a girl. I never could see what saying the same thing over and over again could do for you.) After a long talk about his life and my life he said, "You know, I am the saddest person alive because my mother died last Sunday and I am terribly lonely." Then he hesitated a moment and went on. "I often heard you say when you and John were working that you could not understand why you had not adopted children, and I still see it that way now, because all my life I have been conscious of something missing, you know. I have often heard you say you would like a son, and if you will let me, I will be like your son, because I too feel a lack. I feel I need a mother, someone I can be close to. The priesthood is wonderful, but I am sure it was also my mother's love which always sustained me in the work." And so began a beautiful, beautiful friendship. I hate to tell you this—it pains me so much to think about it—but just this morning I had a phone call from him. He will be celebrating his twenty-fifth anniversary as a priest in June, and I had arranged a party for him with some other priests and friends. But he called to tell me that he will not be here then. He is very, very ill and has been sinking steadily. He told me that he'll never walk again and that he is in a wheelchair now. Isn't it awful that someone so good should have something like this happen. He has a bone disease. I feel perfectly awful about it. Knowing him as I have these last years has been really almost like having a son, a wonderful son for me. It took me so many years to have a son, but I won't have him very long, I'm afraid. I feel dreadful.

The person who has been closest to me beside my husband and my adopted son is my friend Ruth. In all the years she and I were close we never in any way, shape, or form had an argument. She looked after me. She was a very, very wonderful person. If I ever had an attack during the night, I just had to call Ruth and she would say, "Hello, I'll be right over." She was instantaneous—like that. She is a little bit younger than I am. Anyway, one night we were talking about the book *The Cardinal* when she said, "Nan, you are about to be initiated." She wanted me to join her cult. I said I wouldn't join that crazy religion. She said, "Do you actually feel that way about the way I feel? I will concede that Jesus Christ was a wonderful man, but you can't compare him with my living master." When I was reluctant and said No, she told me, "This is the end of our beautiful friendship." My answer was: "I will never forget how kind you have been all these years, but I won't join your religion." And that was it. "Good-bye, Nan," she said. I felt very sad about it for a long time. Several weeks ago I had a terrible fall and she came over and asked if she could come in. So we are back together again. Every single night she visits and we read *The Cardinal* together.

I had been married more than thirty-five years when John died; that was almost fifteen years ago now. Funny thing, but I never knew how many resources I had until I became blind. Now I have talking records of the latest books and magazines. I always used to do a lot of reading. The reason I get so upset about losing money, especially when the women who worked here in the past used to help themselves to it, is that I am now on public assistance, and I've got to keep track of every penny. The woman who came in to try to put me into a nursing home was probably from public assistance, too. I was given fifteen hundred dollars when my husband died—insurance, you know—but my pension was not in effect then, so it wasn't much.

I have no fear of people, even though I can't see them any longer. Now if they ask me questions I don't want to answer, I just pretend I don't hear them. It works pretty well except, of course, you can't act too dopey or they'll have you off to the nursing home without so much as a by-your-leave. I still give parties around here when I get a chance. Real simple food. But I still have friends, you know. I manage to have a good laugh about life, which helps, believe me.

Clarence Martin

Sheffield, Massachusetts

Born 1893

I arrived in snowbound New England on a Saturday afternoon to interview Clarence Martin, eighty-five, in his 1839 farmhouse. The house is located in the historic western Massachusetts town of Sheffield. I entered the farmhouse kitchen, which was made snug and warm by an old potbellied wood stove that stood along one wall. Two blonde little girls, one four and one five, greeted me. Then their grandmother, Ethel Martin, welcomed me and informed me that Clarence was inside playing checkers. Sure enough, there he was—in his old chair by the window, a plant hanging over his head. He barely had time to say hello because he was deeply engrossed in playing a game with his six-year-old grandson. After the game was successfully concluded, he announced in an aside: "I love to play. I always let him win, but not until I've given him a good run for his money." He laughed conspiratorially, his face settling into a wry grin. He wore boots, old workpants, from which now and then peaked a pair of insulated long johns, and a comfortable wool cardigan. A pipe rested in the corner of his mouth as he spoke.

I WAS BORN about fifteen miles from here, in Monterey, Massachusetts, in 1893. I was the seventh child born to my parents; there were ten of us altogether—five boys and five girls. All that's left now is three of us: a sister who is ninety-one (she's pretty lame and blind now) and a younger brother.

My father was a carpenter. He worked up to Crane's in Dalton, Massachusetts, in the old Crane paper factory. You know, that's where they've been making the paper for the money [United States currency] since Revolutionary days. We always had a horse and wagon, a couple of cows for milk, the usual garden, and chickens. That's the way people managed in those days.

The first horse I drove—I guess I was eight years old—was a mustang, and

There ain't no use you wishin' you was younger 'cause you won't be.

she was balky. She wouldn't mind; if you stopped her she might start for you and she might not. I knew that some of the old Civil War men were good horsemen and there were some still around when I was a boy. I stopped to talk to an old veteran—William Maxwell his name was—and I asked him how to manage her. Well, he told me, but first he warned me not to give away the secret to anyone and I promised. "Now you jest take a hold of them lines and you get out and get some dirt and throw it in her mouth. Then you get right back in the wagon. She'll stand there a minute and chew, and when you see her ears come back up you tell her to go and she will." And she did!

Yep, that's when I first started workin' with horses. I didn't even quite finish grammar school. I got my first job when I was thirteen. I'd drive a team between Great Barrington and Monterey, hauling grain and supplies for the Monterey Store Company. A day's work I did. I'd walk to work two and a half miles, get there at seven, get done around four or five, and walk home, six days a week. There was another interesting thing about that job: The man I worked for had been a slave. I'm probably 'bout the only man in this vicinity who ever worked for an ex-slave. London Clark—he was a nice man.

All we had round here were horses in them days. I didn't see an automobile till I was ten years old, and you wouldn't call that an automobile. It steered with a stick and had hard rubber tires and went along bang, bang, without a sight of a muffler. It was all sand roads in those days, and the man would be tryin' to steer it with the stick and, let me tell ya', he'd be busy as can be.

When I was eighteen I bought a horse that was a confirmed kicker 'cause I didn't have any money to speak of. I got a harness and wagon in the deal, too. I knew she'd kicked a lot of wagons to pieces, but I only had twenty-five dollars saved up, so I figured it was a good deal. This farmer had sold her numerous times already for twenty-five to thirty-five dollars. He had a regular business going on, 'cause he'd always tell the people that he'd buy her back if they couldn't handle her. 'Course, he'd only pay 'em seven or eight dollars and pocket the difference. Well, when I drove away I said to myself, "If I can't handle her you'll never get her back from me!" He had her all roped in when I got her, but it was a terrible nuisance to harness her with that complicated rope rig. It'd take an hour to get it on and off and nobody'd have time for that. I drove her like that for four or five days, then I took the ropes off and put a sandburn bit in her mouth—it has a ball that goes in her mouth. It put that ball on the roof of her mouth when you pulled on the reins and forced her head to come up. Well, can't both ends come at once, so it pretty well stopped her from rearin' or kickin'. She'd squeal when you harnessed or unharnessed her. The first time I brought her home my mother come out and said, "I thought when you went out to buy a horse you'd buy a *horse* and not bring home *that* thing." She didn't know how many times she was gonna hear that repeated back to her or she wouldn't have said it. In a month she was drivin' her. The horse wasn't kickin' either; she got used to that sandburn bit and she didn't dare kick. I'd pull them reins, not even hard, and her head'd go up. She was a wonder horse. She'd work and draw, too.

I kept her three years and raised two colts by her. Then I sold her for twenty-five dollars to quite a horse place down here—O'Harrow's—but they hitched her up jest once and she kicked the wagon right to pieces. They didn't have no sandburn bit in her mouth. They thought they'd raise a colt by her, but she got sick that winter and died.

I raised and broke those two colts she'd had and they turned out to be fine horses, too. They lived to be old: twenty-two and twenty-six. Turned out it was a wonderful thing, really, my buying that kicker, 'cause that's what started me shoeing horses. Nobody else would touch them hind feet nohow.

I went in the army in '17, and I didn't go overseas till early the next year. There weren't no cavalry in the army then. I was assigned to a machine gun company. In fact, first I went in the infantry in the Third Division, Thirtieth Infantry. Then, to make up the machine gun outfits they had certain specifications of men. They had to be five foot seven and weigh a certain amount, et cetera, and I met those specifications.

Then they called for horseshoers and I didn't answer 'cause I'd never done any forge work or used the anvil; I didn't consider myself a blacksmith then. Well, they didn't get any volunteers, so the next day they had another call. Again they didn't get any. Then I told 'em I could do the floor work alright (that's what they call workin' on the horse), so they asked would I try it and I said Yes. That was in Syracuse, New York, right on the old fairgrounds.

Before night there was a four-line team up there for me to work on—took all day. In them days they still used to draw all the guns and the ammunition carts with horses, you know. The next day they brought me mules. Well, I'd never shod a mule but it wasn't all that different. That's what I thought I'd do: I thought I'd be a floorsman. But the man in charge said, "No, you can do the floor work alright. Now you're going to fit the shoes." So he had me doing that. Some shoes have to be bigger, some rounder, some more concave or convex. I told him I couldn't fit, so he had to come and help me. It got so I could fit alright. Then a couple of officers came around and told me I'd have to make shoes out of straight bar stock. You take a straight iron and bend it into shoes. It took me about a half a day to make my first shoe, but they didn't say nothing. That man I went in with he'd come over and show me what to do when I was stuck. He wasn't a good instructor—couldn't explain things right—but I learned fast just watching him. I knew that the iron had reached welding heat when the sparks flew, but what I didn't know was that both pieces of iron had to throw off sparks till I observed that I couldn't weld a shoe until the toe piece and the shoe itself had reached the right heat. In three or four days it come back that I'd been made a horseshoer.

Then they transferred me to a machine gun outfit. They give me an outfit of my own—about sixty-five horses and mules I had to look after. I always worked alone. And I could do it alright, too, after a while. So that's how I got my profession as a blacksmith. I stayed with that outfit till the war was over.

What civilian folk don't understand about the army is that you go up to the front lines only for about five days or a week, then you go back, what they call to rest, then another outfit goes forward. So I used to be in charge of bringin' up the guns and the ammunition carts and bringin' 'em back again. The horse and mule-drawn ones, I mean.

One time, on July fourteenth, during about the biggest drive of the entire war, I really didn't see how anyone was going to come out alive, because the sky was full of shells. We lost more men and horses that day than on any other: twenty-one men and twenty-one horses! They gave me the job that night of bringin' twenty-two carts and mules back by myself. We always had to move at night, you know, otherwise you couldn't avoid getting shelled. It was about four miles. I knew enough to see I couldn't make the trip four or five times back and forth that night and end up alive, so I decided to hitch 'em all together in a long line and me up front with the lead mule, and do it all in one trip. As we came into the village in France where we were quartered I heard this terrible racket. The back mules were cuttin' corners goin' round them French stone walls and scrapin' the hubcaps against 'em till the sparks flew. When I got where I was goin' I tied up the lead mule and uncoupled the last one first. When I got to about the seventh, I noticed he'd caught his foot in one of the wheels. The more I tried to get it loose the more he kicked up a storm. Finally I saw I couldn't help him unless I pulled off his shoe (the other mules were gettin' restless). So I went for my tools. By the time I got back he'd gotten his own foot out!

I was the first one to get out of the company, in April 1919. You got your discharge on merit, and I'd never given 'em any trouble. The captain who let me go came from Texas. He was up this great flight of stairs—that was in Germany—and he see'd the whole company was there lined up. He didn't want to let too many of 'em go so he commenced talkin' to 'em and telling 'em they'd have to answer some questions. Well, I was the tenth man from the end, and I saw'd 'em sneak away down the stairs in back of me; they were afraid to have to answer the questions. Pretty soon I was the only man there, so he asked me whether I could answer some questions, and I said, "Yes, sir, I reckon I could answer any question you might ask." I figured I could give him some kind of an answer. That turned out to be the only question he asked me. Then he let me go. The next day I started to Coblenz, Germany on foot with a pack on my back. It was twenty-five miles. Miles didn't mean anything to me then, nor time neither—just keep goin'. But a mail truck came along and they hid me under the mail sacks when they had to go through one of the inspection points. It was forty-five days before I got my discharge. I had to go back through France, and everywheres I went I had to have a physical.

You know'd a year ago I had a heart attack. Yep, I was in intensive care for seven days. Now I don't notice the heart unless I try to do too much, but I know that it will always be there, always has been, you know, since I was a boy. That's not a new thing. I'd had rheumatic fever when I was sixteen, so every time they gave me an exam they'd say, "Is that on your service record?" Well, I hadn't told 'em 'cause I'd forgotten about it when I enlisted, but they sure found out about it over there. Drove me near crazy with the same questions. That was just before and durin' the bad flu epidemic. We was sleepin' on the cold floor with nothin' but a blanket. The woman in the house upstairs died. The one fellow who slept right next to me on the floor got sick, and they took him to the hospital. Twenty-eight miles in an escort wagon. He didn't last more 'n a couple of days. When I got it I thought I wouldn't be noticed if I didn't go down to eat. I didn't tell 'em I was sick. I wondered how long it'd be before they noticed I wasn't there. After a day or so the lieutenant came up to see what was the matter with me. He wanted to send for the doctor or take me to the hospital, but I said, "No, thank you," and stayed right there on the floor. I was mighty sick, but I got better.

I don't know why I've lived so long. My father's father was eighty-four; his mother was eighty-nine. I don't 'member exactly how old my mother's father was when he died; someplace around seventy-four I think. That wasn't bad for those days. Anyway, there ain't no use you wishin' you was younger 'cause you won't be. But I'm surprised to be as able as I am.

I was thirty-three when I got married. My wife was born near Umpachine Falls, in Mill River, in that old red-brick house there. I'd known Ethel most of my life. Later we were neighbors, you know, but we weren't sweethearts before I went off to the army, just acquaintances livin' across the street from each other here in Sheffield. We been married now goin' on fifty-one years. We settled here in this house in '27. We have about five acres and then a ten-acre wood lot over yonder. In the early days it was easy to get a hold of a piece of land to farm. Folks was glad if you worked it for 'em. I'd raise the hay and give 'em some.

We always had the big garden and raised some cows. We like cucumbers; the whole family do. When the three children was home I wouldn't want to go out and pick just three or four. I'd bring in a whole pail full and they'd be gone in no time. We had the three children, in '27, '29, and '31.

The girl lives in Westfield and the two boys live right near here. One's a big-machine operator; he's a workhorse. 'Course the other one is, too; he's a carpenter. They come and help me now. They plow us out when there's snow and plow the garden in the spring. I do the weedin' myself with a hand rake. If you do it right after a rain and keep at it, it's easy. They cut and stack the wood. They're real good to us. They comes once a week, on Sunday, for dinner. The one's been married twice; raised three children by one wife and now he has these three little ones by another. The granddaughter who is good with horses she's married now.

In the old days I always done all my work in the shop. It wasn't till the late thirties I started goin' around to shoe people's horses. Sometimes I'd travel as far as forty miles or more. 'Course there was years when there wasn't hardly any shoein'. During those years I worked right here in the coalyard drivin' the coal wagon. It was about then I started to think about quittin'. I had just enough work to bother me. But then it commenced pickin' up again. They'd call me and say they couldn't get anyone else. I was the only one left and I'd get calls to bail somebody out. So I'd go. After the early forties it was a whole new group of people who called. Before that it was farm horses and loggin' horses—no saddle horses. Then folks moved up here and started havin' pleasure horses. And then it really picked up. Now there are about twenty blacksmiths in these parts, a lot of 'em trained by me. They'd come work with me, some for a few months, and they'd quit. Some worked for two or three years. I learned 'em. People now have more leisure time and more money; that's why they can afford horses.

Folks used to truck a big team as far as a hundred and forty miles to me to be shod. Nobody would handle those horses 'cept me. Never was too much trouble for me to train a horse. I could always get horses to pull or stand or lift their leg. I used different methods with different horses—just like people. You got to know their peculiarities.

During the Depression we was pressed for money, but not for food. We had more then than we have now. We raised our own always. You could buy steak then for ten, fifteen cents, not like today. Ethel used to put up five hundred cans a summer and we raised our own pork. Then we used to have chickens a couple of different times, but Ethel hates to see things shut up so we let 'em run free. Then they'd run all over and get in the garden, so finally we'd have to get rid of them.

I kept on workin' till a year ago; a year and a quarter it was, I guess, since the heart attack. I miss the work. Also, I don't like stayin' in one place all the time with nobody to talk to or anything like that. 'Course I'm pretty deaf now, and that makes it hard, but if folks talk right *at* me, facin' me, I can hear pretty good. All I've had is a crick in my back just once; that's where your back snaps right over. But even the next day I did some work. I'd shod about eighty-four horses the week before! I was quite a while though getting over it. Now what I do mostly is read. They wouldn't renew my license, so that keeps me in more. They say it's the blood vessels in back of my eyes that are causin' the trouble.

But I get around some anyway. One of the people that I learned how to shoe, when he goes horseshoein', comes and takes me along. Then there's one near Thomaston, Connecticut comes up every Monday, or *means* to every Monday, in any case. It's about forty miles from here. He comes up just to take me around and give me a ride. He is an awful nice fellow. He bought a team, a pair of Clydesdales, and now he uses 'em for hayrides and sleighrides down to Canaan Mountain. He called me in to shoe 'em. That's how I come to know him. I drove that team o' his to the church and back for my granddaughter's weddin' last year.

I never cared much for fancy ironwork. 'Course I did some if people asked me to, like workin' on andirons and things like that. But the craft is comin' back. There is a lot of schools around the country teachin' it, but there's only one school I heard of that's any good and that's Cornell.

When you want to git horses to do things it's always the simple thing that works best. Later you ask yourself, why didn't I think of it before? It's pretty much the same with children, but mine never gave me no trouble anyhow. The oldest, when he was little, followed me around all day long. When I was out in the barn milkin' the cows he'd come out and sit there till I was through. When he was a year and a half old my wife had to reach out the window for him; he'd climbed the ladder right up after me where I was puttin' on the new roof. You couldn't keep him away.

When we come here to this place we was the only ones that had small children; now we're the only ones that don't have. I've got friends pretty much all ages now. The young fellas I taught come back a lot. I've only been doin' that since I was sixty-five and gettin' social security. A number of 'em came round at different times, when the shoein' commenced comin' back good, and asked me take 'em on. So I took 'em round with me and I'd let 'em work and I'd tell 'em what to do, but I never took no money. I wouldn't take it, turned it right over to them. I was doin' it for the doin' of it and to keep me out of mischief. I'd just keep enough back for the gas and the tools. It's expensive, you know, blacksmith stock. A lot of 'em were doin' things they didn't like to do when they came to me, like workin' in a shop or bodymen in a garage, things like that. They preferred shoein' and bein' on their own.

The world's a better place now, more convenient, and people are livin' longer. I find I still enjoy myself, especially when somebody comes around, you know. I like to talk. A fella come around yesterday; he'd been a blacksmith. We never seen him before. He came lookin' for a spoke pointer. Folks ask me to sell my tools but I hate to think about it. I want to keep 'em. Never know when I might need 'em. I have a hundred-pound anvil. That's rare, you know. Most people have seventy-five-pound or two-hundred-pound ones. It's worth quite a lot of money. I know one thing: if I don't sell 'em, nobody'll know what their right worth is. None of the younger ones know what they're worth. I like to see 'em around, so I guess I'll keep 'em.

I figure this summer sombody'll come around again and want training. Even after the heart attack I worked with a horse last summer. Some woman wanted to learn how to train her horse, so she brought it over to my field and I'd sit there every afternoon and instruct her while she was doin' it. She was surprised; after a week that horse'd follow her round the field just as nice as you please. That was whip-trainin'.

When that movie Michael made about me was entered at the Berlin Festival (in international competition), I didn't think anyone'd be interested, 'cause it was just everyday business to me.* I didn't think it stood a chance, but then I did think about it afterwards. I remembered that in Germany there's always two men shoeing a horse—one holding the feet, the other doing the work—and that could make somewhat of a difference to see one man doin' it all. They showed the movie two times at Simon's Rock—packed houses, too.

I don't touch television; Ethel do. I do listen to the radio some and most

**My son-in-law, Michael Gottlieb, made a documentary movie about Clarence that won a second prize at the 1976-77 Berlin Festival, and I asked him how making and showing it had affected his life in the area.*

generally to the weather report. I don't care anything about singing. I have the radio on so loud she tells me she has to keep cotton in her ears. I'm supposed to have a new hearin' aid comin'. Supposed to been comin' sometime now. The last one, which was no good, cost nine hundred dollars. We figured out three hundred went to the one man who came, three hundred to the other one who came with him, and three hundred for the company. They were crooks. But this one only cost three hundred and it's guaranteed.

I go to the veterans' meetings sometimes now, but not to church, not since the first Sunday after I got back from the army and the minister was givin' the congregation the devil all through the service. I guess I ain't been back since except to go to a funeral or a weddin'.

I've gotten the highest social security they pay out since I was sixty-five. That's because of what I paid in. We manage pretty good. Can you believe it: when I first bought this place the taxes on it were thirty-seven dollars; now they're over five hundred!

I'll tell ya', the best way to avoid the troubles of old age is not to git there.

I was canning raspberries when I heard the news that my husband had died on a street in Europe. I went on with my work, only saying, "Well, you can't let the berries rot, can you?"

Lady Clay

Oxford, England

Born 1892

Lady Rosalind Clay, Oxford don and mother of a friend in England, received me in her book-lined study, which was cluttered with stacks of periodicals and papers. A French door opened into the garden, and plants were massed by the windows.

I SUPPOSE YOU might be interested to hear about my decision not to go on teaching. I have no one to talk to, to ask advice from; that's the problem. And so I have found the decisions made for me by some sort of an internal process. I have realized for months now that this teaching has got to stop. Yet this college is the only niche I made for myself and therefore, it becomes devilishly hard to leave. I appreciate it so terrifically. The honor that they gave me! It is unusual to have a woman on the staff of a men's college at Oxford—especially Worcester—because it isn't one of the most progressive colleges, you know. The work I got outside of the college was all mere chance. There was no other place where I got in on my own rights, you see, yet now I feel I have to give it up.

The days shorten as you get older. You can't take in difficult reading at night. That means my reading hours are cut. Also, I can only get three hours help a week with this place and it's quite large, you know. Of course, I'd much rather do it myself than have someone incompetent.

Unfortunately, I need the amount of space I've got here. I need a lot of room for all my books and papers. I am the most profuse booklender in Oxford; publications just flow out of here. I am leaving most of my books to the library, but not until I die. My children will have first pick. Charles was a professor at Simon Frazer and for health reasons is now at a university in Florida; he is a bachelor and became a Roman Catholic. Rosemary, my eldest girl, is an historian at Edinburgh on the staff of *The Economic Historian;* she is a profuse writer. She has four children and manages to run her house very well. She brought out a book on the history of Scotland which was picked as the Book of the Year. The next one's a doctor and they have got four sons and a daughter. The youngest, Liz Shore, has four children. She is a doctor holding an important position with the health service and is married to an illustrious MP, a leading star in Wilson's cabinet. Another daughter is teaching Latin at a school in Washington. She studied Greek, but no one wants it today.

I was teaching girls from Trinity College (in the States) for a time, but that has been discontinued because of lack of interest. All anyone seems to want to study these days are future-oriented subjects about which we know nothing anyway. I started teaching in 1915. I used to teach medieval European history up to the first exam [the first set of exams given to an Oxford scholar after he has been studying for a period of time].

I was born here in Oxford, you know, one of seven sisters. (My mother, alas, had no use for girls!) My father was A.L. Smith, master of Baliol College. I was married in 1915 to Edward Murray Wrong, a Canadian and a fellow of Magdalene.

My father made a great pet out of me! I remember my mother knitting and translating from the German at the same time. She was a very able woman. She had a prejudice against our education. You see, it's quite simple: boys are allowed a higher education, but girls must get scholarships. I was always kept terribly short of money. My mother managed the finances. Although she had great intellectual capacity, she spent most of her time in temperance work. My father always said, 'Your mother's idea of economy is to send you off on holiday just short of the return fare!'

After marrying I taught at Summerville for a short time, until my husband moved to Manchester where I taught as well. Seven children were born to us in ten and a half years, though one died. I managed to keep my hand in teaching all those years. My husband died in 1928. He had rheumatic heart disease. It was a difficult, not happy marriage. We became more and more estranged. Just before our last child's birth he took a fatal illness. We were briefly reconciled; then he died.

By 1929 all our savings were lost in the slump. I taught at a great many men's colleges when someone was ill or so. In fact, I never left Oxford for twelve years, filling in jobs for those on sabbatical. But my official connection at Worcester didn't come until 1948. All those years my mind was occupied heavily with my work so, you see, I had no time for tiresome nagging. That's why, I think, my children all turned out well! We were so poor that sometimes we didn't have bedsteads—just mattresses on the floor. We moved sixteen or seventeen times.

In 1951 I married Sir Henry Clay, a long-standing old love. He came back that year as head of Nuffield College. He had been the economic adviser to the Bank of England. No one came to our wedding; we wanted it that way.

My second marriage only lasted three years, but I knew him very, very well. We had been seeing each other for years. I was having a major operation, and it frightened him into proposing marriage. Tears still come to my eyes when I mention Lord Clay, who was my great love. The children all loved Clay, who was also a widower with children.

I have never been paid less because of being a woman, but then I was willing to take on classes which no one else would have touched, as one gets paid less that way, per student. I did lecturing for a time. In fact, I almost tried broadcasting. Thank God, it didn't work out, because my voice is awful. I'm always frightened at the beginning of each new session with students. What I really wanted initially was to be a research fellow, but I always felt I was not accurate enough, that I had not 'learned the method.' I feel I am too random, too impulsive, that I don't have enough critical capacity for research work. Professor Habakuk once asked me, 'Why are you any good at all, then?' I answered (it took me a year to discover the answer), 'Because I'm not a bore!'

This house was bought by Jesus College, and I am assured they will never turn me out. I suppose I will die here. The only problem is that I am getting more clumsy since using my crutches. I knock things over and I'm slightly unsteady. I'll probably break something; or else, as a friend of mind said recently, 'We'll set ourselves on fire one of these days!' College is so interesting that my main regret is the end of the steady flow of bright young men passing through the house. Oh, they will come back to see me (they always do, you know), but it's not quite the same thing. I'm going to teach college entrance people now, but I would still like a very small number of my regular students from Worcester as well. But the problem is doing the reading necessary to prepare myself properly. I don't go to the library because my crutches clank so frightfully. My day is shortened. I tire more easily and everything takes longer. If you have always done everything for yourself you don't want anyone else doing things. 'They' throw things away you need, or they are simply stupid or incompetent. To me all paper is sacred, and I'm not interested in having someone working for me who is careless or madly eccentric. It does seem sickening to give up something you really care about doing for the sake of some little chores. Yet, eighty, I think, is the time to stop, really.

I gave the college long notice of my coming retirement. All they said was, 'Well, I suppose we knew it would come some day.' They were very good to me always. They made me a member of Senior Common, but it is difficult to go there, especially in winter. There's always some nasty patch of ice about between the college and the house. And then it frightens me a bit; you never know whom you are going to meet. Once I said to a young graduate student who was visiting me, speaking about my other young students, 'They make you feel as though they are delighted to see you.' The answer from him was, 'Perhaps they are!'

When I received my honorary degree last year Oxford allowed me to give an enormous party for one hundred people. I chose a tea party, but now I honestly believe a party in the evening would have been better. But then my children would not have been able to come and get back by night. One of them came by helicopter. When I can't sleep I count things, and I was counting them, before and after—all the people who came, I mean. At the party I concentrated on speaking to those who said, 'But I shan't know anyone there.' They ought, of course, to know better; they were nearly all historians!

By the way, I also received an honorary doctorate at Cambridge after the Oxford one, but there was no nonsense about the amenities; for instance, about meeting me at the station. I had to walk to town. They didn't realize the scale I was expecting after my marvelous Oxford experience!

I'm a frightful scribbler—the house is full of my writings. I think I will leave them to the nuns; they are very thorough. My son-in-law Peter said, 'I would like to see your filing habits.' But I suspect he wouldn't! I have never had enough time for pleasure. Now I'll be able to read for fun. I've never done much reading outside my field. I have tried, late at night, but usually I fall asleep. I read detective novels at that time for relaxation but find I don't make much progress.

At the moment I am cleaning up my papers for my family. I have a cremation tag in the mirror of my bedroom. Shortly I'll make another one to take with me wherever I go. One must face one's own death. Ten years ago I had an accident and I have been somewhat crippled since then. The first two or three years after the accident I was much better off, but it is getting progressively more difficult. What I miss terribly is my bicycle!

In the past I had a great garden, especially during the war. I canned everything. I was canning raspberries when I heard the news that my husband had died on a street in Europe. I went on with my work, only saying, 'Well, you can't let the berries rot, can you?' Luckily, I became a good cook, because my second husband was so well known and entertained a great deal. I learned cooking rather late. Someone once said, 'God means you to be a very strong person.' My answer was, 'Well, God might have suited me better for it!' We children once asked my father, apropos of someone, 'Is he nice?' Father answered, 'Well, he's not so very nasty.' I notice this beginning of greater tolerance developing with age within myself, too. I have learned not to say 'it' (the sharp, critical word, I mean).

No one's gone 'gaga' amongst us, so far, I'm glad to say, although everyone is dying off. Four girls and one boy are left amongst my siblings. They began dying like anything about a year ago. My two best friends are still alive. They are botanists, both of them. C.S. Lewis said, 'Friendship is about something,' and it's so true! They used to write me the most enthusiastic letters: 'Do you know what I have just found in the woods yesterday?' I loved getting those letters, but alas, they have stopped writing in the last year. Growing old, I fear. What lies ahead for me you ask. I accept the idea of dying. What I find difficult to accept is that the things you want to do become harder and harder, and it is inevitable that you become more and more dependent and a burden to your children, which I don't want.

I have a lodger and will continue to have one. I only have people in my house who won't do bothersome things; I mean, such as a heavy drinking person would put me off. I have too many visitors almost but not enough of my own children. They are too far away. I would like it if I could find someone who will do shopping and especially someone who will do the ironing. I can't stand ironing. And the gardening is becoming too much for me. I love it, of course; I have always been fascinated by plants. But there is just too much work. My health is relatively good though, considering that I have been on crutches, crippled for ten years, since my fall. I have paroxysmal tachycardia. That's when the natural pacemaker of the heart goes out of hand. It has a threshing machine effect on the heart. You must keep perfectly still and wait till an attack passes, preferably lying down. But awkwardly, so far it's always happened to me on the streets. I think it is the result of tension caused by the increasing number of books which have come out in my field and which I haven't read and feel I must.

The doctor has given me a number to call. He insisted I take it down for help in case of an emergency. Twice I have been very ill in the middle of the night but luckily have had someone there each time. My son Oliver was there the first time; that time I passed a kidney stone. I didn't want to wake him as he was tired, so I waited until morning to call him. The second time I also had someone from the family with me; that was when I broke my hip. I slipped on the linoleum—I was wearing wool socks at the time. Yet, despite these mishaps, I still wouldn't want to stay with one of my children. Maybe with my stepdaughter. Probably because she could say No to me more easily. But unfortunately she's in Wales, and if I went to her I would be cut off from all my friends. I have seen it happen to a friend of mine who moved in with her daughter. She could make no new friends and she was terribly lonely. She only lasted a year there. I have a lot of friends and too many acquaintances. I didn't get along well with my sister here in Oxford, but she dropped in constantly anyway, a most annoying habit. She was brought up to think she was absolutely brilliant, but she hadn't had a new idea since World War One. I have always been told how brilliant I am, but it's not true.

I suppose that I should tell you something about my first marriage. I was too young and I didn't know how to run a formal house, with finger bowls and all. I didn't know or care about such things. I wasn't ready for marriage. You see, I didn't know my husband would expect me to go about with him everywhere he went. My family was not like that. My mother did charity work and was always very busy. She was domineering, but she was busy. My second husband, on the other hand, was an informal man. He used to carry nuts and chocolates in his pocket and at the drop of a hat loved to go out into the fields to picnic under a tree.

You see, in my first marriage I always thought my job was to stay with the children. But my first husband's family believed I should employ a nanny. In their family the children came last, they waited until the grown-ups had eaten, whereas in my family the children got served first. In our house you could always find the pudding with a bit carved out for the baby.

I still go to the hairdresser and have always cared for my clothes and grooming. I used to chastise my daughter Liz for not wearing makeup. I have been told that I was always an intensely feminine and pretty woman, and men buzzed around me! During the war I carried coal and gardened, but I have always loathed cleaning. Through my devotion to my MP son-in-law, Peter, I think my politics have become more and more leftist labour, but basically I was never really a political person. Paradoxically, though I am an atheist, I am also pro-church. Liz, my daughter, says her greatest fear is going off mentally and not realizing it. That's really why she has retired. Now she is living only for other people. She can't bear people all dying off around her.

Rachel Brik

Ulpan Outside of Jerusalem, Israel

Born 1889

Through a friend, writer Florence Cohen, who was also in Israel in 1972–73 and was working on interviews with people in the creative arts who had emigrated from Russia to Israel, I was taken to an Ulpan (residential orientation center) outside of Jerusalem. Florence was to act as translator because she spoke Yiddish. It was there I met Rachel Brik, eighty-four, a Russian émigré.

She was known as Babushka. Although uncomfortably overweight and hampered in her movements by the paralysis that set in after two heart attacks, Rachel impressed one with her warmth and vitality. Her massive round face was punctuated by intense, lively brown eyes and a remarkably mobile, expressive, even sensuous mouth. Despite the fact that neither one of us spoke Hebrew, we managed to communicate laboriously via her Russian-Yiddish, Florence's Yiddish, and my German.

I COME FROM a large orthodox family, though I am no longer religious. We were two sisters and three brothers; I was the secondborn. My father, a rich merchant in Odessa, died when I was twenty-three, just before my marriage. Fifty-four years ago two of my brothers emigrated to Israel. Both are dead now. The youngest and only living brother remains in Russia. He is a brilliant man, with Ph.D.s in three different fields. Though he wants and hopes to move to Israel, at present it is extremely difficult. Both his children—one is a well-known surgeon, the other is an internist—have been denied exit visas, and without them he would be terribly lonely here and quite without resources. The Brik family here has no means to help him. I have a sister in Israel who came in 1948, but she cannot offer us any financial aid either, dependent as she is on her own children and ill besides.

My family and I came here by way of Vienna seven months ago—my son and daughter, their respective mates, and three grandchildren. My daughter's

You have to realize that we people who emigrate from Russia are all very much heroes just for the act of coming.

husband brought his mother as well. As you can see, this flat—a tiny one-story bungalow—is too small. It consists of only two bedrooms and a living room. Our sleeping arrangements are very cramped. We only have five beds, two of them double, for nine people.

We came to Israel only through the efforts and persuasiveness of my younger brother who had been living here for fifty-four years. He was a member of the Stern Gang in British Mandate days and was renowned for his patriotic and philanthropic activities. It was he who brought us to Israel with promises of financial aid and help in job placement and a roof over our heads. I galvanized the family with my desire to see him once more and with my hopes for a better future. I took the initiative.

We had already reached Vienna, leaving everything behind us except a piano and an old family rug that were to be shipped plus a few small random personal possessions, when the rest of my family were given terrible news by the Jewish agency: my brother in Israel had died suddenly, felled by a heart attack. Why didn't they tell me? I would never have come further. But the others chose to continue the journey.

When the plane landed at Lod Airport, Tel Aviv, I remember scanning the long lines of waiting relatives. They were like huge waves of uncontainable humanity that the strong rope and the police seemed unable to keep back. I searched the faces, the stance of each one, looking for a familiar gesture that would metamorphose one of these strangers into my brother. The now reddish-gray hair, the florid mustache, the high color, and the imposing size and weight of the man I hoped to recognize from the often-mutilated and out-of-focus snapshots he had included from time to time in his infrequent letters. Here would be the man who had grown out of the lad I had waved to until he had become a tiny dot on a receding fruit steamer in 1919. But a woman caught my eye instead. I recognized her as my sister-in-law. A woman alone, standing quite still in the agitated crowd, wearing black. At that moment, quite literally, I felt my heart break. They had to come onto the field with an ambulance to carry me to a hospital; I had had a massive heart attack. You see my legs now? I was left paralyzed. Then two months ago I had another attack here at the Ulpan. I ask myself over and over again, Why? Why did he have to die? I came just to see him one more time.

Now we are completely alone. My sister-in-law is indifferent; she does nothing to help us. We have seen her only once since then. My poor brother, if only he knew! Jacov—that's what he was called—was truly a good man. He even helped total strangers.

Tears brimmed in Babushka's eyes. She leaned her head against the chairback and seemed exhausted, pained, as though she just couldn't accept this final irony of her brother's death and her arrival in this strange new land. Her daughter told us she would have to rest. Slowly, with supporting arms, we led her to the back bedroom. The blinds were already down, and Babushka lay back on the old Turkish tapestry bedcover with a deep sigh, closing her eyes. I wondered when I would see her again.

I couldn't bear to question her further, and her daughter was reluctant to allow us any more time with her. But I knew Babushka liked me, and she extended her warm, strong hand to me. "Come back soon," she said. I pieced together the rest of the story after several more visits, each time slowly so as not to tire her.

During the Odessa pogrom my mother's sister and all of her ten children were forced from their cellar hiding-place and brutally killed. Our immediate family escaped that time probably because we were a rich family and we spoke Yiddish, which is similar to German, you know, and because we lived in the German colony, apart from the ghetto. Later, of course, that same fact became instrumental in our persecution during the time of the revolution. We lost everything in 1917.

My husband died because of Hitler. All his family, everyone, was killed. We tried to trace them but never heard a word of their fate. Stalin warned us Jews to escape, those who still could. He sent us to Siberia and, let me tell you, the Russian people were good to us in those days. Stalin said that all Jews must be removed from Odessa in order to save them, so my son and daughter and I took to the woods. Then we began to walk. Sometimes we hitched rides on farm wagons. Finally we reached Siberia.

Meanwhile my husband was serving in the Russian army. God only knew where or on what front! We did not see or hear from him for two years. And then one day he came back to us on leave. We were still in Siberia. But oh, his legs, his poor legs! I couldn't bear to look. They were swollen unrecognizably, with terrible sores all over them. In those days we had no medicines or even any food to give him. He was dying of malnutrition but we couldn't help him. It was terrible. A month later he was gone, in the winter of 1943.

My family here in Israel consists of my son—he is a mechanical engineer trained in Russia as my husband had been—and his wife. My daughter is married to a dental surgeon; it has been difficult for him to find the right niche in Israel since Russian medical training is not considered to be on a par with Israeli. At the moment he is commuting each day to Tel Aviv by motorcycle, where he works as an assistant at the Kupat Cholim Hospital. Then there are my three grandchildren.

We are all frightened to leave the Ulpan, where the rents are low and set by the Jewish agency. We are also very worried by the accumulation of our debts to the agency. We owe for the refrigerator and for the couch and dining set. In our new apartment there will be a stove that we'll have to buy, and the move itself will cost money. Admittedly, the apartment will be bigger, but we'll be subject to rent increases, and it is located on the fifth floor. I wonder how we'll be able to pay the movers to carry the piano up all those flights.

Once I have been lifted—it will probably have to be on a stretcher—up the five flights of stairs, it seems unlikely that I'll ever be able to make the trip down to the courtyard or street again. My daughter must find work to augment the family income, my granddaughter will be off to school each day, and my son-in-law will be at work in the hospital, so my only companion and maybe nursemaid will be my son-in-law's mother, whom I find it hard to live with. She even spies on me. Two Babushkas are one too many in a household. I don't look forward to the move.

Even here, in the rather idealistic setting of the Ulpan, there are the usual personality conflicts that one finds in the outside world. Though the supposed purposes of an Ulpan are to offer immigrants a warm welcome, to help relieve some of their natural anxieties, and, of course, to teach them the new customs and language, we've found that some of the people in positions of authority throw their weight around, which is hard to take after our earlier experiences. This sort of thing adds to our sense of isolation and strangeness. Still, I am glad to be in Israel. No one here runs to the authorities to report a critical remark. It is a free country.

My greatest problem seems to be getting used to this oppressive heat. I suffer from terrible headaches, and I often spend the whole day behind drawn blinds, just waiting for the cooler breezes of evening to blow over the hills.

You have to realize that we people who emigrate from Russia are all very much heroes just for the act of coming! But our difficulties here lie in the fact that we Russians can't ask for anything, and we are not like the Americans, who can easily say, "Go to hell" when something oppresses them. We are used to the yoke and therefore take whatever is handed us.

I wish you would take me with you to America. I have friends there. I am not naive, I don't think it is a "golden country," but for two things—you can get good TV there, which helps to pass the day when you are an invalid, and good people are there who are not Jews. I read about them in the papers. I still read a great deal—books, the papers—and I have a deep love for music. *Es ist schwer ein Jud zu sein!* [It is hard to be a Jew!] *Tanzen kann Ich nicht mehr.* [I can no longer dance.] *Die Gedanken sind da. Aber die Gesundheit nicht.* [The mind is still there, but my health no longer.] When I go two steps my heart begins to hurt and I can't sleep, even at night.

I am not religious but we keep the high holidays—just the festivals. Also, we light the candles on the sabbath. Do you know, in Odessa now there is only one synagogue for the whole city! In my youth there were ten large ones. My father was not religious; he was a Zionist. *Es ist heute eine umgekehrte Welt* [literally meaning a turned-over world]!

On my second-to-last visit I found Babushka on her bed, her hand clutching a handkerchief and resting on her forehead, as though she were trying to push back the relentless heat that was accosting her temples. The headaches had become intolerable the last ten days, during which time a breath-searing, burning desert wind had prevailed.

I don't think I'll survive.

The next time I came to the house it was closed down. The venetian blinds were drawn, but through a chink in the blind I could see that the house was empty. Babushka had moved and God only knows how she would tolerate yet another uprooting.

Max de Cugis

Nice, France

Born 1882

Tennis champion Max de Cugis, whom I met through my French translator, Jacqueline Meppiel, lived in a lovely tangerine-colored Mediterranean villa, situated in a spacious garden. Black cypresses guarded the gates and stood sentinel on either side of the house. An arbor of roses formed the approach to the house. In the center a wide French door, flanked by dark green shutters, welcomed one. A small balcony overhung the front door. The house was located twenty miles or so from Nice in a pleasant old village that is gradually becoming more of a villa-suburb of the city. The coastal mountains lie behind the town and the sea is close by.

Inside, the house had the same air of comfortable Provençal charm: fruitwood country furniture, charming print curtains. A floral design on English linen, well worn, adorned the wing chair of Monsieur de Cugis. Old pottery plates adorned the mantel, and handsome antique earthenware jugs had been turned into lamp bases. Here and there hung a photo: the champion at fourteen in plus fours on the courts of the Renshaw Club, the Davis Cup Team in a conventional team pose. Antique orientals graced the floors and everywhere spilled bouquets of varicolored full-blown roses.

Max de Cugis was a dignified, tall, slim old man, with a patch on his right eye. He wore an impeccably tailored off-white suit of fine wool and an elegant silk ascot. He carried a cane when surveying his "lands," moving always with ease. He seemed in perfect balance, gracious, a gentleman of an era gone by, but somehow not a man who has been left behind. His wife, a pretty woman in her early seventies, bustled about him solicitously and gave off an aura of warmth and sexuality.

DO YOU KNOW I am an old tennis champion? I was quite famous at one time and, believe me, fame has a way of altering your expectations and even meeting most of them. It changes your life. It adds that fillip of excitement

Believe me, fame has a way of altering your expectations.

which, I suppose, tends to make you desirable to women. In any case, I was always lucky in that respect. I loved beautiful women and I had the pick!

My father, who was head of an established firm of greengrocers, sent me to England to boarding school during the summer terms, and it was there I not only learned excellent English (which he held to be important for the future head of an old family business that had a distinguished clientele), but I properly learned the game of tennis. By the age of fourteen or fifteen I had already won the Renshaw Club championship. By 1903 I was champion of France. Altogether I won forty-eight championships: four times I was champion of Europe, nine times singles champion, fourteen times doubles champion (with the same partner), and seven times I won the mixed doubles championship. By 1906 I had three Olympic gold medals, won in Athens, and the fourth one I won in 1925 in Antwerp, playing doubles with Suzanne Lenglen, a fine player.

In looking back on my life it wasn't just the winning in itself, exhilarating as that admittedly is, which made it seem such a magical time, but the effect of all this on my life-style. I still feel it today, incidentally—the doors that were opened to me. These were the real rewards of playing well.

To give an example: In 1908, while playing for the championship in Germany (it was quite normal for the victoria of the crown prince to be sent to fetch me), the empress herself made the cocktails for us. I was given an intimate glance of their life that day. Later that same long summer evening I played the crown prince and beat him. That was a bit ticklish to handle! Another time I was staying in the Grand Hotel—I think it may have been Ospidaletti—when, while putting out my boots to be cleaned, I spied down the hotel corridor a man I instantly recognized as the King of Spain (I'd seen him at matches; he was a tennis buff). He was tiptoeing gingerly down the hall to what I knew to be the suite of a woman of fashion, his latest paramour. Of course, I kept my counsel and breathed no word of it. Later, on the courts, I met him. We became fast friends. But I am sure my discretion didn't hurt my reputation.

Oh, but it wasn't all just encounters with royalty; that would have become a bore. Too much protocol! But it was rather the opportunity I was given to travel, to meet up sometimes with bizarre situations. I enjoyed it all! I must have had the right personality for such a life because, I tell you, I took to it almost too naturally. For instance, I remember a funny incident; it stands out in my mind's eye. In Biarritz, in 1910, I was invited to join the then hydroplane champion in his plane. This superb mechanical contraption consisted of two wooden levels of wings, some ropes, a twelve-cylinder Renault engine, and a box to sit in. But what made it amusing was the starter: Two oxen were hitched to the ropes. These poor dumb beasts faithfully pulled us along the beach until suddenly the wind caught us sooner than expected, and instead, the oxen were pulled by us into the water. All ended well, because their trainer managed to unhitch them quickly enough, thank God!

My last championship, except the doubles I played with Suzanne Lenglen, was in 1923. I started to play the game at the age of four. My English school was Woodford Green in Sussex; I joined the Connaught Club for tennis there. My father's mania for languages was at work when he sent me off to Spain as well. But my father was a sensible man, and when he saw my tennis talent he encouraged me.

You know, I was captain of the Davis Cup Team in 1925. On the way back, on the old ship *Berengaria,* the Ballet Negre was on board, coming over to Paris. I met Josephine Baker then. She was quite an amazing woman. What vitality! I enjoyed such encounters.

In 1923 I stopped playing because I was forty-one years of age. I don't like to see a great player moving downhill, and so I decided to change careers abruptly. I took over the management of a beautiful, large old farm. My godfather, the well-known portrait painter François Flameng, had a two-hundred-forty-acre farm, which he allowed me to cultivate. I suppose all that disciplined athletic training and later the hard physical labor of farming has kept me well. Always in the fresh air! These days I cultivate my roses. Did you see the allée of rose plants leading up to the house?

During the First World War I began as a soldier, second class. I spent two years in the Argonne, slugging it out in the artillery. Then I was offered the chance to take the examination for officer's training. I commanded in the Sanitaire service and had fifty American boys under me. I was given a higher command in 1917 in the same service but now all French. In 1940 I had two German prisoners of war working for me on the farm for two years. In '45, just after war's end, one of them returned and set fire to my mill. Everything was burnt down—house, barns, sheds, everything! I had to sell some woods in order to rebuild just a little house for myself. I still own it and I rent it now. I wanted to move down here, to the south of France, where the climate is good. I have some rich American friends who made it all possible. They bought this house here in Provence in the name of their daughter, but meanwhile I am allowed to live in it. I have been here since 1950—twenty-three years.

I still cultivate my garden; I only have someone to mow the lawns. You know, when you are ninety-one years old you become lazy. The years weigh heavily on your shoulders. But I can't complain. I sleep well and I'm never sick. I haven't smoked in my entire life and so I'm never out of breath. That seems to be a curse of old age for most people. All my family have reached a ripe old age: my father eighty-eight, my grandfather ninety-three, my mother eighty-seven. There were three boys and two girls in our family. I'm a grandfather, you know. But they all live in Mexico. My granddaughter is very petite. When she came to visit she seemed like a gypsy to me. She is married to a man seven feet two inches tall. Ridiculous!

My first wife had spinal meningitis. She was cured after a year of intensive care, but for the last four years of her life she had to be put in a mental hospital. I don't know whether the meningitis had affected her brain.

During World War One she served as an assistant in a hospital. There she made friends with another young woman, who later lost her husband (I think it was around '47 or '48). So my wife persuaded her to settle down here. She bought an inexpensive little house right next to ours. We became close friends, and when my wife died we married. Keeps you young! We have no problems.

My new wife is a splendid cook. In fact, my second marriage is much better than the first. She is affectionate, practical, and looks after me most beautifully.

My first wife was altogether too independent, but she was bright and talented. For instance, she invented the idea of the accessory bag—the little felt bag also—and, of course, with that she founded a very successful business.

I felt I had to stop playing tennis altogether after '54 because I had a cataract operation. They operated on me four times in one year. One eye makes tennis impossible.

Once I played against Gustav the Fifth. He was a terror! Cheating and cheating in tennis and in bridge also. Yes, the king never paid for anything. But I had a sense of humor, so I didn't mind too much about his cheating me. I might do it, too, if I were king. Nowadays I spend most of my worktime in the garden, but it is an immense amount of work. Lots of things to do: water, cultivate, weed, replant, fertilize, spray. I grow flowers, tomatoes, lettuce, parsley, potatoes, and other vegetables.

Of course, my wife expects me to go marketing with her. In France that takes time, too. She buys, I drive and carry. Luckily my eyesight isn't so bad but that I can read and I watch the color TV. I watch all the matches.

Last time I was at Wimbledon was in '61. They invited me to come to celebrate my fiftieth-year jubilee. I was treated like a veritable king. Nowadays I am forgotten, but in my own time I was popular—with women, too. Oh, I was terrible, terrible: chasing the women in the opera, the singers, the dancers! But they've all remained good friends. That's an art. To stay friends.

No, I don't resent the end of that world for me. The transition came slowly, so the wrench wasn't too bad. And I love the country, living here amongst my roses in the hill country, with this beautiful clear light. No, it's a great privilege.

I am a real egotist, you know. I have taken life as I wanted it, and I have no regrets. Of course, life is quite different now, but what has been, has been. When I want to be happy all I must do is plug in the memory of the glorious life I had. *La Belle Époque:* it is finished. We can't go back but must accept the life we live now. Sometimes I'm disgusted by the prospect of how life-styles have changed. I know I was lucky to have been born in an easier period, when things still had grace. I was first married in 1905. In those days it seemed a fortune to be earning one thousand francs per month. On that we managed a maid, a cook, a car, and a chauffeur. Unbelievable now! No, I regret only *la belle vie.* I was received and wined and dined by all the world, like a young grand duke. We used to wash with milk or champagne—truthfully. What waste that seems now.

I remember in Saint Petersburg, when I was playing there in the early part of the century, I had three servants, a chauffeur, a whole house, and even a troika with three horses—one for riding. Now they play just for the dollar. It is disgusting. Look what happened: sixty-seven players boycotted Wimbledon because one of their number refused to play the Czechs. Absolutely disgusting! It has all changed, but I enjoyed the best of it.

JO SMITH

When people get older they are the same kind of people . . . only more so.

DWIGHT SMITH

My thinking hasn't changed a great deal over the years, maybe because I have a closed mind or because I am smarter than I think.

Jo and Dwight Smith

Claremont, California

Born 1899 and 1900

Dwight Smith, seventy-five, and Jo Smith, seventy-six, had been introduced to me by a mutual friend who had long been active in the geriatric field. She felt not only would they be interesting as a couple living in Pilgrim Place, an unusual retirement community for ministers of the United Church of Christ, but that they would have so much to contribute to the whole subject of aging, since they themselves had been working and were, in fact, still active in the field of geriatrics. I found them, two humorous, lively, highly articulate people, in a charming little house filled with books, rugs he had hooked, nice antiques, mementoes, and a fine cat by the name of Magnificat. It was part of a whole community of such little houses, some free-standing as theirs was, others attached, with a central dining hall/meeting house off to one side.

JO: I STUDIED nursing at Saint Lukes in New York City just after I graduated from Mount Holyoke. I wanted to be a doctor. My family was willing but there was no money, and in those days they didn't give scholarships to girls. My father was a corporation lawyer, but he was also in real estate. I went into training in the fall of 1921. There were five of us college graduates who went into nursing; in those days nurses were just an upper servant, and to have a college graduate go into that sort of thing was considered demeaning. All five of us stuck together even though we were in different hospitals. I went into surgical nursing, and then I taught at Yale School of Nursing.

I met Dwight at a college prom. He went off to China, where he taught English for two years at Yale in China. This was in central China. He came back in 1924, and we married in my first year of teaching. We were going to go back to the Orient in 1927, but this was when the trouble was going on, so consequently we did not go back. That's when he went into the ministry, where he spent twenty-six years. We had two years in Edinburgh while he got his doctorate.

DWIGHT: When I first went to college I thought psychology was big stuff. While I was still in college I decided to go to missionary school. I was asked to teach in China to see how I would take to it. This really was a program that preceded the Peace Corps idea. Yale in China was started basically as a medical school, but students had to study in English, so I went out to teach English to the Chinese schoolchildren who would want to go on to medical school. In divinity school I was expecting to go back to China, so all my studies were about China. Then I had a chance to go to Edinburgh to take my Ph.D. degree. There I took church history and wrote my dissertation on Robert Browne, who was the founder of Congregationalism.

JO: When we were married I was teaching nursing at Yale, and that's how we ate. My mother, who was very much an invalid, lived with us. In other words, we couldn't have married unless Dwight took us both on. She paid the rent, and we paid for everything else. With anyone else but Dwight it probably wouldn't have worked. We kept the house full of young people, and Mother had a ball. She was able to take care of herself during the day. She had three strokes one after the other, which affected her mentally. However, she did know that Cynthia was on the way, which gave her a big thrill. She moved to Washington with us, and that is where she died at age seventy-two.

When Cynthia was born we were in Billingham; it was during the Depression. What I did there, of course, was to make sure the family existed. Dwight had his first church there. When members of the congregation got sick I used to nurse them. It was very rough. I was out of the house a lot, and Dwight was in it. I taught Red Cross home nursing classes until my children finally said, "Do we have to?" because they were always being used in demonstrations. This was all part-time volunteer work.

When we were in Olympia the war came and everyone deserted the Welfare Department. They asked if I would do this medical social welfare business. I got a Presidential Citation for the aides that I trained.

DWIGHT: During the wartime years the March of Dimes got Jo and a public health nurse to go to Warm Springs to learn the hot pack treatment so that they could come back to teach it.

JO: I left Poppa to take care of the whole family while I was there for the summer. Now that's accepted practice, but in those days women leaving the family for job training was unheard of.

I never was a minister's wife. I didn't go around making proper calls or anything. One summer while the war was on there wasn't any gas, and all the people who had means had a shack on Mud Bay. They couldn't go out, and so they said please keep the Sunday school going because otherwise they wouldn't know what to do with the kids. One Sunday only I was there to look after two hundred fifty children. In desperation I sent one of the kids to fetch Dwight, and together we dramatized the story of the good Samaritan from the pulpit. The two hundred fifty kids sat rapt, just listening to this coming over the

PA system. Later we were asked to do a small radio show.

Subsequently, we used this material on the local radio station live, and it was a great success. All this was being done free. Then the National Council of Churches heard about it, and they sent me to Chicago to take a course on radio. We got a Peabody for that program. Later, in New York, I worked for the Riverside Church radio station for a while.

When we moved to Boston fame preceded me, and the council of churches asked if I would put on a program. There were only about twenty children there (I was used to working with over two hundred), so I took my son Andy, who was about eight, and another child and I appeared in a program called "Mother, Tell Me a Story." There were just three voices—I would tell a story and the kids would interrupt. The thing went all over New England—this was the Boston WEII station. We got another Peabody for that. The program lasted as long as we were in Boston—about four or five years.

We also did one together called "Junior Roundtable," which was an absolute scream. That was on WLAW. We did it for about a year. Because we didn't have a Sunday school of our own, we involved everybody else's Sunday school. We asked various churches to let us have three kids, and we would discuss every kind of topic with them. They would listen to the kids who were appearing the Sunday before them, but they were not rehearsed. We had an audience, as this was live. During one of the programs I asked if anyone had heard President Eisenhower's prayer during his inauguration, and one of the children said, No. She was the daughter of a famous Harvard professor, and it caused him some embarrassment.

The program we liked best we took to New York with us when we moved again; it was called "Mr. and Mrs. Smith." We did it at midnight on Saturday nights. We used to have guests—some of the Boston Symphony Orchestra, for example. Dwight used to sign off with Big Ben striking midnight and by saying, "Let us enter the new week together with God." We never identified ourselves except as Mr. and Mrs. Smith. We had the most enormous following of truck drivers. It was beamed all the way up to Nova Scotia, and they listened like crazy.

Though I started my professional life as a nurse, I had been working with the welfare department in Olympia, Washington. When we moved to Boston in order that Dwight could accept a new assignment, my social work supervisor said, "Why don't you go ahead and get a degree, because you have a talent for this sort of thing, and you'll never get any farther without it."

I went to Boston University School of Social Work—I was fifty then. By then our children were in graduate school. The school didn't flicker an eye that an old lady was looking for a degree. I took all the courses I could on a part-time basis, then the dean said that I would have to "fish or cut bait," that I'd have to take my year of supervised field work and some courses on a full-time basis. I said I couldn't do it. I had a part-time job with the Tuberculosis Health Association that brought in a little money and we needed that, what with all the kids' expenses. "Well," the dean asked, "if I get you a scholarship will you continue?" and I said it would depend. I was being very negative. Later he said the Soroptomists of New England were offering a scholarship to a student who would specialize in geriatrics. I asked, what's geriatrics? He told me it was a matter of old age. This was twenty-three years ago, and it was an unknown field then. The scholarship was astronomical—it paid all my tuition, for all my books, for transportation of any kind, and provided a small salary. It was an offer I couldn't resist.

Then Boston University had to look around like mad to find courses that even mentioned old age. The only group work placement that Boston University could find for me was out at Hecht House in Dorchester. It was the Jewish Philanthropy Community Settlement. I was out there for half a year, and I had the time of my life. I think I was the only gentile within a radius of twenty miles. They were so good to me; I just loved it. They had one little group of old people and one worker assigned to it. To have a student assigned to it meant that we practically doubled the attendance of the group. The group grew, and once the thing got started it was its own best advertisement. That's how I got into geriatrics. Then, in case work, they had to put me to work with Family Service Society and assign me to all the cases that dealt with old people.

DWIGHT: In Boston I was the minister of Mount Vernon Church, which is right across the basin from MIT. It was a handsome church in a wonderful location, but there had been social changes in the Back Bay area that the church never had been willing to contemplate. It had been built by the generosity of well-to-do people, and that area of Back Bay was full of families of means who had enough puritan conscience and/or who felt guilty about the way their ancestors had gotten their money, and so would come through fairly generously. They would get together every year and find out what the deficit was and write out the checks to cover it. But this is ruinous for a church, because the membership of the church never accepts responsibility for itself. Later these families moved away and the area filled up with students and old people. But these are groups that can't support a church. They need the service but they can't support it.

JO: At that point in time my husband was also propositioned to move to New York as general secretary of the John Milton Society for the Blind.

DWIGHT: As editor of the *John Milton Magazine* I wrote an editorial every month. Bill Goldberg gave us the money to start it in 1969. The society has published a Braille magazine since 1962, but this is a large-type edition of the Braille magazine. This is for people who have a sight impairment but who are not completely blind.

JO: We moved to New York, and I had my degree. I went to visit a friend who was heading up the department of aging, and she asked me to do a six-month survey on foster homes for the aged. It is really wonderful to be in with the pioneers in any field. I worked with Bill Posner. What he was actually doing was what the Community Service Society wanted to do. I handed in my research and I think they must have filed it, because they never did anything with it. By that time I was out of a job, so I went to see Geneva Matthewson, and she said, "I hope you are looking for a job. Get in touch with Henry Street because they are looking for you."

DWIGHT: After graduating, the first job of any importance that Jo had was there with the Henry Street Settlement in New York, where she started the program for elderly people. When the time came for her to leave for a new job, she was given a farewell party by the Good Companions of Henry Street. The chairman had come from Israel and had selected a seder plate for her and explained that it was a new industry starting in Israel—making antiques.

JO: I retired from the health department when I was sixty-five, but they kept me on for a few years.

The job I enjoyed the most was the one I had with the Queensbridge Health Maintenance Clinic for the elderly, which was the prototype for the HMO's that are around the country now. I was part of one of the original four that were set up by the federal government to see if the concept would work.

Retirement carries a reaction of grief with it. When we settled here in the retirement community, I fell back on my nursing. I went back to our little nursing home here, which had only forty-two beds, and I said I would like to teach a course to nurses' aides (I had to go back to school to get a teaching certificate; this took about one year). I was set up in Claremont High School with an evening course, whereupon I went to the doctor who ran the nursing home and suggested his aides come along. Then I got other nursing homes coming in. The bad ones don't want me and the good ones want me back again. One of the local colleges heard about it and asked me to set up a program there. It has made the nursing home personnel more understanding of the patients they serve.

A minister is underfoot all the time, so retirement is not really that different. We are doing pretty much the same thing now as we always have. When I started teaching this thing it became obvious there were some people in these jobs who didn't know what they were doing. I suggested that I ought to be followed by a younger nurse who knew all the most recent techniques—these kids ought to get a course in basic nursing skills. The nurse discovered they needed some reaffirmation on their own basis, and so Dwight follows with another course on psychosocial needs. The aides themselves actually asked for this.

DWIGHT: We are really scab labor, because Jo does not have the right qualifications for college teaching; also we are too old to get proper college contracts.

JO: Despite that we're teaching here in Claremont in the various community colleges and high school adult programs. One of the themes I talk on is the concept of the Silver Age. It is a concept I swiped from a British social work journal. The precept is to stop thinking of old age as a slump and to start thinking of an intermediatory stage called the Silver Age. This can start with women when the youngest child marries and leaves home and there is a change of role that starts. It isn't so much a matter of keeping someone going but of preventing something from happening. For instance, taking care of health, then, will often save you from being one of the five percent who are institutionalized later.

This summer Dwight and I are going over to the men's prison at Chino to teach a course on creative writing on a volunteer basis. We are wild to try it.

Shortly, we'll be speaking at a conference on consumerism. I feel sure that somehow we can relate your topic of self-esteem and determination, Dwight, to that topic. Generally speaking, there are a lot of old people in the audience when we speak at these things, and I really believe that the stereotype of the old person is perpetuated by themselves. I give them the old rousements, and we try to shake them up a bit in their thinking.

When we moved here I said I am going to destroy my past, so I destroyed all my scripts thinking he would destroy all his sermons. So we moved out here with none of my scripts and all his sermons. The sermons were thrown out just the other day. Sermons get dated, too.

DWIGHT: Sixty percent of us here in this retirement community are from the United Church of Christ. Here we belong to local churches whatever they may be and once a week we have a fellowship meeting. Depends on who's doing it, but since most of us are frustrated because we no longer have a flock, God gets pretty well instructed sometimes during grace. I realize now that I believed in social activism throughout my life. I voted for Norman Thomas for years, though my father was a Republican and a doctor who was against socialized medicine.

The Congregational Church believed that every person can speak to God. My thinking hasn't changed a great deal over the years, maybe because I have a closed mind or because I am smarter than I think. In my first church I conceived the idea of having a family forum. But we had to cancel it because my board of directors wouldn't agree. During the war I even appeared in *Time* magazine on a picket line. Again, this led to some squabbles with the board.

JO: It's strange but true that it is easier to imagine oneself dead than being old. Sometimes we walk—about half a mile a day. But we don't exercise, although we should. I am practically blind in one eye and I can't hear out of one ear. It's insulting. I feel like a damn fool. They think it is due to a blow I got on the head when I was on a freighter going to Sweden; there was a terrible storm and I fell on my head. The doctors think this is what caused it.

DWIGHT: Everyone who lives here in Pilgrim Place has lived elsewhere. One neighbor was in South Africa, another in China and in Turkey, another in India; they are very interesting to live near. Jo and I perhaps chase around more than some others, but a number of them do volunteer work of various kinds. Some visit the prisons, some do recording for the blind, some do aide jobs in public schools. There is a good deal more going on than shows on the surface. And we have lectures and discussions and films.

JO: One of the things we hope will develop in the future is that a doctor will be on call. We have all been expected to make our own arrangements. This same thing is true with legal advice. We are also trying to move things along for home care. We have a relatively small nursing home facility, but people are there who we think should be in their own homes if we only had home care available. Although this is a marvelous place, some of the social problems have not yet been worked out. I can go over to the outpatients' department to have my blood pressure checked. They also have a pincushion club for those who need injections.

Most of us are paying very reasonable rent, and we are charged for two meals a week whether we eat them or not. You see, if they are going to keep the dining room open they have to have an income. They only supply lunch, a midday meal, but will bring it on a tray if you are unwell. We have our own laundry room and are free to come and go. We are night people rather than early morning people. We almost always watch the eleven o'clock news and then have a drink and go to bed around midnight. The average age here is around eighty, and most are alert and lively. There are no rules about when you have to be in. As a final point I'd say I think that when people get older they are the same kind of people they have been only more so.

Well, I tell you, I'm just glad that I am here and able to see everythin' the Lord lets me see.

Margaret Miller

Letohatchee, Alabama

Born 1893

I took some photographs in Alabama a few years ago for the American Friends Service Committee, and when I wanted to do an interview with a rural Southern Black man or woman I asked them for help. Out of this came the following interview with Margaret Miller.

I WAS BORN not too far from here, in this county. I was born in 1893, so I am eighty-two, yes ma'am, on the thirty-first of July. I haven't got a brother and sister livin'—nobody livin' but me. I had four—two sisters and two brothers, that's all I knowed. I don't know nothin' about my daddy; he and my mama was parted. He worked for the Crayhills—that's 'crosstown, by the railroad somewhere. My mama she stayed over here. She worked the farm and cooked out for the white folks.

My mama's name was Tillie Douglas and my papa was called Jake Douglas. I saw him sometimes—once or twice. I stuck to my mama till she left me. She took care of me and I took care of her till the Lord called her. I don't know whether she died before my brother or not—when you get old your memory goes. When I was young the old people used to come and sit around the porches, and they didn't have to worry none 'bout things like rememberin' everythin'.

My mama told me her mama left her and went to Tampa, Florida. Her own mother never did see her child but once. She gave it to her mama as a Christmas present. So I never did see my grandma.

I was raised up with my brother's chillun, who were older than me. We grew up around here with lots of other kids, but we never got into any bad crowds or nothin' 'cause we had the school and church. We used to swim and fish, and we'd hunt for partridges. That's all we did, but now chillun don't think of doin' things like that.

There used to be plum trees along the road here. You could sell berries, plums, and apples. In my lifetime the folks from up North bought this land; then they give them colored folk time to pay for it. They had night classes and Bible studies, and then let Christmas come and everybody got somethin'. They took the chillun out of the fields and sent 'em to school and even fed 'em. At that time chillun knew nothin' but going to school and that the teachers loved 'em. Those Northern folk was good people. They was some kind of Episcopalians.

They called the school they'd started Calhoun School. The older lady, the founder, was named Charlotte Thorn. She brung all the white teachers from up North, New York and about, to teach us.

It was a good school then. We had from kindergarten up. Picnics we had and a Southern flag and everythin', but it's all cut out since. My baby, when he finished, was one of the last boys goin' to that school, and that was in 1939. It used to go right up to the twelfth grade.

I didn't get no further than the eighth grade, then I quit. But I liked school. Mama didn't have nobody but me at the time; I was the baby. I never did see but two of my mama's other chillun. (My sister, who is older, died when her baby was four years old.) My mama was strict alright; she sure was. But I got along well with her because I was the only one left home with her. After my sister died she tended her chillun until my sister's husband married again and took them off her hands.

When I was seventeen I had went to Pensacola in Florida to visit some kindreds, and I met my husband there. I come back to Pollack, Alabama, and that's where me and him married, in 1911. I was eighteen when I was married. I stayed down there awhile and went back to my mother when I started havin' chillun. He was a good man. He worked on the track with shovel and rake. Sometimes he worked way down the road, and when he didn't come home for a spell I'd take one or two of the boys and go down to Louisiana to be with him when he was workin'. I liked it down there. We lived in railroad workers' houses. I'd usually stay a month or so. We did all our buyin' and things in New Orleans.

As long as he was in the railroad I did my travelin'. I have been to Orlando, Florida; Jacksonville, Pennsylvania; and I've been to Detroit. All that was on passes. After he died I mostly stopped goin' because of the dim stations. Besides, now they done cut out all the trains.

My husband never lost his job durin' the Depression. You know, he helped Roosevelt off the train down there in Louisiana. We liked Roosevelt—he was a good man. I made quilts in Roosevelt's time and I still have them; I also made mattresses. Everybody made their own bed tickin' then, during Depression days. Roosevelt was a good President, not like Nixon. Cared about poor folks.

I had eighteen children all told, but I haven't but one livin'. Just one son. I lost two sons about three years ago—one lived in Pensacola and one stayed here. And the baby, I lost him in the army. The others died when they was little.

My husband workin' on the railroad at that time was my help. That's why, to tell you the truth, I never did too much work, not for others. 'Cause of him I didn't have to get in the fields like a lot of other womenfolk, who had no money comin'. We did farm some. Me and the chillun would farm a little and raise corn and cotton. My mama was livin' then, and she helped me with the kids. Most of the folks stopped farmin' around here and that's when all them woods growed up. Before you could see everywhere, just fields.

My mama bought ten acres of land in her lifetime, and my sons bought some more when they came out of the army. (None of them got married till they come out of the army.) We still have thirty acres, but we don't farm it anymore. We have a few cows now, that's all. I been tryin' to get my son to farm it but he won't.

My church where I goes is back yonder in the woods. It's called Salem and it's a Christian church. The other little church you see on the hill is a Baptist church. I go there on a preaching Sunday, which is once a month. Our preacher now has other churches to take care of. They tell us old folks to go to Sunday school, too, but there is not so many chillun as there used to be. There is still a lot of members in our church, but they don't pay their dues. But those old-time hymns sound as good as ever, yes, sir.

Our church is an old-time one, with old pews and lanterns, but things got broken and taken away. We fixed our church up again and we just got electric light put in. They had old-time medicine bottles they used to dress the graves with and these have all gone, stolen or broken.

All my kindred, my husband, my mama and three sons are all buried there in the churchyard.

My mama died right here in her house. I can't tell you how many years ago. She helped me with everyone of my chillun. I stayed right with my mama, right until she died, yes, ma'am.

This here house will do if I live. But I'm gonna try to get it fixed. You know how the wind blows. I'm going to have to get something done to it if I live till the winter comes. This is not a warm house. My husband has been dead soon to be eighteen years. He died right here. We married in 1911 and we stayed together until death parted us. I remember my grandson was born just after he died. Now I got twelve grandchillun. I don't see them a lot 'cause they're too far away. The oldest boy is in Michigan, one is in Montgomery, the other one is nearby here. Then I have two daughters-in-law livin' here.

My two sons built the house after World War Two. They was both in the war. Nobody teached them how to do it, but they built all three of these houses. I have been livin' in this one since they built it. I added nothin' but a bathroom to mine. I use tubes now to bathe instead of just the bathtub, in case I slip. I have a boy stays with me nights and sometimes, when I fall out of bed, I have to call him to pick me up. Lucky I didn't hurt myself them last two times I fell.

I gets up early every mornin'. Many mornin's I look out and they is all gone. 'Course they gotta go to school and work. And I am still here. Can't walk good no more. It's my legs that worry me the most, but I try to walk a little every day and that helps. Loosens 'em up. When I go to church now I don't get up and down until it's time to leave. I've had them legs for over a year, but I can do a little better since I lost a little weight.

The preacher told me if I ever get sick to call him and he would come. He is faithful. I don't have no good appetite to eat. I eats a little meat and eggs and things. I have a refrigerator; that helps. I have to cook my food myself and, do you know, I miss many a meal. I just don't care to get up and do anythin' like that. If I call them and tell them they bring me somethin'.

I don't have nobody to come and clean; I do myself. I do my own little washin'. I have to keep busy doin' somethin' for myself. My grandchillun I nursed from babies, but they don't have time for their grandma. I go to my daughter-in-law and spend the day there. She is lookin' after her son's baby and can't leave her house. I go down there and sit with her, then come back here. She takes pains with me—she is a good woman. I can't walk fast, and she stays right with me. Her name is Martha Jane.

When I could see pretty good I made the patchwork quilt there on the bed, but when I got so I couldn't see no more I just had to leave it off. I ain't finished it. A few weeks ago I had a bad hand, and I can't use my thumb for pushing needles. I don't know myself what happened to it—it just come and swoll up and the nail come off. I had to go to the doctor and he lanced it. It's kinda sore now. Every time I go to my doctor he tells me to get Medicare, but it's not understood whether I can get it. If I can, I sure need it.

I had cataracts in my eyes. I had the operation over ten years ago. They took them off of both my eyes at the same time.

I had another operation before my husband died, and every now and then it worries me. I gets a pain, but I don't tell no one. I would like to go to a higher up doctor and see what it is, but it costs too much. That's why I want the Medicare right now. My doctor is workin' on my blood. I was kind of stout before I started takin' the pills he gave. I don't care for drinks no more. Don't know whether that's the pills.

Most all day I sit here in the house, as I am not able to do nothin'. My eyes have got so I can't see enough to go out by myself. In the old days I used to read my Bible every day until my eyes done got so bad. Now the little letters all run together. I have been in around this house now a year. This knee is bad, so I have to walk with a stick. I have everythin' wrong. Somethin' goin' on all the time. I got arthritis, my knee is bad, my eyes, too. I have been goin' to the doctor. I got so I couldn't bend my leg and put my stockin's on. And I'd catch a chill whenever I went out anywhere. I have to wear stockin's when I go out now 'cause at my age you have to wear them when you go anywhere. But at home I don't wear any. I have the cramps often, so I wear this coin to help.

They always say the Lord makes a way for you. Alma is thirty years old, and she helps her old grandma all she can. She tells me that I cannot get food stamps, that I get too much money (two hundred dollars) to get these other things from the government. Alma may be right. She lives yonder in the trailer with her sister.

I don't get no welfare check, see. I gets my little pension check from my boy that I lost in the army, and I gets a little social security check off my husband on the railroad. His ain't nothin' much, but I thanks the Lord it come when I gets my water bill and my gas bill. They wants big money. Great big money. It be seventy dollars every three months when I gets my bill. I have to stint myself to keep paid up. I got a gas stove to cook; I heat by it, too.

Ever since I have been in the world this area has been colored folks, but now they are lettin' in some whites here. That ain't makin' no trouble. But if many more come in I'm goin' up the road a way. We just been livin' out here, nothin' to bother us. It was a big place then and a lot of colored folks had their homes here, but it ain't so now. Still, there are quite a number of acres left for us. Everythin' is just alright. We live together alright.

Trouble is most of the folks from here gone up North. I don't think they'll come back from up the road yet awhile. If they live long enough 'course they might. But mostly they don't come to visit until death hits and that's too late.

I visited my sister's daughter last Monday and we talked about the old times. We talked about how the kids would mind the old folks when we was young. Her brother, who lives with her, can't walk as he doesn't have a leg. They lives way out in the woods alone. It'd scare me. I worries about her and I can't get to see her. She is just six months younger than me.

At night I always close all my windows 'cause I get scared. I can't sleep unless I close them all. It be hot in here, but I have to bear with it. I have my door fastened and windows and all. When my husband was alive I didn't lock up then. He wasn't scared. I go to bed anywhere from six o'clock on. Some nights I sleep good, some nights I don't. You can't never tell who will come in.

Well, I tell you, I'm just glad that I am here and able to see everythin' the Lord lets me see. I thanks God every morning. Sometimes the pain makes me get up early and sometimes the pains ain't too bad. I listen to the stories on the radio and I thinks too much.

As my wife and I grew older we became conscious of an ever-increasing need to be close. . . . We became inseparable.

Wachtmeester Johannes Lambertus van der Scheer

Zutphen, The Netherlands

Born 1886

I found Cavalry Sergeant Van der Scheer sitting under a grape arbor in his garden shelling peas. He lived in the small rural town of Warnsveld, not far from the city of Zutphen in Gelderland, Holland, which lies near the German border. His well-kept, trim, little brick house dates back to the time when this was all farmland. He was wearing a sleeveless undershirt, which showed off the strong musculature of his tanned arms. His back was unusually straight for a man of eighty-seven and his eyes were bright and clear. One thought of him as a man in his sixties. I had been introduced to him through the local doctor, who was a cousin of mine.

I WAS BORN in Zutphen in 1886, went to school there through the eighth grade, served in the cavalry in this region, and was married here. Later I worked in the government tax bureau in Zutphen. I've lived in this same house since 1921 and have tended the garden every year since then.

Over there, on the horizon, you can see the steeple of the church I attended as a small boy. In my day it was compulsory for everyone to attend catechism class, though I haven't been a very good churchman since. My father, on the other hand, was a strict Christian all his life.

I'll tell you a story: I was a very good swimmer as a boy, fourteen or fifteen years old; one day I swam in a big meet all the way from Arnhem to Westerbonen. The pleasure boat took twenty-five minutes over it, so you can see it was quite a distance. I won second prize; it was a nickel-plated watch, and I was, of course, very proud of it. When I came home that afternoon my father asked me where I got the watch, and I told him, forgetting for a moment that I should have been attending church, not swimming in a meet on Sunday morning. With a stern look my father took the watch and smashed it.

Another time I was learning to ride my bike. It was Sunday and the minister of our church happened to walk by. He stopped to ask my father whether he knew it was Sunday and why was I allowed to ride my bicycle on the sabbath. Well, my father spanked me there and then. But that was his way, stern but just.

At seventeen, in 1903, I joined the cavalry. The money wasn't good in those days, but I was born with spurs on my heels, just like my father. He had started in the cavalry also, although later he became a policeman. I was the eldest, so that when my father died very suddenly of pneumonia, leaving eight children—five boys and three girls—I was expected to help out. But my cavalry earnings were small, so my mother, with one brother, set up a small store. At forty my mother became blind, though she lived till she was sixty-three. Two of my brothers died in early childhood, at four and five. My last brother, the one closest in age to me and the one with whom I used to have to share a bed when I was young, died at fifty, leaving just me and two sisters. One is seven years younger and one is fifteen years my junior.

I met my wife while dancing, when I had just become a *Wachtmeester,* a sergeant, in the cavalry. She was employed as a kitchen maid in a good house. That's where she learned to cook so well. At first her "people" tried to put a stop to our courtship. They didn't want a proper girl in their household to go out with a "Hussar" [cavalryman]. My wife was a very pretty girl and in those days employers were concerned with the moral tone of their employees. Luckily my lieutenant played the violin and my wife's mistress and master played instruments as well, so they used to have musical afternoons playing trios and quartets. One day my wife was bringing in the tea things when the mistress said to the lieutenant, "She goes out with a Hussar," but he answered, "Yes, I know; it's my under-officer, the master of the watch, and he's a fine upstanding fellow." After that she was allowed to go out with me. But getting to see her often was another matter. In those days girls had a free Sunday only once every three weeks and Thursday evenings from eight to ten. If she was just five minutes late she was reprimanded.

We were both impatient with the long six-year wait before we could marry; it was a cavalry regulation for noncommissioned officers. So I decided to join the police force in Amsterdam, where they needed recruits and this rule didn't apply. I was very anxious to speed up the time of our marriage. But I only lasted in the police three months, though I managed to have some funny experiences while serving.

I was assigned a beat with another policeman, who knew his way around the city. One night he told me to look up to a well-lit window which had opaque glass panels at the bottom and was clear at the top. "There," he told me, "at quarter past ten, when the shops close, you will see the most beautiful woman undressing and stepping into her bath. All we have to do is get back here on time and climb up on that little shoemaker's shed which stands in front of the house." (One used to find such little stores in front of many buildings in

Amsterdam.) Sure enough, at the appointed time we arrived and there, precisely at ten fifteen, the good woman began her ritual of disrobing. We were so excited by her enticing silhouette that we decided to get a better look (I was twenty-four at the time and that explains my enthusiasm) and climbed up on the shed. I wasn't looking at my feet but rather at the titillating sight which suddenly came into focus for me through the upper pane. When stepping forward I didn't notice the little skylight in the roof of the shed, and with one clumsy step and a shattering crash my foot went through the glass and I fell, with a loud clatter, onto the tin roof. We ran as fast as lightning back to our stations on Prince Hendrik Gracht. Just then a frantic phone call came through complaining of peeping toms. We were duly sent off to investigate our own crime! We were most sympathetic with the poor woman and promised her we would write up a report and do everything possible to apprehend the culprits. Which, of course, we never did.

I'm afraid I was too outspoken for the police force. You could only be a policeman if you were willing to follow orders blindly. The end of my police career came one night when I was called up before the police high commissioner and was accused of having disobeyed orders. Of course, I knew perfectly well that they have to have discipline in the police, just as they do in the cavalry, but it's just that I liked being a cavalryman and not a policeman.

We were finally married in 1916 and were we happy! My wife was a real woman, but she never shammed emotions or playacted. In the mornings when I left I always kissed her good-bye, and again at night when I came home. But she never played silly games with me, like hanging all over me for others to see. She loved me deeply and I loved her. I never went out at night but she was waiting up for me. She'd be sitting in her rocking chair, looking out the bedroom window.

Our daughter and only child was born in 1918. I received a telegram at the frontier saying that my wife's confinement was imminent, and I was given a few days leave to go help her. But before I could saddle up, the order was countermanded. We had a minor revolution here in Holland at that time. Some people wanted to depose the queen, so the cavalry was sent into Amsterdam to protect her. We were ordered to surround the palace with our wagons turned backwards to keep the mob from storming it. The crisis lasted only ten days, but it was long enough for me to miss the birth. I never saw my little one till she was ten days old.

From 1903 to 1925 I remained in the cavalry. Then in '25 our particular service, at least in this area, was disbanded. The army was being mechanized. At that point I had the choice of going on a pension or being transferred into another part of the country. I didn't want to be separated from my family, so I chose the pension.

In the last war I was in the Dutch underground. The act I'm most proud of as I look back over my life was saving the lives of two English pilots who had parachuted onto a haystack out in a field, here in back of Warnsveld village. I was one of the air raid wardens in town at the time, and I was just about to leave my tour of duty up in the church tower when I saw two strange shapes against the moonlit sky. Parachutists. Knowing just about where they'd land, I rushed out on my bike to try to get there before the Germans spotted them. Luckily the other two wardens on duty that night were sleeping as usual, so they didn't see what I saw. These two *Lumpen* were paid workers.

I could see that the spotlights had already caught the two parachutists in their beams, and it would just be a matter of minutes before they'd get to the landing site. I'd already seen plenty of dead men before in my life. When I got there I found six or seven of them burned unrecognizably. There were usually nine men in a bomber. Seven of them I could account for, dead. When I got to the eighth one I found him badly wounded but alive; the ninth was definitely alive. I didn't waste any time on the dead ones but rushed to pull the two who were still alive into a dense thicket. I stuffed handkerchiefs into the wounded ones' mouths, hoping they wouldn't groan. I ran back to the plane just as the Germans arrived. I pretended that I had just gotten there myself. I had gathered the parachutes under my arm already and led them to believe I had rushed to the scene to collect them. They asked me about the rest of the crew, and I said they must have burned up completely. I told them I found only seven dead men, and I carried the seven parachutes to prove it.

I had an accomplice, who helped me drag the two off the field later that night. (Just a few days before the Germans retreated at the end of the war they executed my friend as a member of the underground.) We brought the two men to a courageous lady with a big house, who nursed them and hid them away in a false attic of her house until they were well enough to make it back to the front, which by then was close by, at Maastricht. Of course, the Germans suspected all along, I am sure, that my friend and I were in the underground. As the war wore on I was regularly getting warnings from various people on our side to go into hiding. Then I would go stay with a farmer I knew, hidden away in the false bottom of his haywagon.

I had a gun with thirteen bullets in the cartridge. I was determined to use it if ever they caught me. I wasn't going to give them the pleasure of doing me in, and I was certainly going to take a few of them with me. I'm glad I was never forced to use it because they would have taken hostages from that farm village in retaliation for harboring me. That's why I never told anyone what I was doing, not even my wife; it was too dangerous to involve them.

I was the first person in our town to be dispossessed from their house by the occupation forces. They quartered some soldiers in it. I was told I'd have to be out by December thirty-first, and I wasn't allowed to take anything. I went to a friend, a farmer, and asked him whether I could borrow his wagon. He said Yes, but he didn't think the horse could pull it, since that day the streets were sheer ice. So instead, I harnessed up the sled and asked him to help but he wouldn't; he said he had to go to church. "Whenever the Germans whistle you run, but when a good Hollander asks for a hand you have to go fold your hands in prayer. *Pot Verdikkie,* I'll do it myself" and with that I moved off. I took out everything in the house in several loads and left it with neighbors.

When the soldiers returned and saw that the furniture had been taken, they rounded up all my things they could find in the surrounding houses and put them back in the house. They said the house had been robbed. I said, "Like hell; that's all my furniture and I took it." So they called in the commandant. He was a pretty reasonable fellow and said, "Alright, make a list of everything there in triplicate, then when our men leave the house they will notify you, the owner, and you can check to make sure it's still all there."

Two months later I'm told by neighbors that the soldiers are leaving, in fact, have left my house, so I go back to the house via the back door. But a huge fat German is standing there; I tell him I've come to check my furniture. I show him the papers. He says come back at six. (He was in the corps that built tank obstructions and things like that.) At six I'm back with my brother-in-law's big handcart and my brother-in-law to help. We ring the bell but no one answers. I finally remove the grill and climb in through the cellar window. I walk through the house. Everything looks disheveled and broken, the walls are filthy with graffiti. I go up the stairs, first into the front room, my daughter's room, next to the spare room, finally into the master bedroom. I look in. There, sprawled naked all over my bed, lies the fat German with a woman in his arms. I yell, *"Heraus! Drauss!"* He grabs his trousers from the chair and runs down the stairs and out.

Even while hiding out from the Nazis I used to sneak back here occasionally to see my wife. I'd throw stones up at her window from the back garden late at night. She'd know it was me. Then I'd bring her a bit of food from the farmers, and we'd exchange news and spend part of the night together.

But toward the end of the occupation they quartered more soldiers in our house, and this time my wife and child as well as I had to be on the run. We hid out in a deserted farm village, where my son-in-law came to me one day to warn me that the Canadians were coming soon. They thought they might shell the town and I'd better get out. I sent my family away, but I decided I'd be able to convince the Canadians I was a patriot, so I waited for them. Meanwhile, I spent my time searching the chicken yards and gathering up all the uncollected eggs I could find to give to the Canadians as a welcoming present. Finally, a big tank pulled up at the door where I was staying, and a tall brute of a guy jumped out with map in hand to ask me for instructions. As I'd been in the cavalry, I'd given this whole matter a good deal of thought. I knew they'd be wanting to know where the big gun installations and pillboxes were, so although I spoke no English I was able to draw in on his map a good number of the German installations for the entire region of Zutphen and Warnsveld; I'd kept my eyes open while traveling around on my bicycle.

The next day twenty Canadians came marching by with their corporal, and they brought me a note from the captain on the tank. I had managed to acquire a gun that one of the NSBers [collaborators] had left standing when there was a shelling in Warnsveld, so when these Canadians indicated via the map that they needed someone to lead them across the back country and along the canal, I said, "I'm coming," and with that I grabbed my gun. In order to get to one of those hidden German gun installations I mentioned, you had to follow along a ditch and then to cross an open field. But once there you had a perfect view of the gun installations from behind. The Canadians were marching nicely in a row, like sitting ducks, so I indicated for them to separate and crawl on their bellies—in fact, I got behind a hedge. It was a good thing, too, because the first one in line was shot down as he started out across the field. After that, believe me, they hit the ground. I had a round of one hundred shells in my cartridge, but by the end of the afternoon I had none left. The next day we got some reinforcements, but that poor corporal who had come up with the first twenty troops was badly wounded by a grenade. We helped him back to the farmhouse when we returned at night after the first day's shooting. There were bodies everywhere you looked. The Germans withdrew and the Canadians eventually took the town, though there were still German snipers about. One hid out in the church tower; another shot a Canadian on the street, but we couldn't isolate the direction of the shot at first. When we found the house where he'd been hiding we threw in grenades, but he had already escaped. We saw him running across a field with a Canadian jeep after him; they caught him.

You had to be firm with the Germans. If you insisted on your rights they pushed you around a lot less than if you just passively gave in. For instance, I never handed over my bike or my radio, though we were ordered to do so, and I got away with it. I used to deliver food from the farmers to some Jews who were still in hiding in Zutphen. I managed that because I was an air raid warden, so I had a permit to be on the streets. When I wore my old cavalry boots and riding breeches I looked quite a bit like one of the NSBers, so they let me pass.

After the war I went back to the tax office and worked there until age sixty-five. I retired for good in 1951. Since then I've done occasional odd jobs for the tax bureau and have looked after temporary projects for some of the organizations to which I belong. Taking care of my house and garden was always time-consuming. I've shingled and mended the roof, puttied the windows and painted them, rebuilt the fence, plus taken care of this large garden. My wife used to can everything; now my daughter does it. The garden manages to keep us in fresh vegetables most of the year.

At first, some people tried to talk me into coming back to work part-time, but I said no thanks, because I've been waiting for time to do what I want since I was seventeen, in 1903. I have been retired for twenty-five years and since then have been getting two pensions: one from the tax bureau and the other, the old military pension, I've been collecting since 1924, when I retired from the cavalry. Together they amount to twelve hundred guilders per month, which is less than half what I was getting before retirement. My aggregate salary then was twenty-four hundred guilders per month. And that was in the days when money was still worth something. My only complaint with our pension system is that it encourages sloth. Every Netherlander who has paid up the premiums during his or her working life is entitled to a minimum monthly AOV [social security] payment of six hundred fifty guilders. However, if your pension is well above this figure, they reason that you don't need the full amount of social security as well, so they deduct a good part. In my case I get only about a quarter of the six hundred fifty since I am a widower. Also, my yearly vacation allowance is cut from the usual three hundred fifty to about one hundred guilders. So, in effect, you are being penalized for working hard all your life.

It is just lucky that I own this house. Would you believe that the annual taxes on it have gone up from one hundred eighty-five guilders in 1921 to twelve hundred today? In those days the house stood close to a wood, and surrounding it were pastures divided by small canals. That was before they reclaimed the land and none of these suburban houses were built yet. It was a small town then and much friendlier; everyone knew one another.

It's no longer *gezellig* at home. I've lived alone here since 1969. My daughter tries to help me and does a great deal. When my wife died, at first my daughter came over two or three times a week to visit, but I knew she couldn't afford the time. She and her husband run a busy bakery shop and do all the baking themselves. They are up at four thirty A.M. to start the ovens, and after dinner they still have to mix the dough. The bell rings for the first customer at eight A.M. and never stops ringing until six o'clock in the evening. All I ever did when she came was to sit there crying. Now it's much better, and I go over to their house for lunch every day.

Yes, it is ironic. As my wife and I grew older we became conscious of an ever-increasing need to be close. During the course of our lives I had often been absent of an evening. There were many organizational meetings to attend, but toward the end I gave up all such functions. We became inseparable. For instance, even if I had errands to do in town I would rush through them just to be back home with her as quickly as possible. Yes, I had known her exactly sixty years when she died—since 1909. We understood each other very well all those years, and paid each other mind.

It is almost six years ago now that my wife died. For eight months I nursed her night and day. I slept next to her here on the couch. We brought the bed downstairs, and I never left her side except to fetch her a cup of tea or a bite to eat. My daughter relieved me now and then as much as she was able. It was terrible to see my wife lying there so completely still, helpless, staring at us. She no longer spoke, and the only movement she was capable of was an occasional restless motion of one hand, as though she wanted something. Finally, it became too much of a strain for us. She wasn't getting better, and we had to put her in the hospital, where we visited her twice a day.

A few weeks after her death I ran into our family doctor. "Well, what are you planning to do with yourself?" he asked. "Move into the residence for the elderly, where you won't be so lonely?" "I'm going to stay here, right in my own house," I answered.

Yes, it's little things that make it hard to bear being alone. When I used to work in the garden all morning, by ten thirty I'd know that any moment my wife would be outside the kitchen door under the arbor calling me in for coffee. There is a club for the old right here. I could go but I don't, because all they do all day is sit, play dominoes, and drink tea. It bores me, to be honest.

Most Sundays I make the round of the old people's residences to visit a number of widows—seven of them. They are always glad to see me, though they are a bit old for me. Two can't walk, one is a bit mixed up above, and with most you have to shout to be heard. I've noticed that the old women are always clustered together chatting and making cups of coffee or knitting (unless, of course, they're senile), whereas the men sit off in corners by themselves. My difficulty is that I feel like a fifty-year-old man, though I have to admit I tire more easily than I used to.

I've never thought of remarrying, but I have been looking for a likely widow who would share a living arrangement with me. I had hoped to find a military widow. I put an ad in the paper and, believe it or not, I got twenty-seven answers, but nothing worked out right. I visited three of them in their homes. The last one I invited out here to visit me because she lived in Rotterdam—too far away for me.

One of the widows was a very personable, attractive woman and I found her sympathetic. We got along well and everything was moving along so nicely that I took courage and felt I could reasonably, without being insulting, ask her when she would like to come here and move in. "Move in?" she asked. "But I thought it was clear that you would move in with *me!* I have a beautiful apartment in Rotterdam. I made my husband a promise on his deathbed that I would never move from our flat. He wanted to be sure I would always be there, so I just can't leave." Well, I couldn't leave either, not my garden and my house and the neighborhood where I know all the nice, quiet bicycle lanes. My life is here, has been here, and my daughter and grandchildren are an important part of it. I wouldn't want to leave them. So, sadly, we parted. But we both knew that it could have worked out between us. Maybe we made a mistake, but you can't teach an old horse new tricks.

Another woman who visited wasn't bad at all, but she had a son who brought her over in his car and somehow made it clear to me that he would be part of the bargain. He immediately took over and ordered us around. I wasn't about to put up with that. I hadn't lived eighty-four years for nothing. She wanted very much to come live with me, but I just didn't trust her son or her daughter, who had come as well.

I have established a daily routine in the last few years; I go bicycling over to my daughter's for lunch before noon and on the way I work up an appetite by taking a little ten- to fifteen-kilometer roundtrip in the countryside. On Sundays I manage to do at least forty kilometers on some of the back country roads. I also do gymnastics—pushups and chinups—every morning. I still enjoy life and I try to take it in my stride; that's the real secret.

There is a nice girl living here who rents my daughter's old room. She cooks dinner for both of us when my son and daughter are away on vacation and every night she makes my supper, which is a big help. She has a boyfriend, who comes over three or four nights a week, and I don't want to impose on her, so we see little of each other. But it is good to have another person, a young cheerful person in the house. I know I'm lucky. She has her own life to lead and so does my daughter. I don't want them to sit here with me of an evening. They're young and have their own interests, and I have *had* my life, believe me I have.

Not that I want to die, but if tomorrow morning I didn't wake up again I have to admit I wouldn't mind. It's the damned loneliness; that's what gets you. Sometimes I sit here at night for a whole month with no one to talk to of an evening. You go to bed alone; the next morning you get up alone, dress yourself, and never say a word to a living soul. It's no way to live.

I'm a member of the winter clan.... I don't dance anymore, but I advise the young people on the ceremonies, as they were passed down to me.

Steven Trujillo

San Juan Pueblo, New Mexico

Born 1899

I asked the old man who came to the door of the sun-baked pink adobe house in San Juan Pueblo whether I could talk to him, and he said, "No, I'm sorry; my son-in-law died very unexpectedly last night at the young age of thirty-eight, and they are about to do an autopsy." He asked if I was going to be there tomorrow, and when I said No, he said, "Oh, alright, let's do it quickly." I asked him about the baskets he made that I had heard about in Santa Fe.

I WAS BORN in 1899, so I am seventy-six years old. Just this last school year I started on a new job. I spend all day, nine weeks at a time, moving from school to school in the various towns around this area. I teach the schoolchildren how to make baskets, and I talk to them also about how they should behave, about their people's traditions, and the need for working hard in life. "Don't be lazy." I teach them values. I tell them also how things used to be.

I'm a member of the winter clan—there are two kivas in our pueblo—my grandfather was one of the well-known chiefs [spiritual leaders] of the pueblo. It is a voluntary job; it is not hereditary. I don't dance anymore, but I advise the young people on the ceremonies, as they were passed down to me. I am the oldest one in our kiva, and I used to perform the cloud dance, the turtle dance, the buffalo, the dog, and the Comanche. Our big feast day is the Feast of San Juan on the twenty-fourth of June.

I got married when I was twenty-eight years old, in 1927, and I have five children and seventeen grandchildren. One of my daughters lives with me, and my little grandson lives here, too.

I was sent to the Indian school in Santa Fe. When I came back for a vacation, I looked for my father but I couldn't find him. My father had died while I was away, but no one had let me know. My uncle asked me, "Where have you been staying?" (I had been moving around from one family to another looking for my father.) My uncle decided to take me under his wing. From then on in, I lived with my uncle, and it was he who taught me everything I know. I used to watch him going down to the river and picking up these willow wands of a certain length and thickness. He cut them when they were green and worked them into baskets. I also saw him making belts, and weaving. I always helped him with gathering the willow shoots and also with the farming. We plowed everything by hand. It used to take two days just to travel by wagon to Santa Fe. Everything was done with horse or mule. Now there are advantages to the car and the young people are not interested in learning the old ways. They often don't want to take the trouble to do things which are hard any longer, like making your own basket. Still it is coming back slowly but surely.

My grandfather used to instruct me in the dances and I obeyed him. But nowadays the young people don't have that kind of respect for their elders. They are more interested in moving ahead in the world. Many of them, of course, go to high school and on to college and buy a house elsewhere and leave the pueblos. But some of them come back because they feel happier among their own people.

The pueblo was basically Catholic. My father and grandfather were Catholics, too. My grandfather said, "Our Lord and the Gods of our fathers are one and the same God," and that was very moving. There was no conflict for him. I went to Indian school through the third grade. I like to write. [I noticed his handwriting was beautiful—a calligrapher's hand.] I've learned what I know from living.

Making baskets all started in 1951 or so. I had a nephew who was digging for old ruins, and he asked me if I knew how to make baskets. I answered, "Yes, my own uncle used to do it." So I went to the river that same day and started working five wands in and five against each other, and I tried to weave them together. But that's not how you do it. You only take three and three and weave them together. Gradually with time I have figured it out and have retaught myself how to make them. My uncle used to sell the big baskets for seventy-five cents, but now I sell the little ones for fifteen dollars and the big ones for twenty-five dollars.

Until a couple of years ago, before I started teaching, I was farming. I knew how to make gourd rattles and Katchina dolls; we used to grow the gourds ourselves. Since retiring from Los Alamos, where, in the fifties, I worked in the salvage department for a while, basically all I've done all my life is be a farmer and a craftsman.

I feel fine—no problems. Still teach five days a week and then quite often I walk down to the river about a mile and cut the willow wands I need. Only I don't have much time to make the baskets because of the teaching. After I've eaten, talked to my family, or gone to the kiva, there is no time left.

Though I'm fine, my wife hasn't been very well lately. She has a dull pain in her side which never goes away. I'm worried for her. The doctor gave her a shot and called it by a fancy name. But I still don't know what her sickness is.

I built this house for her myself. Started long ago when we got married. The front part came first, and then I added on the side and the back, and finally the kitchen. It is a fine adobe. I've got an old wagon, and over there, in that round oven, is where we bake the bread. We rarely buy tortillas, only when we're pressed for time. We've lived here in San Juan Pueblo all our lives.

Now I have to teach children who speak the languages of different tribes. I teach anyone in the public school who wants to learn. Some really love it, but some don't. I concentrate on the ones who do, because I feel it is important to pass on my knowledge.

Most of us Pueblo Indians today really talk the same basic Indian language. At least we can understand each other. One time when I went to see the snake dance in Hopi country I was talking my own language and they understood me —maybe because my great great grandfather came from over there.

I enjoy talking to people. I don't feel the way a lot of the others do in the pueblos about speaking to the white man. Since I've learned to speak both Spanish and English, I have no trouble talking to anyone. Maybe also because I worked away from the pueblo for a while I think like my grandfather, who understood that the different peoples are one people and different gods are one God. I've always known that there are good people and bad people in this world.

I continue to work each day in the pottery and the garden.

Alice Sordet

Ferney-Voltaire, France

Born 1889

The Swiss journalist Camille de Bellet-Sauge introduced us to Alice Sordet. She took us to Lifas, the pottery in Ferney belonging to Alice Sordet. The word Lifas is a contraction of her first name and that of her former husband, Bonifas, with whom she founded the pottery in 1922.

I WAS BORN in 1889 in Geneva, Switzerland. My mother was a painter of modest reputation whose name is still remembered by the older generation of painters in Geneva. My father was a banker, my favorite uncle a well-known photographer by the name of Boissonas (which may have had something to do with my choice of photography as a second vocation during the war). I got my art training at the Beaux Arts School in Geneva, where I met my future husband, Paul Bonifas. His father was a fine engraver of gold watches who also wrote poetry. Paul and I got married in 1917. Shortly after our honeymoon we went to Paris with the intention of establishing ourselves as potters there. That was between the years of 1919 and 1922. While in Paris we became intimates of Le Corbusier, Juan Gris, Jean Cocteau, and many other interesting artists and writers. We exhibited our pottery at the Salon d'Automne in 1927–28, and our work is represented in the Musée d'Art Moderne, Paris.

In 1922 we decided to move to Ferney, partly because the children were coming and our parents wanted very much to be near enough to enjoy their grandchildren. We chose Ferney specifically because it has a history as a potteries town dating back to Voltaire's time, and it is noted for its fine clay of a superior consistency and color. We were confident we would find an old farmhouse with the requisite space for our work and for much less money than in Paris.

We had three children: one son, presently professor of microbiology at the University of Lausanne; one daughter, a teacher in Lausanne; and our youngest daughter, who recently joined me here with her husband and is taking over the management of the potteries. This daughter, who followed in our footsteps and in fact married a ceramicist as well, was sent by UNESCO, together with her husband, to teach pottery in various African nations and in Mexico.

During World War Two I had to run the potteries single-handedly. My husband stayed in Switzerland to be with our eighteen-year-old son, Valentin, who was determined to continue his medical studies despite the outbreak of war (otherwise he would have been conscripted). There Paul met a young cousin, who fell madly in love with him. It went to his head, as one says, and he began an affair with her. She got pregnant and persuaded him that he should leave me.

Clare, my potter daughter, had stayed here with me at the start of the war, so the family was physically divided. It proved to be very difficult for me to get any kind of fair legal representation across the border in Switzerland. But, thank God, I was legally the sole owner of the pottery and the house. Despite my reluctance, in fact unwillingness, to plunge into a divorce, Paul went ahead unilaterally. We were unable to see each other to communicate properly, and so he proceeded precipitously with the divorce and married the girl in a matter of months. Soon thereafter a second child was born, and right after the war they moved to America. She whisked him off to Oregon, where he had been offered an appointment as professor of ceramics and master ceramicist in residence. But, alas, not long after their arrival there he died very suddenly. He was forty years older than she!

In order to be able to live during the war I was forced to develop a more lucrative and essential profession than pottery, and so I settled on photography, about which I knew at least something through my Uncle Boissonas' tutelage. During the day I photographed German soldiers, while at night I ran a clandestine office, taking "identification" portraits of underground workers and resistance fighters who had need of forged documents. The Germans finally got on to me, and if the war hadn't ended when it did there would have been another outcome to the story. They were about to arrest me I found out later.

The pottery started in one small building, and little by little it has grown to its present size. It also includes five apartments for the young potters working here and, of course, the various workrooms and kilns. Also our showroom.

Thank God, I've always been very healthy. I continue to work each day in the pottery and in the garden. I do my own shopping and cook my lunch and dinner, so it keeps me busy. No time to think about the state of my health. Until two years ago I worked full-time at the pottery—eight hours a day. Now it is a little less since my daughter has taken over. But it is still I who do all the fine hand-painting of the ceramic figures and objects produced by the factory. I manage to get to the museums and galleries. I take long walks and I read a good deal. I still love to travel. Usually my daughter, the one who is a schoolteacher, accompanies me. Our last two trips were to Cairo and to the Balearic Islands. I particularly love Greece. But my children are the real center of my present life.

When I think back on my marriage and even the time after the divorce, I think I can say truthfully that I had the best years of Paul's life. We remained friends, you know, and never lost our respect for each other. I suppose that came from our long years of partnership in the pottery. Our life together had been full of intellectual and artistic ferment. An exciting time. Together we met Lorca and Dufy, discovered Spain before it was spoiled, knew all the exciting early painters and writers. Do you know, the irony is that shortly before his death Paul thought seriously of coming back to me. I often think about it and suppose I would have taken him back, but it turned out to be too late.

Lord, that period during the war was a difficult time of my life: to be alone, without funds, living under the yoke of the Germans and then to have to go through such a personal trauma as that heartwrenching separation. I suppose I was lucky in that my children pretty much took my side during the divorce and also afterwards. I certainly developed a good deal of strength and independence from the experience, but it was a hard price to pay.

My life nowadays is pleasant. I enjoy having the young apprentices from the pottery round me. It's enlivening, stimulating to see their interest and enthusiasm for their work. And, of course, I am pleased to have my grandchildren about and my daughter and son-in-law across the terrace, five steps away. In that sense I am very lucky. I still enjoy friendships with the young, maybe because all my life I have had friends younger than myself.

Since my official retirement two years ago, my daughter has made a number of changes. In the interest of efficiency she has hired a secretary and has rearranged the office. It was difficult at first when she took over because I had to share my workroom and kitchen with her. But now the situation is improved since I am again alone in the old house and my daughter has her own newly rebuilt house adjoining mine. Admittedly, Clare is making the whole thing run more smoothly, but she tends to be so efficient sometimes that she almost appears to be just a bit officious. I realize it is hard for her, after I have run the pottery single-handedly for over forty years, to take over from me. At times I feel ignored and "pushed into a corner," even though, obviously, I don't suffer from the usual complaint of old age—loneliness. In the midst of this extended family situation that obviously does not become a problem.

Alice Sordet lives in a lovely centuries-old farmhouse constructed with massive beams. The house stands in the center of Ferney, which remains in the shadow of its famous eighteenth-century citizen, Voltaire. She lives comfortably and in easy proximity with simple, beautiful old things: a provincial chest, her mother's delicate paintings, nicely faded oriental rugs, and what interested me particularly were the many late nineteenth-century photographs by her uncle Boissonas—poetic ladies dressed in flowing robes by the pyramids, a charming group portrait of three generations of the family attending the circus, and then some romantic shots of veiled dancers á la Duncan—this last done with very much an art nouveau feeling and in soft focus. Flowerpots hang from the old farmhouse beams and everything has an air of intelligent easiness and informality.

Alice is a handsome, pithy, energetic lady with crinkly, steel-gray hair, a ramrod-straight back, and flashing black eyes through which one immediately senses her quickness of mind. She is surrounded by family dogs, birds, and a general air of pleasant chaos. I found her sitting at a big table that was standing outside, on the wide second-floor veranda-deck. She was engrossed in painting a beautiful ceramic peacock. The piece was to be fired one more time before it would be taken down to the displayroom. Her hand was steady, and she looked intensely involved and full of pleasure in her work. She wore the characteristic sturdy mountain boots of the Swiss and a big apron. An old shepherd dog rested his chin in her lap while she was painting, while a mongrel golden retriever sat expectantly by her side. A parrot was perched in a cage hung from the rafters. One of her granddaughters, age seventeen or eighteen I would say, made a sudden appearance, having come to chat about her university course. Then one heard drifting up the stairwell the crisp patterns of a Mozart sonata for piano. Apparently one of the assistants was practicing, Alice explained. "Talented in more than one of the arts!" What an alive household I thought, centered around this remarkable artist and matriarch.

Desiderio Gallegos

Mora, New Mexico

Born 1884

My meeting with Desiderio Gallegos was made possible through the American Friends Service Committee. Gallegos' grandson was a close friend of Luis Torres (they were both activists in the Mexican American Movement in New Mexico), and Torres had worked with the Friends, who in turn suggested his name to me.

I WAS BORN in 1884, on the sixteenth of November, in a place called Ute Creek, New Mexico. I was the second son until my older brother died when he was eight and I was six. We kept sheep. Right from the start I herded sheep with my father. That's all we did until I grew up—in fact, until I got married at the age of twenty-seven: just take care of sheep.

In those days there was still open rangeland and we could roam anywhere we wanted. From the age of seven on I had to take care of the sheep alone. My father would run the base camp and I would come back to it regularly. Some days I would have to go further to find forage, depending always on the season and how much rainfall there'd been. Later, of course, my two younger brothers joined me herding, though often they had to take their sheep to other ground. We also played together, but the main thing in our life was herding sheep.

We used to camp out in the open with the sheep, even in winter. For a long time, it seems, we had no wagon. When we were finally financially able to buy one we used it to move up and down the trail along with our sheep. We also slept in it. We ate well, mostly beans and some meat—mutton or rabbit. We knew all sorts of things about the use of herbs and medicines. I remember we used to make a salve out of the pitch of a tree mixed with lard. Whenever we had sores or infections we'd cure them with this salve. We never went to a doctor. We also used to dye our own wool and weave it ourselves.

When I was sixteen I went to Las Vegas to school for a year. I already knew how to read and write in Spanish. This was because our mother spent

When you are out alone with the sheep for so long you learn how to be solitary. Then you don't mind it so much anymore.

the last three years before she married at eighteen in a convent school and she had taught us. But she died when I was thirteen years old. It was my father's idea that I get an education. I stayed with a paternal aunt, who offered to feed and clothe me while I was there. The money we'd saved only lasted a year and I had to return to herding. But I liked school and I continued to read and study as much as I could. I always liked history, particularly the history of the United States. But I studied other things as well. It was my father who influenced me to become a Democrat, which I have been all my life. When I registered to vote the first time the party was weak, but I saw the day when it developed into the strongest party. My father said, "See, I told you so!"

One of the noticeable differences between those early years of my life and today is the elders' control over the young. I was under my father's direct supervision until I was a grown man and declared my independence in order to start my own ranch. I wanted to get married. I had met the girl, a neighbor's daughter, who was to become my wife. Of course, it was my father who arranged the actual marriage, but I very much wanted to marry her. Nowadays people are free before they know what to do with their freedom. It's not good. Mind you, I didn't necessarily *like* being under the rule of my father, but that is the way it was and we accepted it. We were much more respectful of the old than people are today. But there are advantages for us today: My father died at eighty-nine years of age and never received a penny of assistance from anyone —social security or welfare or church services. Today we get help from the government. With my daughter working and her house all paid for we manage pretty well. This even though my son-in-law is ill and cannot work. My daughter is a school teacher and my grandson is also. Besides, he is an organizer for the Mexican American movement here in the Southwest.

But I want to tell you about our marriage. After the feast we moved right onto our land, though there was no house as yet. The foundations were in and we stretched a tent across them. First, we had to dig a well and then together we built our house. It was an adobe house. We were very happy. Just when we had built up a good life for ourselves and our children had been born, my wife died. I've never married again. Oh, I tried at first to marry my wife's sister, but she refused. I wanted her to take care of the children. I don't understand why she wouldn't marry me. After all, I asked her as much for her sake as mine. But I never loved anyone else except my wife. Oh, there was once a pretty, rich widow with a child, but she did not want to take care of my children.

My youngest daughter was two when her mother died, and she went to stay with her grandmother until the grandmother, in turn, died, when my daughter was six. Since I couldn't keep the ranch and take care of the children, I sold my sheep and moved to Pueblo, Colorado to work in the steel mills there.

I earned very little money in those days: four dollars a day. Sometimes we worked seven days, sometimes six. The nightshift worked seven days a week. It was a straight hourly wage with no overtime. I didn't have money enough to hire a housekeeper, so I had to put the children in a convent school. Once a month, on Sunday, I used to take them out for walks in the parks of Pueblo. It was a convent rule that I could only see them that often.

There were many nationalities working in the steel mills. I worked as an assistant on one of the big cranes and enjoyed the work until the Depression came; then they started cutting back the number of hours a day we could work. They never laid me off entirely, but you couldn't make a living on just a few hours of work. Besides, I was disappointed; for a long time they had promised me a better job but they never promoted me. I worked hard. But I never missed the sheep; that had been such hard work that once I left it, I forgot it.

I decided I'd be better off back in New Mexico, and I thought I'd like to try my hand at farming. I no longer wanted to raise sheep and had become interested in planting. We settled down here in Mora. This very land we're living on now belonged to the widow woman who had married my grandfather. She made an agreement with me that I could farm the ranch and share the produce from it with her. It was not a set agreement, but only that I would give her what I thought was fair, depending on that year's harvest.

After a number of years of farming I decided to raise some cattle as well. It was around that time I met a man called Dan Cassidy. He was an experienced cattle rancher, but at the time he was raising sheep, though he knew little about the art of sheepherding. We decided we might as well make a swap. For five years he would take on my herd of cattle and I his sheep. In five years time we would both have doubled the number of head to be returned to the original owners. It was a good agreement. I started with one hundred of his sheep and gave him back two hundred; my twenty cows became a herd of forty. But when the time was up I decided to sell most of my cattle, except for very few we kept for our milk. Those cows you see over there in my uncle's field are part of that original herd.

After the five years were over, I didn't want to go back to farming. Besides, my daughter and her husband were buying this land from the widow woman. I was sixty-five by then and it seemed a good time to retire. I was glad not to have to work any longer. I went on welfare. Started with twenty-eight dollars a month, but it's gone up over the years; now it's ninety dollars a month.

I decided to move to Mora from the farm, because one Sunday when I was walking the three miles to Mass a man picked me up and asked me why I was walking such a distance. I answered, "No transport." He was the welfare case worker and he suggested I move to the center of town. He said they'd pay my rent and enough extra for heat and light. So I thought, why not? I rented the little house I lived in for over twenty years until I couldn't manage so well anymore because of my weak legs.

I still go to Mass every Sunday but by car now. My daughter drives me. You ask whether I am a Penitente and the answer is yes; I've been a Penitente all my life, but now it is changed. During the forty days of Lent I used to walk the three miles to Mora to go to Mass and the three miles back. I guess I've always been healthy, and maybe that's why I've lived so long.

How do I feel at ninety-one? Well, you can see for yourself. My legs are weak; they give on me. I try to ride my Exercycle every day to strengthen my legs. I have a gauge on it which tells me how many miles I've done. I've gone nine hundred miles in four months. The hearing aid doesn't help my hearing. I don't even wear it. I can't hear.

I left my house in Mora pretty much on the insistence of my daughters, who felt I should no longer be alone. If I had good legs I could still manage, and I could come and go as I please and wouldn't be dependent on anyone. I would prefer that. Now my daughters prepare my meals and take care of me. I can't do much and there isn't much I like to do anymore. I watch wrestling on TV, and if I get a ride into town I go to the post office or the store and to Mass. Sometimes I read a magazine. Every once in a while I get on a bus and go to Las Vegas to see my grandchildren. D'you know, I have forty-two great grandchildren. I had twelve grandchildren but two died.

I wasn't getting to know the great grandchildren as well as I would like to, so I started a system to get them to visit me. I opened savings accounts with five dollars in them for each child, and I told them I would match what they put in. Each year I have a party for all the children. I have been doing this for about fifteen years, and I've taught them how to save money.

My main worry now is not having enough money to take care of myself. I will soon receive one hundred forty dollars from social security instead of the ninety dollars I used to get from welfare, and if I am careful with my money I can just manage.

In the days when the land here was still open, anyone could enter it and *domicilio,* that is, homestead. They'd settle on the best land, near available water, but the rest was left for us to graze our sheep. Gradually the farmers settled on more and more of the open land. By the time I left there was still enough grazing land, but problems between the sheepherders and the cattlemen were beginning. They carried arms, and a number of the conflicts ended in violence. There was law enforcement and the courts but that was too slow, and arguments were often settled with a gun.

Once, near the land where I was raised, there was a big cattle company. One winter there was a particularly severe snowstorm. The cattle were huddled together, and in their panic to seek forage and shelter they stampeded, and a great majority of them suffocated or froze to death. That storm broke the company and they had to move out, leaving the rangeland free once again.

Shortly thereafter my father's stepfather brought five thousand sheep down from Colorado. Everything went well because he could find grazing for his sheep. As a matter of fact, the grass grew almost two feet high that year because there was so much rain. They could cut it and store it for winter. But prairie fires were always a danger there. In one of the worst fires, which swept across large tracts of land, my father's stepfather lost all his sheep, and so he, too, went broke.

The luck shifted one way and then the other. My life was like that, too. First, to have such a good woman and then to lose her. There were a number of widows who wanted to marry me, and my daughters urged me, but when you are out alone with the sheep for so long you learn how to be solitary. Then you don't mind it so much anymore.

I mostly stayed on my own path of painting . . . because that is the thing I feel I was supposed to do in life.

Dorothy Brett

Taos, New Mexico

Born 1882

I had heard of Dorothy Brett, an English painter and close friend of D.H. Lawrence, ever since, at the age of eight, I had spent a memorable summer in Taos, invited by Mabel Dodge Luhan, who had made "Tony's House" available to my father, William Scott Pyle, a painter. In '75 I was given an introduction to Dorothy Brett by her friend Enid Hilton, whom I had just interviewed in California.

I stopped at the Taos bookstore to inquire. There it was suggested that I contact John Manchester first, as Dorothy's health at ninety-one had its ups and downs and he was her close friend, next-door neighbor, and also the guardian of her gates. He agreed to speak to Dorothy for me. In his house, where I stopped to introduce myself, I was able to absorb the powerful and mystical mood of her canvases that were hanging on most of the walls. I spent a delightful hour with her that first day and came by again, while she was having lunch the next day. She was, at ninety-one, a fascinating and still extraordinarily vibrant and charismatic woman with that English upperclass felicity of language. But also, she had the directness and power that was learned, I imagine, from living so long alone in this ancient, wide American Indian land of desert and mountain, arroyas and cottonwood trees; this land that she had recaptured in brilliant color, with power and insight in her painting.

Since her death I have reread her book, Lawrence and Brett, a Friendship,* *and John Manchester's enlightening introduction and epilogue, which give the book a fascinating new dimension in its own right as a study of Brett but also as an important addendum to a further understanding of Lawrence. Manchester writes in his introduction that Brett "was a soul image to Lawrence, a counterpart to his own inner feminine side. . . . Frieda (Lawrence's wife) . . . might very well be a projection of an archetypal*

*First published 1933 by J.B. Lippincott & Co.; reissued 1974 by Sunstone Press, Santa Fe, New Mexico.

mother image, either good or devouring, but it was Brett whom Lawrence chose as a soul image." She was the subject of a number of Lawrence's stories: The Princess, The Last Laugh, *and* Glad Ghosts. *The character of Jenny in Aldous Huxley's* Crome Yellow *was also modeled after Brett.**

I WAS BORN in London in 1882 of a rather distinguished family. My father was the Second Viscount Esher. He was a free lance—he headed an office which looked after all the old parks and houses in England. He helped arrange the coronation of Edward the Seventh around the time when my sister and I were presented at court, and then he retired and wrote. He was a very charming man; he could charm the birdies off the trees, I can tell you. We had a house in London and another about five miles from Windsor. I have two brothers and one sister, Sylvia, who later married an Indian raja to become the Ranee of Sarawak. She wrote a book about it called *Queen of the Headhunters.* Naturally, she spent a good deal of her time there in India. One brother was in the army and the other was "in the city." He was supposed to be a businessman but he didn't like working.

I grew up during the latter part of Queen Victoria's reign; the queen was a marvelous woman. I used to go to dancing classes at Windsor Castle that had been arranged for her grandchildren. Her youngest daughter had married Prince Henry of Battenberg, and the children and she had a famous dancing teacher to the castle once a week to teach them. The local children—gentry, that is—were asked to attend as well. The old queen would sit on the sofa quite benignly, dressed in the little white cap she wore, but everyone was always frightened of her. She wanted to be nice, but because she was a queen everyone was terrified.

I didn't go to school; I was educated by governesses and by my father. My father had traveled so much as a boy he wouldn't travel with us, but he talked about his own travels often and he sent us off on educational trips. My father's father was a judge: Lord Chief Justice of the Court of Appeals. My mother was a hausfrau.

When I was a child our family used to go to Scotland always in the fall. I fished a great deal and I painted. We had a very, very nice house painted pink near a certain part of the moors where I went fishing and the boys went shooting.

It was a British general who got me into the Slade School—The Royal College of Art (still the most prestigious and established art school in England). He was a neighbor of ours in Scotland, and he asked to see some of my drawings. When I showed them to him he was impressed and said, "You promise you'll go to the Slade School when you go back to England." I asked, "What about the family?" He answered, "I'll handle the family," and he

*Introduction by John Manchester to Dorothy Brett's book, *Lawrence and Brett, a Friendship* (Santa Fe, N.M.: Sunstone Press, 1974).

wangled it. That fall I went to the Slade School. But what was interesting was that I had great trouble getting in. They said they didn't like girls from my social background. They wanted only people who were going to earn a living. The school was for prospective teachers, but I got in and I stayed for four years. My style has not changed, just the subject matter.

My parents did not take kindly to my entering the Slade. It was an entirely new world for me, the people I met there. I was there six years, and then my father got me a charming studio in London. I was in that for quite a while, but most of my friends lived in Hampstead, and as this was about an hour away they all begged me to move there. So I got a little house in Hampstead, which disappointed my father, but I said, "That's that."

I had many friends and we had a very gay time—parties, charades, a salon where all the artists and painters would meet—people like Katherine Mansfield, Mark Gertler, John Middleton Murry. It wasn't until later, when I became friends with Ottoline (Lady Ottoline Morrell), that I met Aldous Huxley and Leonard and Virginia Woolf.

My parents wouldn't accept my new social life. If they had joined in and met these people it would have been a lot better. My art life was tiresome to them, but I had to pursue it come what may. So it was perhaps a wise thing not to burden them with me. I think that grown-up children are an interference to parents, and they should go off on their own.

I don't feel I grew away from any of the family at that time, but perhaps they felt it to be so. All we did was just have a lot of fun, though sometimes there were a few awkward moments. But I didn't have many "excursions." I mostly stayed on my own path of painting, because after all, that's what I wanted to do and that's what I have done with my life and that's what I am going to do until I drop, as they say. Because that is the thing I feel I was supposed to do in life, and there it is, as simple as that.

I first met Lawrence when I was thirty-two. The second time I saw him he had been in Australia, then he came over to London. I had a tiny house in Hampstead at the time where I had "Thursdays," you know, a sort of salon. Mark Gertler, who was a painter friend, brought Lawrence around to see me. He and Frieda came together to one of my Thursdays. (I had just about six or seven people come each time. It was very exclusive; no one could come who wasn't invited. The evenings were always very nice and very gay.) That's how Lawrence and I first started in London. Then the three of us came over to America together.

I didn't know what I was coming to when I came over here. I didn't know anything. Lawrence had wanted a whole group of people to come over, Gertler and Koteliansky, but they all backed out except me. And I've stayed ever since. Of course, I have been back to London, but I felt just like a ghost in my old world. I loved the freedom from any inhibitions and social problems which pertains here. In London, you see, I had left the social world, thank God, and went into the art world. Though I was, of course, almost ostracized by the social world, it did not bother me a bit. Later, as my paintings began to sell and I was accepted as an artist, attitudes toward me changed.

I have lived here in Taos since, I think, 1924. This house, which I built, went up quite quickly but not until I had lived up on the ranch for more than ten years. You know, you get the Indians and they get busy on building. They get the trees from the hills there. Up at the ranch we'd cut the trees for a building ourselves; Lawrence loved that sort of work. The thing was to get the money, because you knew that money was so hard to get hold of. But I managed. It cost seven thousand dollars. Could you imagine building a house for that now? We made the adobes ourselves. They were fourteen by seven by four. You can buy them, of course, but it is much cheaper to make them. You have to use old dried-out straw. Everything was transported with horses in those days and the road to Santa Fe was sand and washed out constantly when it rained.

I settled here because of Lawrence and then became a friend of Mabel—Mabel Dodge Luhan—the writer and heiress who had moved to Taos, bringing many painters and writers with her, and who then married the Indian Tony Luhan, scandalizing her family and displeasing the Pueblo elders. Anyone who comes here to talk to me always wants to know the salacious details of my relationship with Lawrence, but I tell them they can read about it in my book. I don't feel like talking about it over and over again.

If Mabel hadn't been such a boon and a blessing here they (the Pueblo I mean) wouldn't have allowed her marriage. But she helped so much. She was so generous. You have to understand that the Indians had been abused so terribly. You don't just walk into a person's country and take it. As you know, England did so much of that in the past. But exploitation is diminishing all over the world. You can no longer walk into another's country so easily and just sit down and say, "Alright, now it's mine." There's much greater awareness of the rights of the native population. Mabel understood the power and dignity of the Indian.

There was a lot of feeling against Mabel in the town at first. They felt she was high-handed, but they've come around. Mabel gave them the hospital and, can you believe it, the town refused it. So what did she do? She knew an order of nuns and gave it to them. They ran it for a long time until they sold it to the people who have it now. Do you know, people died on their way to Santa Fe on that road. They died before they got to the hospital. The hospital here was a boon and a blessing and a necessity. Then there was the problem of getting the Spanish people in; they were scared of Anglo medicine. Finally, an old Spanish man was hospitalized and came out alive, and that started the others going. Now everybody goes. It is accepted and it saves many lives.

I think Tony and Mabel had a real love affair at the beginning and at the end, too. Sometimes she got feeling frustrated. Tony couldn't read and write, and she felt strangled. Then she couldn't get out when she made up her mind to go. But the whole thing readjusted and finally was alright. The Pueblo had been horrified at first, but when Tony went to speak to them he managed to charm them all.

I met Leopold Stokowski here when Mabel lured him down to Taos and invited me to a luncheon party to meet him. We kind of clicked, you know. And then that fall I went up to New York and to Philadelphia to hear the concerts. I had only heard them on the radio. So I went up to Philadelphia and I stayed with an old friend. I went to all his concerts, which turned out to be very interesting. After the first one he invited me to go to tea. So I went to see him, clambering up the steep stairs to his nice little apartment, and there I found him with his secretaries. We had tea and he asked me what I thought of the concert. I said, "I thought the music was absolutely beautiful, and your top coat was immaculate" (it came from London), but I added, "One thing was ugly, very ugly, that I really didn't like and that was the chairs! When you all got up to go away for the recess you left a stage full of hideous, cheap wooden chairs, with thick legs." It had never struck him. I said, "There was the beautiful harp, the cellos, and double bass, lovely instruments, leaning against hideous chairs." The next time the curtain went up the audience applauded the lovely gilt chairs. I mean very nice gilt chairs with well-made legs—something you could look at and not feel sick about. The audience had suffered but did not know what to do. I did it and did it properly.

I am always painting; I have never given it up for a minute. Some mornings, like this morning, I didn't paint because I didn't feel too good and I never touch painting if I am not feeling right, because you make a mess of it. Since I try to paint every morning I feel that in the afternoons I can do what I like. I go downtown. In the old days I used to ride or fish, but now I don't think I could get on my horse without a chair. The whole thing is a little bit beyond me now, don't you think? In the past I had a darling horse named Prince. But now everything has been spoiled here by too many cars. It is not the same. This landscape matters to me very much because I painted it and the Indian life I found here.

Did you ever read a writer called W.H. Hudson? I have always felt that if you feel a hesitancy about going to see someone, just overcome it. That's happened to me often in my life. I had a very interesting friendship develop out of overcoming just such a fear. I sought out Hudson and he became a friend of mine. He was a very shy man, tall and very handsome, but in the end a dreadful thing happened: I had made some drawings and paintings of him which I had put into storage in England when I moved over here. My second brother, in a moment of complete idiocy, was asked by the firm that was holding them for me if they could burn them. Since I hadn't bothered with them for many years, he said Yes without consulting me or considering the work in question. They burned up everything I possessed; it was irreplaceable. My brother was terribly upset when he realized what he had done, but it was too late; everything was gone.

Now my neighbor and great friend, John Manchester, looks after my paintings. He has most of them at his gallery in Taos. In fact, he has become the guardian at my gates. Do you know that one of my portraits, the one of Lawrence, is in the National Portrait Gallery in London? Some of the others are in museums over here. John's an extremely nice person, very intelligent and well read, though somewhat of a recluse, I suppose, because he is such a shy man. He has helped me a great deal with the second printing of my book.

I have made no plans for the future. I will wait and see what happens. You can make lots of plans and what happens? It all goes in another direction anyway, so there you are! And you go with it and that's that. For instance, my coming here to Taos for six months and I have been here ever since. So what's the good? It's just daydreaming to make plans; anybody can daydream. The only thing is I don't want anything unpleasant to happen that can be avoided. Besides John, who is always nearby, I have this excellent woman who has been kind enough to stay and look after me. She also drives me to town. And then there is my darling Danke Schön [her beloved dachshund, who at mention of its name, jumped right into her lap].

Anyhow, I think things will be controlled from above. I am sure a higher power takes care of our lives. I even think there are probably other mortal beings in the universe. I developed these beliefs from reading and from meeting people like Gurdjieff and Jung. You know, you can't live in this Indian country without becoming aware of spirit powers.

I was always interested in spiritual ideas. When I was still in London there was a great Gurdjieffian thing going on in Paris and Katherine Mansfield and I went over. When I first entered the hall, Gurdjieff was sitting there and I was introduced to him, but he never got up to greet us, so I didn't say a word, just stood there. I thought, "Hang it all!" But finally he did rouse himself and we shook hands and talked. Then I started going to the lectures, which were certainly very, very interesting. He called on what were then known as the "performers," who came on to the stage and were told to hold a very painful pose until he told them to relax. The purpose of that was discipline. I followed in every way I could, books and exercises and things. I was always fascinated by it. But I think the trouble is that, like everything, it gets into a certain groove of habit. You learn to sit in a certain posture that may be painful, but somehow you don't get what you want from it. You torment yourself by taking aching positions that don't get you anywhere at all.

I have been interested in Buddhism a good part of my life, but that was strongest while I was in London. When I came here I became more fascinated with American Indian concepts of the gods. I believe in all religions; they just have a different way of putting it, that's all. The object is just the same. I no longer go to meetings because it's a waste of time anyway since I can't hear.

I used to have a magnificent ear trumpet, but it was a nuisance having to hold it up. It was made of tin and was a wonderful thing. Nowadays my telephone is amplified, so I can hear perfectly. I keep in touch with my friends all over the country. John even suggests that my life-long deafness might have helped cause some inner shyness, which helped in the end to keep Lawrence and me apart. But we loved each other, you know. I am very lucky still at ninety-one and have been all my life. I just get into bed and am asleep in half a tick. I wake up very early, when the sun comes up. I hate curtains. When I got into a hotel room I would always take the curtains down and put them under the bed—couldn't bear them. With them up you couldn't see the sky, the stars, the moon, anything. I hate a dark room. Maybe this goes back to my childhood. When I was small my brothers would deliberately frighten me at night. Then some of the servants thought it was funny and did the same thing. I never sleep in a dark room. You know, actually, the night is never dark unless it is stormy with heavy clouds. When I lived up on the ranch where Frieda and Lawrence lived, I slept out on the porch, so I am used to sleeping in daylight. The daylight doesn't wake me up; only the sun does when it comes on my face. I was at the ranch for ten years, a good part of it alone, before I built this house, and now you see I still sleep out on this glass-enclosed porch so I can see the stars.

I am really very well except for my knee, which I banged on the gate some months ago, although I don't fuss about it. If I don't wake up one morning, it really doesn't matter.

I am the oldest deputy at the National Assembly. But why should that be particularly noteworthy? Why the oldest? I could be the heaviest, the lightest, the tallest.

Virgile Barel

Nice, France

Born 1890

Virgile Barel was eighty-three when I interviewed him in 1973; today, at eighty-eight, he is still serving as a member of the French National Assembly from the Alpes-Maritime District. He is the author of Fifty Years of Fight, *is also a long-standing member of the Communist party.*

My translator and friend, Jacqueline Meppiel (who knew Barel and had introduced us), and I climbed the stone stairs of the solid old middle-class apartment house in Nice where Barel and his wife live and work. They received us in his study. Barel, a rather short, intense Frenchman, charming and dynamic, welcomed us warmly. His wife, unusually young looking, was an attractive woman in her early eighties.

The walls of the study were lined with books, interspersed by paintings and lithographs done by friends of the Barels who were incidentally also the masters of modern French painting: several Picassos, some Legers, and, I believe, a Matisse. Large plants filled the spaces behind chairs and the couch. A door stood open to the library annex, which contained, besides books, a beautifully organized file system of all the pertinent party and government reports, statistics, bills. A young assistant was doing research while the interview was being conducted. Madame Barel was working in the annex part of the time but joined us for some of the conversation.

Barel had no interest in supplying us with a personal life history. His energy was so clearly focused on his work, on politics, on the present problems and the future of France, and on world issues that it didn't seem right to try to deflect him with questions of a personal nature.

I AM THE oldest deputy at the National Assembly. But why should that be particularly noteworthy? Why the oldest? I could be the heaviest, the lightest, the tallest. People are always surprised. They say to me, "How can you be so alert at your age?" I tell you, I premeditated my old age most carefully. I led a wise life, never smoked, only drank a little wine, got as much sleep as possible, and I never ate too much. It is an example of personal hygiene governed by good instincts.

The main preoccupation of my life and the problem that still weighs most heavily on my mind is the death of my son Max, who was tortured and killed in 1944 by the Nazis. He was to follow in my footsteps. His convictions were very close to my own. There you see his portrait by Picasso, a close friend of mine. Presently I am concerned with the Klaus-Barbie trial and am waiting to hear the decision of the Supreme Court in Bolivia. [Barbie has since been acquitted.] It is close to my heart. I think the parallel of the two lives, my son's and Barbie's, is obvious.

In spite of my age and of the fact that people often think that at this stage one has lost one's intellectual curiosity, I am assaulted by a need for action. My intellectual curiosity has, in fact, increased. Ideas come to me at every moment. At this point in time the main subject of interest to me is the Third Age, as we call it in France. I have just made a report to the National Assembly entitled "Third Age and Leisure."

However, the optimal organization of the Third Life is still to me a matter for study and inquiry. Certain points seem clear, though. (In considering what I am about to say, you must remember that we are living in a capitalist regime and that I am a Communist.) Point one is that society should be organized in such a way that no man or woman has to reach retirement in a state of exhaustion. That is, no more slavery to the machine, no more debilitating working and living conditions or poor transportation. Life should be organized in such a way that work is bearable, and when one gets to retirement age (sixty to sixty-five seems right for men and fifty-five for women at the present time), when active and directly productive life comes to an end, one should not have to worry about material security. The end of life should really be the Golden Age.

The prospect of retirement should be a joy not a fear. Therefore, it is society's duty to be responsible toward old people (and I mean this not in the sense of charity).

A second point would be that there must be no break in the rhythm between the working years and retirement. The retired worker should be able to maintain a social occupation. In the USSR retired workers return to their factories just to keep in touch. A solution must be found for this without increasing unemployment amongst the younger workers. One must not forget that aged people can make valuable contributions to society. I am often told: "But you are a Communist, you are for retirement at age sixty, and yet here you are, still working at eighty-three!" There are many like me.

There are so many ways of handling retirement. One can stay with one's family but that is sometimes difficult. It can bring reciprocal restraint. One can live alone or as a couple, but to do this successfully one must be financially secure. Or one can go to a retirement home. Lots of old people have money enough to do so, but retirement homes have become sources for speculators.

These homes are often "luxury homes," where a lot of money is required from old people as a condition for entrance. In a sense, old people have become the "raw material" for speculation. Very few retirement homes are accessible to the masses. Finally, there are Third Age villages, where people can buy their own small bungalow. One such village exists at Serre [Alpes-Maritimes], but people there complain about being isolated.

I think the main problem lies with those who wish to live on their own or as an isolated couple. For such people it is important to have places where they can meet, to have collective activities. But how? That's a problem.

As for myself, I am in good health, and that's a basic condition to enjoying the Third Age. I am a living example of what I would like for others; my Third Age is the continuation of my active life. I look forward to death with serenity. My only wish is to keep all my faculties and never to become a debilitated, gouty, and valetudinarian old man. But to wish is not good dialectical materialism. Let us say that I try my best to remain useful to the collectivity. I keep on fighting for the working class.

How can a workingman reach that sense of plenitude in his old age, that same sense of fulfillment which you often find in the third age of intellectuals? Only through carrying on with some meaningful activity, not necessarily the same activity one performed throughout the working years.

In conclusion, I think that the development of society, the march of progress, the increase in class consciousness, the improvement in the living conditions of people, the progress of medicine—these make the finding of a solution to the problem of aging imperative. But capitalist regimes try to solve that problem to their own advantage and at the expense of the working classes. I would just like to point out to you by way of example the incomes of old people living on social security in your country. It should be a duty for a capitalist, as well as any other regime, to provide a happy Third Age to all those who produced its wealth. I am convinced only mass action from the party and the unions, for example, can force a regime into doing so.

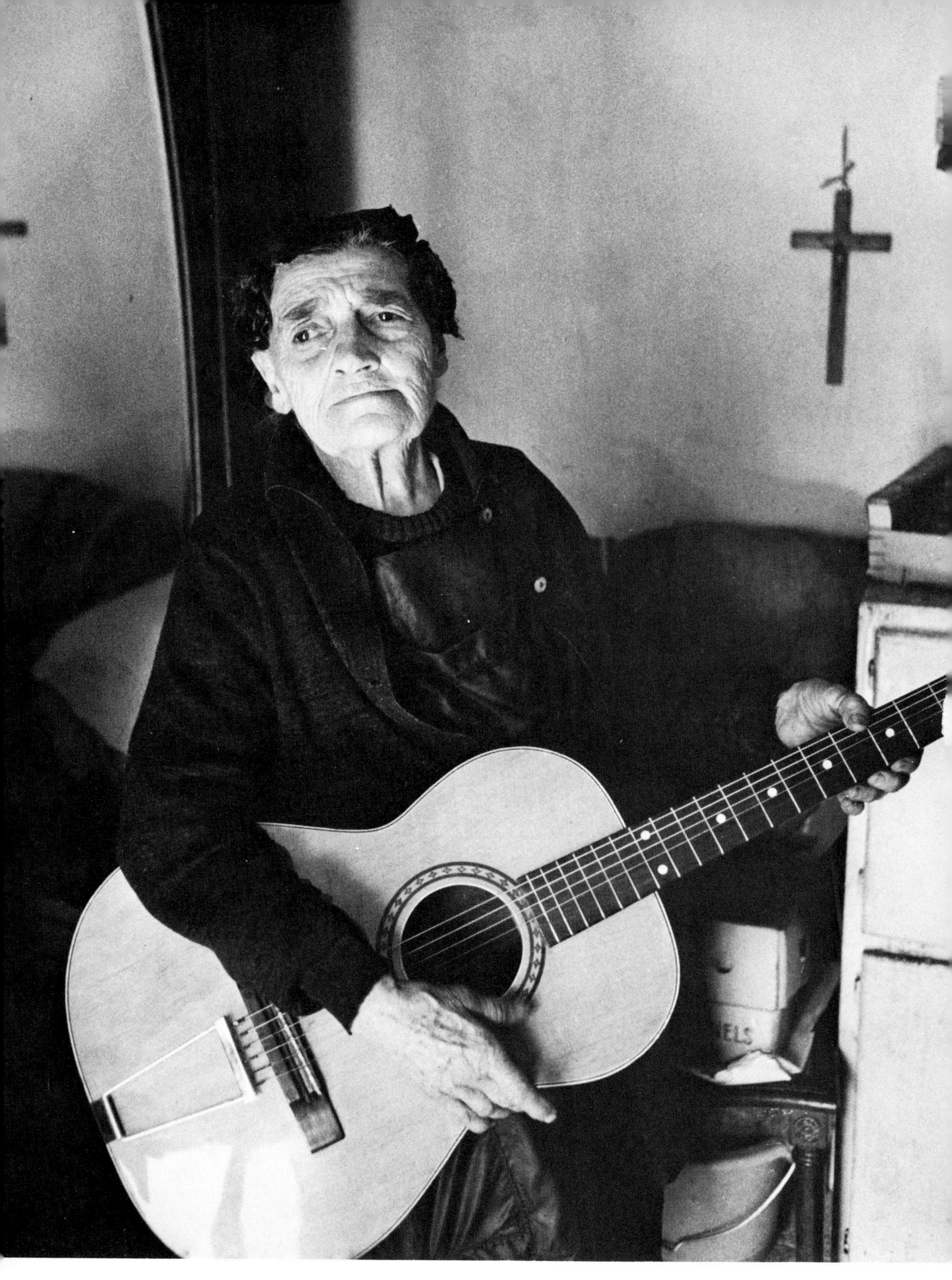

My guitar teacher must love me, because otherwise he wouldn't come every week. Not up six flights!

Marie Rose Scudelari

Nice, France

Born 1890

After a year spent in Israel I returned via ferry to Marseille. Here Jacqueline Meppiel met us. She was to act as translator and had arranged a number of interviews for me.

Marie Rose Scudelari, a lemon vendor in the Nice Market, was the first. We found her at her stand and followed her through back alleys to her door, then climbed up the six flights of marble stairs to her small flat. She seated herself by the window, one hand draped over the guitar that lay on the round table by the window. An extraordinary view stretched out behind her: In the close foreground rose the elegant golden dome of a baroque church, behind it a pattern of sunlit walls broken by deep slashes of shadow. The variegated angles of red-tiled rooftops were punctuated here and there by a stately black cypress or a stretch of green shrubbery. It was truly a "room with a view." "I'll die here," were Marie Rose's opening words.

Marie Rose was a rather wrinkled old woman who was troubled by two horn-like growths the size of Ping-Pong balls on the back of her head, which she camouflaged with two little black velvet bows. Her eyes were bright and flashing, and despite her infirmities she took obvious trouble with her appearance. A charming pink cameo closed the neck opening of her neat, old-fashioned black calico dress. She wore the characteristic black boots of the French vendeuse *of an older generation.*

BOTH MY PARENTS were Italians, born in Spezia. They moved to France when I was two years old. I was one of six children and have sold lemons at the open market in Nice since I was twelve years old. My sister is a *vendeuse* as well. She is also still alive. The nuns in a neighboring convent used to feed us when we were little because we were so poor, but an education they *didn't* give us. I am totally self-educated; I taught myself to read and write. I'm a poet. I still write, especially the lyrics for my songs.

She led us through the clutter of shallow old wooden lemon crates, which were piled in all corners of the small flat—even on the daybed in the second room, to a tiny balcony. The French doors were flung wide.

You see, I can look down on our padre and the children in the schoolyard. Of course, he can't be bothered with such poor people as me. When I'm sick he leaves me alone. Nobody comes—not even my sister; her legs won't take the stairs. Just my cats, *eh mes chéries?*

Three cats had been alternately rubbing themselves against our legs and stalking with disdainful air across the kitchen sinktop or now and then reminding us of their presence by tipping and upsetting the precarious balance of the stacked citrus boxes.

Une belle vue, n'est-ce pas? That is why I chose it. I always have to look at something beautiful. It feeds my soul. You see, I am an "artist."

[Marie Rose brought me back to the big round table and picked up her guitar.] I played for Monte Carlo television. They did a whole hour interview with me playing and singing my own songs. They liked me very much. Tomorrow I have to go back there to be paid for the performance. After that, people started coming to the lemon stand just to hear me sing. One woman even gave me six thousand old francs for a gift just because she liked my singing. In one of my songs I say,

Au soir de vie
Mon coeur reste jeune.

It's true; I feel no older. But I have to learn to play the guitar properly. I used to play the banjo, but then I exchanged it for the guitar. Now I wish I'd never given away my banjo. I played it very well—better than the guitar.

Marie Rose sang in a romantic turn-of-the-century manner with accompanying gestures, a little artificial rose held to her heart and her eyes cast dramatically upward. Her voice sounded somewhat wavery and hoarse, but her delivery was superb. She sang with the absolute conviction of an artist, while energetically strumming her chords—almost any chords—which often had little or no relationship to the melody.

I have always sung. I was a chanteuse but never in cheap cafés. I have too much self-respect to be a demimondaine, though I always had lovers. I used to go dancing every night till two or three o'clock with a man who was a hustler. But he was a marvellous dancer. We were good friends, but one day he tried to kiss me. I slapped his face! He was alright for dancing but not for kissing. I never got married, because in marriage you have to stay with the same man. I'm always in love. Always. It's my forty-year-old guitar teacher I love now. He is very handsome. Every Tuesday he comes to give me a lesson. He sits next to me on the couch, puts his arm around my shoulder or on my knee—we kiss—but that's all. I've suffered very much by love, by men, that is why I sing and write songs.

[She pulled out a dog-eared notebook and began to read:]

Mon coeur reste jeune, ma foi
Aimes toujours comme autrefois
Si je souffre, je sais pourquoi.
De chanter ne m'appraise pas
Les idées changent tant fois
Si je souffre, je sais pourquoi.

My guitar teacher must love me, because otherwise he wouldn't come every week. Not up six flights! The other day a fifty-year-old man came to see me at the market. He said, "Get rid of that other man, the guitar player," and I said, "What are we going to do together?" He said, "Eat and drink together." I answered, "For that I don't need a man."

Le coeur est jeune! C'est drôle ça, eh? My last serious amour was when I was forty-five, but I've had others, less important, since then. The guitar player tried to make love to me, but I was afraid. *"Le peur qui me refrain."* I've always been afraid of the maladies. But I've always been healthy. Only once I had to go to the hospital for five days with the flu. It was during a bad cold spell one winter recently. I got sick selling lemons in the open market, always outside in that awful numbing cold. I have medicine for bronchitis, and usually I manage to look after myself. If I ever do get sick, everyone is too busy with his or her own concerns to come up here to look after me. All my life I have had lovers but no friends.

Each day I go straight to market and straight home again. I never eat meat and don't drink much wine. The fish, alas, is no good anymore. The sea is too polluted! The good fish now is available only to the rich. The second-class stuff they can keep! I eat pasta, eggs, cheese, and, of course, lemons. [She stuffed two lemons into her bra and offered us each two.] That's what I always did when I was young. I had no breasts, but with the lemons I was so proud of my chest!

She was rummaging through a shoe carton full of old photographs of herself. As I spied a lovely standing nude, she deftly managed to shuffle it under and pulled out a more "respectable" one, a really lovely romantic portrait. There were innumerable others in many different poses and costumes. She must have been a photographer's model, I thought.

I was my father's favorite. I loved him very much. He always called me Bella Rosita because I was so pretty. It made my mother furious with jealousy. He was a good man but poor. He couldn't support us six little ones on the meager salary of a water company worker. At first, when I was very young, fourteen or so, I didn't like sex, but then I grew to like it. I was in love with an eighteen-year-old boy, and one beautiful day we went on a picnic, two boys and two girls. While the two boys were sleeping off the lunch I went to meet my other lover. He was the son of the mayor of Nice, forty-four years old, and a real gentleman. He had told me to meet him at a fine hotel on the Boulevard des Anglaises. He was very rich. It was he who took all those photographs. He was a fine photographer but, of course, only an amateur. My other friend, when he discovered that I was gone, became jealous and came chasing after me. One day he saw me talking to the mayor's son and slapped me on the face in a jealous rage. For two days he waited outside the hotel in which we were staying, and I was afraid he would shoot me. But my friend spoke to the manager, and I was able to escape through the back entrance.

My friend was a man of the world. He bought me jewels and clothes and set me up in a villa. He was a very handsome, fine man. I wasn't faithful to him though; I couldn't be. It ended one day after two years because I couldn't stay with one man. *C'est les chats. Ils sont amoreux.* I'm an artist and that is the way we are! As far as love is concerned, I'm terrible, ooh la la. "They" used to give me jewels, but I never made any money off "them." And no one thereafter supported me. I still like to sell lemons; you get a chance to talk to lots of people. My customers cheat me, but I don't care.

I get a pension of two hundred dollars every three months. I don't go to the cinema and I eat at home, so I don't need much. I own my own home. In fact, I bought an extra room across the hall and gave it to my sister, but she doesn't like the long climb, so she rents it out. That way I'm not bothered having to pay taxes on the earnings.

When I was young I took singing lessons. Then fifteen years ago I learned to play the banjo. But really I am a poet. Last year I even cut a record in Monte Carlo. I am not a sad type. *Je suis très gai!* I make everyone laugh. I like being alone. If I had a bigger apartment I'd only have more work. Now my loves are my work and my guitar.

I have called one of my cats after an Italian bicycle champion and the other, a girl cat, Cinderella. I've already spent two hundred francs on the cats just to feed them. But I had to get them to keep away the rats climbing up the drainpipes. Everyone I know is dead. Only my sister is still alive. Though I do have two little grandnephews, but I hardly ever see them because they live in Paris.

I go to church every week; I'm a very good Catholic! In fact, through prayer I can cure people. Tonight I'll go to Mass. I'm spiritual, and material things count nothing for me. I believe that only the soul and the heart are important. Only God interests me. I have a great faculty to love, but I don't think people are worth it, so I give my love to God. Ah, but you've given your love to many men, you'll say! Yes, you're right, but now I know they're not worth it. God is the only person, the only presence. I love what is beautiful; that's why I love this view and my little rooms. You know, I'm as old as from the day I was born until today. It is all a continuation. But the years really don't count. [She repeated her prayer.]

Ah Seigneur, je suis votre Poète
Faut-il que pour vous aimez
Je le répéte?
Le temps est trop court, il
Me faut l'éternité.

Zvi Ariel

Kibbutz Givat Brenner, Israel

Born 1906

Kibbutz Givat Brenner, founded in 1928 near Tel Aviv, had a membership of around 1,800 when I visited there in 1973. During the three days of my stay I ate in the communal dining hall; stayed at the guesthouse; was shown the various nurseries, the school, the library, and the music rooms, the newly built wing for old people who need nursing care, the small hospital and clinic, the various machine and woodworking shops, the bottling plant, the orchards, the studios of the two resident artists (one a sculptor who had escaped to Israel during the Nazi occupation of France, the other a painter—both in their seventies or eighties). There was a craft shop for older workers (those no longer able to do the heavy agricultural or industrial labor), where matting was being woven on hand looms to be used for blinds and table mats, and also a bookbindery that employed older workers.

I was taken on these rounds by a woman, helpful and informative, who was one of the social workers responsible for the care of some of the older kibbutz members. The majority of these persons are still in their own little houses but need some nursing care or other attention, such as the regular distribution of medicines and food or simply moral support. After following her on her daily round of visits we stopped at her father's house. She had arranged for me to interview him.

Although Zvi Ariel came to Israel in 1935, he changed his name to an Israeli one only five years ago. He greeted us at the door, followed closely at the heels by his devoted German shepherd, Tessa. He was wearing comfortable sandals, and his clean white shirt was open deep at the neck, in the fashion of Israeli men. He was tanned and slim.

I AM A relative newcomer to communal life; it's only because my daughter and son-in-law were full members that I was considered for associate

Here [at the kibbutz] it is no dishonor to grow old, and one isn't alone and abandoned as is so often the case in the outside world.

membership in Givat Brenner. You know, kibbutzniks may have their parents live on the kibbutz (though not as full voting members) if there is a real human need, either economic or medical, that can be clearly established. Quite often these requests are denied because the committee feels there is some other means of support at hand: perhaps another son or daughter with financial resources and/or a large enough house.

If an application is accepted, as it was in my case, the kibbutz assigns one an apartment. I now live close to my children, I have work which I love, and I feel secure because I know my needs will be looked after by the community and my children should I become ill. And yet, I am quite independent. Like all the kibbutz members, however, I have to work for my keep. I make toys for the kindergarten and nurseries and picture frames for people's houses. Also, I repair venetian blinds and make furniture, bookcases, and so forth, on order, in the kibbutz woodworking plant.

I noticed that in Zvi's small three-room apartment one room was entirely devoted to his animals. A large tropical fish tank with interesting colored light patterns playing on it stood in one corner. In the other there was a hamster cage with two little hamsters running on their treadmill. The walls of his home were hung with examples of his decorative iron work, and handmade wooden frames displayed his pictures to advantage. Zvi's creative energies were in evidence in the entire house: he had made the stools and the bookcase, and had created indirect imaginative lighting effects and interesting lamps out of bits of scrap iron and wood salvaged from the kibbutz shops.

[He shook his head sadly.] My father died during World War One, when I was very young, only nine years old. I was the middle child in the family. German soldiers occupied Lithuania, as they did again in World War Two, and we suffered from terrible hunger, especially during the last part of the war. For four years we had to subsist on a ration of only one hundred grams of bread a day and no meat. Of course, we foraged and when possible smuggled right under the Germans' noses. One day, I remember, I was caught with two bottles of ale on me. But I never told them where I got those bottles. I kept insisting that I'd begged for them so long that someone, a total stranger, had finally broken down and given them to me. I stuck to my story with such determination that they never found out the truth, and they let me go.

As children we were forced to attend the loathed *Zwang Schule,* enforced school—I don't know how else to translate it—where we were exposed to German culture and had to learn German or else our bread rations were cut. Also, we had to gather reeds down in the marshes and bring them to school so that we could weave them into clean pallets for the soldiers' bedding.

Altogether, I attended school for seven years, then, at eleven, I had to go to work to help support the family. My mother was unemployed and my father was dead. It was war, and prices were staggeringly high. Right from the start I was lucky to find a job in the electrical works that was operated by the Vilna city government. I'd always liked mechanical and scientific things, so I had a natural aptitude for electricity. When I started, the Germans were running the plant; later it was taken over by the Lithuanians. After I was married I continued to work there until we emigrated to Israel, but I was chief electrical engineer there only during the last sixteen years of work.

I was married at nineteen. My wife and I had a nice four-bedroom apartment. Two servant girls helped with the household chores. At that time two thirds of the population was Jewish, one third Christian, but the higher posts were all held by Jews. Figuratively, I only had to snap my fingers and point in order to have my six assistants materialize and take over the actual manual work.

Besides the electrical post, I held another job—representing the Phillips Company of Holland. I also did private repair work in my off hours. Yes, my wife was well provided for. She never had to lift a finger except to look after the children.

When our boy was two and our daughter eight we decided to move to Israel. My wife had no desire to emigrate, and in some ways she proved right. We had a very hard time there at first. I had been a Zionist for many years, but what prompted our final decision to leave everything behind and go to the homeland was an experience we had on the street one day. In one of the papers I was mentioned as one of the Jews who had unjustly been awarded a most lucrative and prestigious post in the electric plant. As I was the best qualified for the position, I realized the danger signals inherent in such anti-Semitic thinking. Somehow this minor incident clinched my determination to get away. The earlier pogroms were still fresh in our memory. I proved to be only too right, but none of us could have foreseen what was to come in even our most fearful nightmares.

I handed in my resignation. The burgomaster at first refused to let me go. He threatened me and pointed out I'd have no pension and no severance pay since I was leaving by my own choice. In the end the burgomaster relented and I was given my severance pay.

We came here to Israel as only the few lucky ones have done: with some money in pocket, bringing our own furniture, and carrying excellent work certificates. Yet we had a very difficult time. We were warned by some that the agency handling new immigrants' arrivals would deposit us, like cattle for the slaughter, out on an open field next to our pathetic bundles of possessions with no roof over our heads and no job or food. We couldn't, we wouldn't believe these tales, but they turned out to be only too true.

Eventually we managed to find two rooms—you couldn't call it an apartment—in Mea Shearim, the orthodox quarter of Jerusalem: two miserable rooms in a damp, dirty old house. The rabbi who rented us these quarters, after first buttering us up with compliments about Lithuanians being the finest and the best Jews, proceeded to charge us six months' rent in advance before he would even let us examine the contract. We had to pay extra for everything: gas, electricity, even water! He required us to keep a completely kosher kitchen; no cooking on Saturdays. This meant we had to buy everything double, pots and dishes, for the meat and the dairy products, because our own things were still out on the high seas.

My wife became more and more depressed. She cried constantly for her family, the life she had left behind, her beautiful things. If we asked the rabbi for any help he refused us, even straw which we needed to make sleeping mats for ourselves. We had no choice but to sleep draped over our luggage. At least this kept us off the cold stone floor.

Then one day the ship brought our things. With tools and the letter of recommendation and certificate in hand I went immediately to the Histradrut. But the answer was monotonously the same: "No, we have nothing for you today. Come back in three days."

On the walk home I saw what seemed to be a rubbish heap, with old bedsteads and a broken-down closet in the back. I pulled out two dilapidated iron bedsteads, and we stuffed straw sacks for the mattresses. Then I managed to buy a bit of scrap lumber, with which I was able to hammer together two benches and a primitive table.

I went back to the Histradrut one more time and again elicited the same discouraging answer: "Come back in a few days." I wondered why they put us through this monstrous endurance contest; why had the Zionist organizations wanted us to come if there was no work? But I had no choice except to go back to the same humiliation. The next time I felt angry, and there was really nothing to lose in being honest. With fire in my eyes I asked them, "What do you expect me and my family to do here, starve?" That day they let me work as a common laborer, pulling heavy rooftiles off a truck. They paid me eighteen piasters a day for working from dawn to dark. I wasn't used to such a hard grind. My back was severely strained and my hands were full of blisters. Still, it meant food in our bellies. So the next day I returned, but I was told others' turns had come and I would have to wait. I had to wait a whole week. Our savings were dwindling dangerously low.

We had no relatives here in the country and, except for one old man from Vilna, no friends to call on for help. I began to wonder whether I'd done right to expose my family like this for the sake of a principle and some vague premonitions of danger.

Our situation became intolerable when the devout began to throw stones at my little boy because he stood out in the crowd of Hasidic children, with their sober black clothes, hats, and sidecurls. They took to calling him a goy.

My wife and I couldn't eat; we were sick with worry and began to speak to each other in desperate terms. We really felt death would be preferable to this way of living. When our goods finally arrived many objects were broken, the crystal was smashed, and many things had disappeared. Somehow that was the last straw, though we knew, of course, that "things" aren't that important.

For weeks we struggled to establish a life here, to lift ourselves a little above our miserable condition, but it seemed as though the more we struggled, like a person in quicksand, the farther down we were sucked. Then early one sabbath there was a knock at our door. I got up from my mat and cautiously opened the door. I was expecting more demands for money from the rabbi, but who should be standing before me but my cousin, my long-lost cousin. He looked slowly over the sleeping bodies, and I could see in his eyes the pity he felt for us and for our miserable state of poverty. Tears slowly welled up. Speechlessly we threw ourselves into each other's arms. Suddenly I broke down and sobbed like a child, and he comforted me. "You who were the best, the richest in the town, and look how I find you!"

My cousin had heard of our arrival and had been searching for us. He had come to Palestine many years ago and spoke fluent Arabic. At that time he was serving as the head of an export firm, and later he became the director of a hospital.

He took quick stock of our situation and immediately went to rouse the rabbi, our landlord. With threats to kill a few devout inhabitants of Mea Shearim and on the sabbath, too, unless the landlord agreed to release us from our restrictive, unjust lease, he made plans to have an Arab horse-drawn wagon bring us and all our worldly goods down to Tel Aviv that very day.

My cousin had a friend who had an apartment in Tel Aviv, which he let us have for two pounds and fifty-two piasters a month. Next door there was a large workroom, which I was able to get for two pounds seventy-two per month. Believe it or not, when I sold the electrical business a few years back, still in that same loft, it was worth three hundred thousand pounds. We lived well there, and our fortune changed once I was able to do my own work again. I ran an electrical shop for eighteen years, then, after my wife died twenty-five years ago now—I had used up all my savings for the huge medical bills—I sold the electrical business and all the tools. I turned my shop into a workroom from which I went out to do apartment renovations. Often I was simply given the keys and told to go ahead, given complete carte blanche to renovate the apartment in question as I saw fit.

Here in the kibbutz I still work, of course, like everyone else, but now I am doing mostly carpentry. Officially, I am supposed to work five days a week, but actually I work more like six or seven. I do the work of three young men! They give me all their venetian blinds to fix and frames to make—sometimes intricate gilded ones. I work in metal, too, making various decorative objects for people. But my favorite occupation is making toys for the kindergarten children. As I told you, I've been living here now for the last five years, and I really believe kibbutz life to be the best possible way of life. Here it is no dishonor to grow old, and one isn't alone and abandoned as is so often the case in the outside world. I only wish I had had sense enough to come long ago.

I was forty-two years of age when my beloved wife died. She was forty-one. It happened during the worst part of World War Two, when bombs were dropping on Tel Aviv. The bombings scared her so much that her weakened heart began to fail. She couldn't breathe, and my daughter and I had to spell each other, operating a hand-bellows to keep her going. Even after all these years I am certain there is no better woman left in the whole world! I go to her grave every year, and by following my example I hope my children will do the same for me when I am dead.

While the war was on we didn't hear from our families, but the news of the atrocities became known to most of us in Palestine, certainly by the Jewish committee and the allied leaders. In the city of Vilna all except a small handful of the nine thousand Jews were killed by the Nazis. The name of the camp where my whole family perished is Vilkavischki—my mother, three brothers, uncles and aunts and cousins, all except one cousin who escaped. He managed to crawl under the wire. He told me how my brother's wife was killed while clutching her newborn baby in her arms. One Christian seminarian, also a prisoner but one who survived, spoke to my sister just before she was killed. She refused a chance to escape because she would have had to leave her little children behind. He saw how they all had to dig their own graves before they were shot.

After the war and my wife's death I never wanted to marry again, but I was lonely. I should have followed my instincts and not the advice of others, not even the well-meaning advice of my daughter, who was afraid I'd be too lonely without a wife. My second wife came from Romania. We were married what now seems a short time, but while it was going on it seemed endless. In all sixteen years she never once cooked me a meal. She was no housekeeper at all; she just loved luxury. Did she know how to spend money! My God, she drained me dry. It was her attractions that held me in that terrible marriage.

Then I found out that she had had three or four men before me! She was a very pretty woman, but like most pretty women she was spoiled. She lived high on the hog, spending, spending, and lying her way through life. One day we were fighting and she left as a defiant joke, but I turned the joke around on her. I wrote her that "if by tomorrow I don't find a letter from the rabbi about a divorce in my letterbox, I won't answer for your safety!" That is how these matters are handled in Israel, as a divorce is a religious not a civil question. I meant it, too. I was at the end of my patience. She complied but not without buying off my lawyer first. I don't wish to know how! I ended up having to pay her money, but it was worth it just to be rid of her. She is now married to a seventy-six-year-old man who is sick. She'll get his money, too.

The worst thing about living with her was that I had to feel ashamed of her. My daughter never knew the truth. I had too much pride to admit how bad my situation had become.

Now sometimes I lie in bed and wonder what life is all about, just to end up alone like this. The TV can't talk back and neither can the four walls. There's no one to answer me. You know what my daughter said to me recently? "I love you and really want you to be happy and to have a good full life so much that I hope you will find a woman with whom you can share things." My daughter is a good woman, generous like her mother. So now I go to the cinema with a friend. And who knows? I have plenty of friends here on the kibbutz and others who still live in Tel Aviv.

My daughter includes me in all the family events and festivities; and my son is a good son, who comes twice a month on the sabbath to see me. You see, my life is full. One rich American woman even wanted to marry me, and there are others, too, I suspect have designs on me. You know, there aren't that many hale old men like me left when you reach sixty-nine. But essentially I've been alone here now for four and a half years.

The kibbutz was not new to me when I came. I'd been visiting friends here since we first arrived in Israel, thirty-nine years ago. In fact, I was good friends with some of the founding members.

I am happy in Givat Brenner. When I first got my apartment it wasn't nice; the floors were caked with dirt. But I cleaned and painted everything, rewired it, and then put in all these handmade fixtures. Usually I eat one meal at the canteen; for the other meals I bring home produce from the kibbutz commissary and cook it myself. I have my grandchildren nearby and my good dog, Tessa. My two hamsters and the fishtank with all sorts of tropical fish and turtles give me a lot of pleasure. So, you see, even at home I'm not alone. Luckily my health is good. I get up at five every morning. In the evenings I watch TV or read the Yiddish paper. There are plenty of books at the kibbutz library, also lectures and films. I especially enjoy reading about politics, though actually I've never taken much of an active part. But I'm still very much interested in what's going on in the world. Peace—that's the most difficult thing to achieve and remains always my most fervent hope. But to realize it I feel we mustn't give away even an inch of our soil.

Kathleen Lynch

Sarasota, Florida

Born 1898

Kathleen Lynch asked the receptionist in the beautiful, well-tended lobby, with its large sweep of glass overlooking the gardens, the pool, and beyond the bay, to show me the bank of elevators. I got off at a high floor and found her door. Her room and the adjoining bathroom were well appointed and pleasantly furnished, the walls painted pale blue. It was bright, with a lovely view of the water. Ms. Lynch herself, a gracious, soft-spoken, attractive woman in her late seventies, welcomed me to a comfortable chair.

ON MY FATHER'S side, as my name indicates, I am of Irish descent; of English on my mother's. The Puritan New England strain can effectively kill any other, and so it has been with me. I was born in Littleton, a town in the White Mountains of northern New Hampshire. When I was three years old my father, a successful merchant, died and my mother never remarried. My first distinct memory is of the day of my father's death. My childhood was sheltered, uneventful. Books were my favorite companions. During my undergraduate days at Mount Holyoke College I was a hardworking, delighted student, reaping the usual benefits of academic industry: sophomore and senior honors and Phi Beta Kappa in my junior year. Many years later my adopted daughter surmised correctly: "You are at home in the classroom and nowhere else!"

Aided by fellowships, I earned an M.A. degree from Columbia University and a Ph.D. from the University of Michigan. Brief teaching experiences at the University of Wisconsin and at Vassar College were followed by forty-one years of teaching at Mount Holyoke College, where eventually I held a chair, becoming Mary Lyon professor of English. I served my turn as chairman of the department of English.

I helped support my mother in the latter part of her life; in fact, she lived with me and went to Columbia with me when I was studying there. Later she came to the University of Michigan as well. In my mother's time if a widow

I have had a long and full life . . . and hope to make a dignified exit.

did not remarry she would never think of taking up a career. She had a very good mind but did not have very much education.

My mother never wanted me to get married. I never understood what her psychology was; I think she herself had been quite happy in her marriage, and all I can say is that she just did not want me to get married. She was an independent person and was active in the community with clubs and church. She died in 1951.

I retired when I had to, at sixty-five. I was not unreconciled to retiring, but it still came as a shock. Mandatory retirement, it seems to me, is a matter of economics, because there are always plenty of young people coming along who are longing for academic posts. I think you need to retire to make room for them. In any case, some people would linger too long.

One facet of my preretirement life was my research in seventeenth-century drama. My first and best book was *The Social Mode of Restoration Comedy,* first published by the University of Michigan in its Language and Literature Series. This book was followed by a number of others, the research for which was undertaken in England and in Ireland during sabbatical leaves and was made possible by various fellowships and grants, including a Guggenheim Fellowship.

Before my retirement I was in England on a Guggenheim grant, working on a book about Roger Boyle.* I had had the fellowship for a year and was about to ask for another year when I was called back to be chairman of my department, and this held me up somewhat on my book. It was not published until shortly after I retired.

After retirement I lived on the island of Madeira for about eight years before I came here. I couldn't afford to live in Holyoke, Massachusetts, and as there were no taxes levied on foreigners in Madeira, I chose the island for my retirement. I had been there a number of times already; as a young woman I walked across the entire island once, and I loved it. I found a charming little cottage, which I was able to rent, and later moved into a new apartment building.

I discovered, as I was getting older, that there were no good doctors and no good dentists in Madeira, and the English residents, who made up the greatest number of foreign residents, were often transported to England on stretchers if anything ailed them. Or they died in the local hospital because good help was not available. I thought it would be better if I did not spend my last years under those conditions. I was sorry to go. I had many good friends there amongst the tightly-knit little colony of expatriates.

There wasn't much culture in Madeira, though; no good library, no English films, no theater except once in a while a traveling company. Madeira offered cheap living and beautiful scenery. It is a very lovely island and I really didn't want to leave. I could get to England so easily and that is my favorite place.

I stayed in Bournemouth once, in a residential hotel for elderly people.

**Roger Boyle: First Earl of Orrery* (Knoxville: University of Tennessee Press, 1965).

This represents one way of life for the aged, but it is grim. Many elderly people left alone, of course, do stay in these hotels, but if they get ill they are rushed off very quickly to a hospital or nursing home. I am told the old people's homes in England are well run, but that they are designed for people who have no resources. I would not have qualified. England makes life for its elderly poor cozier than that of royalty. I love England and would have preferred to end my days there, but it is simply not possible economically.

I found this home, Plymouth Harbor, almost by accident. I remembered that the people who had lived in my bungalow before me in Madeira had done some research on homes, so I wrote to them and asked for some information. They sent me some brochures, and I chose this one without having seen it. I had to wait for three years after I registered. I might not have gotten in that fast except for something that happened in London. I spoke to two ladies at breakfast one morning at the hotel where I was staying, and one of them asked me what I was doing. I said I was waiting to get into Plymouth Harbor, and she said she had been living there for two years. She came back, was very active with my case, and managed to get me in faster than I had expected. She is now my next-door neighbor.

I am not a great lover of Florida. I agree with Henry James, who said that Florida offered nothing but a few poaching places around the coast. This is more or less how I feel. I think that Plymouth Harbor is one of these poaching places. It's in a lovely setting. I haven't many contacts outside this place. I gave a talk with slides on Madeira earlier this year. A lot of my old students turned up, and through them I have now been able to make new acquaintances.

I—a single woman—was romantic enough to adopt a child. It wasn't easy. It took two and a half years of effort on my part, and I had a great deal of trouble doing it. I couldn't get anywhere with the Massachusetts agencies, so I consulted New York State. I was told I could adopt a child of school age who was a problem child, but I didn't want a problem child. This adoption saga will show you how much accident enters into one's life. Someone came into the zoology department at Mount Holyoke for a semester who was an exchange teacher and who had adopted children from an orphanage in New Orleans. She said she did not think I would have any problem there. You see, I was a "spinster." She put me in touch with them, and they said they would be delighted to help.

I discovered that the Deep South was the place to go at that time, because they were much less rigid than the others. They presented no problems and asked what sort of child would I like, what age. I said, "Perhaps a baby a year old." I really didn't know, so they selected a child for me, and I was to go down and see it.

The baby that they chose for me I really didn't like at all, though it was a perfectly healthy child. There was nothing wrong with it, but I didn't like it. I didn't know what to do and finally said, "I don't believe I want this child." And what do you think the head of the organization said to me? "No one ever wants the child we pick out for them. Why don't you go into the nursery yourself and pick one out." So I went into the nursery and I looked around; the babies all looked alike. They were three to six months old and were kicking up their heels, looking at the ceiling. And they all looked exactly alike. I looked around and I didn't know what to do. I thought, this is very bad. They will think I'm not serious. Suddenly this baby crawled down to the end of her crib and poked her head through the bars (my daughter has a very narrow head) and smiled at me. I thought this was very encouraging and said, "I will take the child that smiled."

When I got back to Massachusetts my friend asked me how I did. I said, "I took the child that smiled at me," and she asked how I could do that, because it could have been just gas on the stomach. However, I did it and I didn't care to know about her history. I guess I could have found out something about it, but the delightful ladies who ran the orphanage (it was a private charity) didn't keep the records very carefully, and I had a feeling I would probably get the records of another child. I thought it was just as well not to be confused by all this, so I asked for nothing. But I couldn't take the child then because I was still teaching and had to wait until the Christmas break. She was three months old then; I had to wait until she was six months.

When I went down at Christmas vacation they told me, "Your baby is in the hospital; she has a very bad cold." But they let her out of the hospital anyway and brought her back to the orphanage. There she was put in my arms —I, who had never held a child before. That same day I got on the plane, which was occupied entirely by men reading newspapers. They looked at me with aversion—marching down the aisle with a child in my arms. There was no stewardess on board—just a steward. This was long ago. I was forty-three and I had never traveled by plane before.

I made the trip, but it turned out that the baby had whooping cough. I took her straight to the doctor, and he said, "I think the next twenty-four hours will decide whether she lives or dies." Thank God, she had a light case, though she has always been a little delicate since. In order to continue with my teaching I had to hire a nurse for five months, but then it was the summer vacation, and I thought I could take over. I did have a maid, which was a help.

Our home was a pleasant house, surrounded by an apple orchard, and blossom time was always a special joy. My daughter's favorite schools were not in this country but in England, when I was on sabbatical leave. She had several seasons in summer camp and was often my traveling companion.

I had difficulties at times, but no more than many parents, I am sure. When my daughter was a teenager I used to think of Thackeray's remark that "To be father and mother both is too much for anyone." I educated her and found her a junior college in Virginia called Southern Seminary. There she majored in Latin. Later, while she was living in Guam, she ran a kindergarten, which I might say she did very well. I don't think for a moment she wanted to become a college professor. She is very happily married and is happy with her children. She is not particularly introspective; she is just as outgoing as she was when I first saw her.

Her husband is a young naval officer. I don't see them very often because they have been located in such remote places. When her little girl was born I went out to Asmarah, Ethiopia to visit. Her husband was stationed at a small communications center there. My daughter is a very adaptable person and she loves these changes. They are coming to visit me this June. I adore my daughter.

I entered this home about a year ago. About one third of us here have been teachers or have been in business or in government posts, although quite a few of the women have survived their husbands or have not been in business life at all. There are very few men here and just a few couples. The average age is about eighty. We have an infirmary here which is very well run but, alas, too small. There was some talk several years ago of building a separate infirmary, but this was when economic conditions were very much better than they are now. Terminally ill people go to the infirmary, or if they are able and have funds for the purpose, they can have nurses in their apartments.

This is not an exciting life, but I don't know how much excitement I could expect at this time of life. I have a sort of obsession about Sundays; I am always glad when they are over. I tend to write letters whenever I have a spare moment, as I have a lot of friends who live out of the country. That's at least one pleasant occupation for a Sunday afternoon.

I led a discussion group here, which met twice a month, on the letters of Henry James, but the interest wasn't great and I haven't offered or been asked to repeat the seminar. I had a professor once called John Erskine, a delightful man and a fine lecturer, who was very fond of the seventeenth century, particularly Suckling. He had a way of reciting some of Suckling's lyrics that I have never forgotten. When I went to the University of Michigan I told the director of my thesis that I would like to do something from that period, remembering some of the things I had heard from Mr. Erskine. Then later I went on to William Congreve, who was much more interesting, of course. When you are a graduate student you are looking around for something of interest. At Columbia, where I took my master's degree, things were systematized, almost surprisingly so. You had to write a thesis, of course. I was told to go to the department secretary and to look through a list of available topics, then I was told to choose a subject that wasn't in the book. It gets a little more complicated as you go on.

My Ph.D. thesis was entitled "The Social Mode of Restoration Comedy"; it was published by Macmillan and was reprinted many years later, but never in paperback. When I was in the Library of Congress in Washington I looked to see what they had by me, and they had one copy of the thesis; I don't think it was authorized. French romances of the seventeenth century were my source. I taught eighteenth-century literature and the history of drama.

We have quite a number of evenings of one sort or another, when people come to speak to us. But I am in the situation of not having a car, so it would be hard for me to get anywhere outside the home. I suppose I am interested in lecturing occasionally at one of the local colleges. I feel one of the great handicaps in this country to be the lack of public transportation. I will not ask people to transport me anywhere because I do not believe in doing that. What really grieves me is the lack of a good library in Sarasota. However, ground is being broken this week for a new one, which will be open next July. We have a Plymouth Harbor bus that takes us to town, but we have to walk once we are dropped in town. It is said because the bookmobile comes here once a week that it does not seem necessary or desirable for our bus to take us to the library and compete with the bookmobile. I find most of the ladies wish to go to the hairdresser or go shopping. As the library is quite in another direction, I rarely am able to go, since I can't walk any distance.

My health is fairly good, though I have all sorts of minor elderly ailments. I have a spur in my right heel at the moment, which annoys me. It makes it hard for me to walk on the pavement. Though I still read a good deal I have trouble with chronic conjunctivitis down here. It may be the constant air conditioning —you know, we can't open our windows. But since I don't like to read in too great a hurry (I like to savor the author) my eyes haven't been much of a problem. I tire easily; that's the major complaint. Still, one of the assets of this place is the swimming pool. I do make use of it, and I am sure it has contributed to my state of health. I suppose it is the practical aspects of life which loom a little too large when you get older, because you are constantly reminded by your physical limitations of obstacles to doing things. They loom a little larger than they should.

This is a nonprofit organization. We have an active residents' committee; some very capable women who have been here since the beginning form the nucleus. They have had a good deal to do with determining the way Plymouth Harbor operates, and the trustees have accepted their suggestions. The original board included a number of Congregationalists, but it is not sponsored by the church.

I was very lucky. There was an invalid who lived next door to me in Holyoke. When she died she left my daughter a third of her estate. She knew that after I had educated her I would not be able to provide for her, and she wanted to do this. She was a wonderful person, and she set up a trust fund for my daughter and left me a bequest. This made it possible for me to make the initial payment here. A college professor in a small New England college does not earn a huge salary, you realize.

I think you are a different person at different times of your life, a different person in the classroom than you are outside of it. And you are different when you are pursuing academic interests than you are when you are no longer pursuing them. Now I am what you would call aged. I don't think you are unlucky if you have had intellectual pursuits; you can always draw on them, so to speak. But I miss the stimulation, the challenge of my work. It saddens me that I cannot afford to go back to England. I cannot travel—I can't afford it—but I know this is to be expected in these circumstances. Nevertheless, I regret it, for I still have research I would enjoy doing, friends I would enjoy seeing.

I like what George Meredith said about old age. He was confined to a wheelchair after having been a very active man, climbing mountains in Switzerland and such things. He said, "We, who have loved the sweep of the winds and the motion of legs, we come to this? But for myself, I will confess it is the natural order, there is no irony in nature."

I have reached my final home in Plymouth Harbor. I have no hobbies, but I have many friends. I adore my daughter and am happy with my grandchildren on those rare occasions when I see them. Books interest me as much as ever, and solitude always refreshes me. I have had a long and full life. I grow tired rather easily and will welcome the end whenever it comes and hope to make a dignified exit.

Gheorghe Sarbu

Poiana Tapului, The Socialist Republic of Romania

Born 1894

I was introduced to Gheorghe and Maranda Sarbu through a friend. The Sarbus, a handsome couple, live in a simple little mountain house among open fields that extend to the forests of the Carpathian Mountains.

I WAS BORN in 1894 here on Samora Hill. The Hungarian border was ten kilometers away in those days, but this was always part of Romania. There were only twenty houses in the village then, ten of them on this hill.

After my five years of elementary schooling I was apprenticed in the local pepper factory for three years and then began serious work, twelve hours each day, six days a week.

Both my wife and I are orthodox. We still practice our religion but not as seriously as in earlier days. We keep the holidays, but we don't find our peace in religion but in our daily life. I never concern myself with envy; I am a philosopher who believes everyone gets what is right for that person. I help others and enjoy them. I have found people are destroyed only by themselves, by this envy and self-seeking, their restlessness.

When the first war began, in 1916, I fought against the Germans. I was in the front line in Moldavia and in Austria. It was a nightmare. I don't know why I didn't try to desert—many did. This area was called the "triangle of death"—it was hell, such butchery. I came back here once but was sent out again to fight the Hungarians. The French, the English, and even the Americans came to our aid, otherwise Romania would have been beaten.

I was unbelievably lucky I was not killed or wounded. But I got typhus from the lice. After 1918 there were eight hundred thousand dead—and most of them died from typhus.

After the war's end I stayed in a village in Moldavia, where I worked as a

Maranda married me, I think, because I was such an abstemious man. . . . I won't quarrel with her and I won't let her thrash around in bed.

mechanic in a small factory making hydro airplanes. Then I came to Constanţa. I found work in a veterinary hospital, where they were doing research in vaccines. I was a mechanic there, too. Altogether I worked for forty-three years of my life. I have received decorations for my good work. At sixty I retired and got my pension. I used to work days and parts of the nights, too, at the veterinary institute—an example for all of a conscientious, good worker. I never took a day of holiday while working, and I've never been ill or missed work except for the typhus. I believe honestly when I have no more work I'll die!

All my life I've known it's important for the good life to sleep well and long—also to be moderate in sex. Even now I sleep for over eight hours. My mother lived to be eighty years old, but my father had a stomach illness and he died at forty-six. I myself am careful. I don't drink or smoke.

This is my first marriage. Maranda married me, I think, because I was such an abstemious man. She decided to marry me when she discovered this, in contrast to her first husband. We've been married twenty-eight years. She is more nervous than I am and gets more easily excited. When she does she is told by me, "Be quiet, my dear." I won't quarrel with her and I won't let her thrash around in bed.

Her brother in America left her all his money, but we got nothing of it—ten thousand dollars it was, after selling his house and bar. It would have been more, but the brother was a drunkard and squandered it away. He never once gave us any money for the care of their mother. Still, what difference does it make—we were never destined to get any of it anyway.

I love animals, especially my sheep. I keep eleven ewes and one ram. I go for long walks into the forest with my little wagon to gather wood. Also, I clear the paths. I've taken to storing and caring for the building materials of my neighbors because we have much more room here.

What I don't like is having to worry about material things. I enjoy most the peace and quiet which enables me to think about life, about its meaning. I did most of the work of building this house myself, but I also had workers to do the plumbing and some of the electrical work. I like to putter. We both love our flower garden and the vegetables and the fruit trees. But it's a big garden and much work.

I can't bear noise and unnecessary stress, the noise of a restaurant, for instance. I'd rather eat at home in peace. I like only to hear a bird in the tree, not the noise and cacophony of humans in a crowd. In the evenings we read together. She is copying whole books now in her own handwriting, because books are hard to come by in our country.

We just manage with our garden and the sheep on our joint pension. If just nothing happens to one of us first! We're happy here.

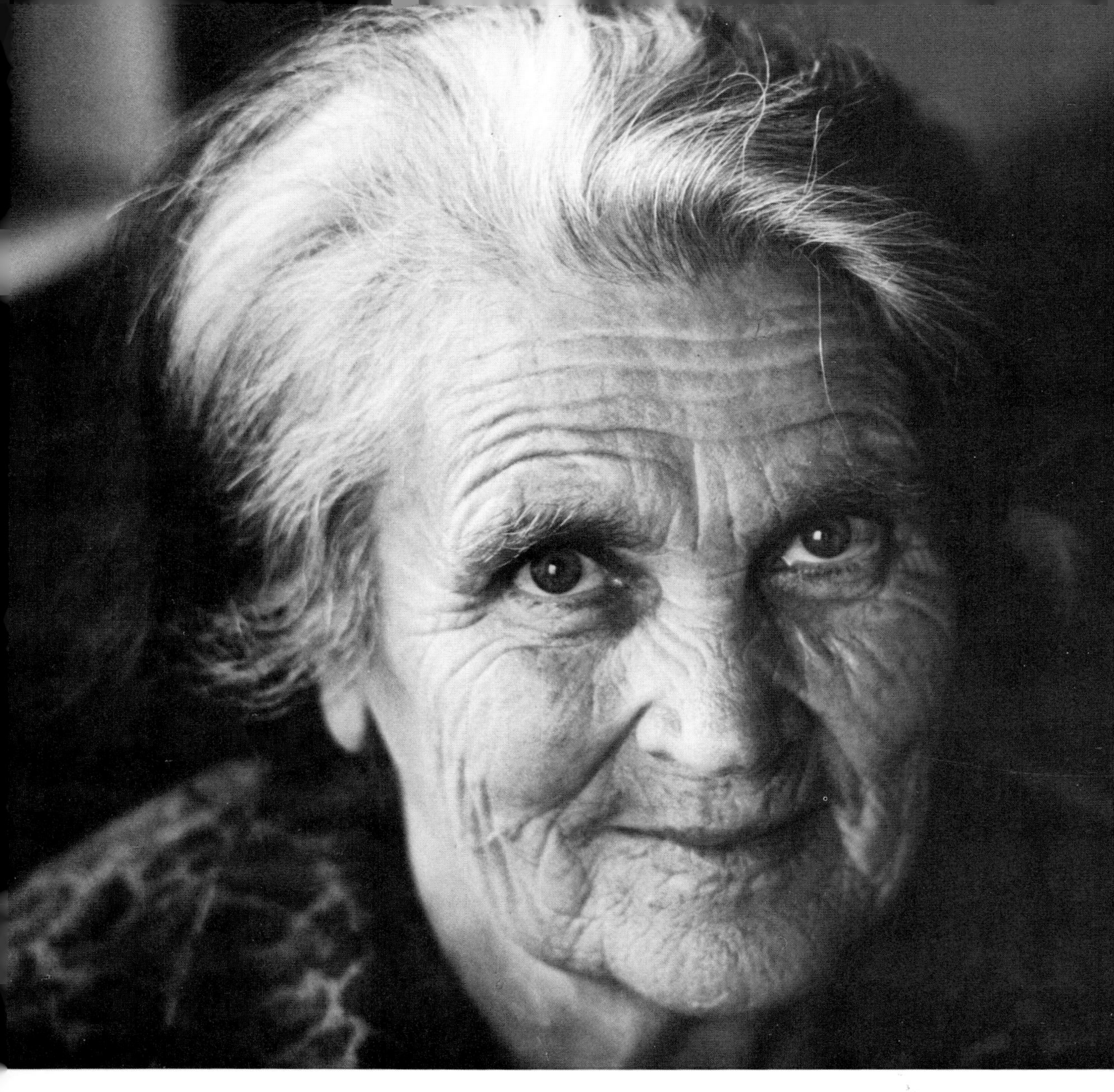

The essential point for older people is having . . . a set of necessary tasks that have to be done, like feeding the sheep or bringing in firewood for the stove.

Maranda Sarbu

Poiana Tapului, The Socialist Republic of Romania

Born 1899

I WAS BORN in 1899 in Bucovina, on the northern border of Romania abutting Russia, which was under the rule of the Austrian empire until 1918. My mother lived to be one hundred fourteen years old, but my father died in World War One while fighting against the Romanians. I had two brothers. One brother emigrated to America in 1912 and died there. The other died of kidney disease right in Bucovina at the age of sixty.

I was married at twenty-one to a man who turned out to be an alcoholic. I finally had to leave him in 1929 because he became so violent. I was thirty. We were divorced, and shortly thereafter he died. I had one son by him in 1925—Dumitru Tudorache—my only child.

I worked as a practical nurse in Constanţa to support him from the thirties to 1945, when I met my present husband. When he was in his late teens my son worked as a technician of medical apparatus in the same hospital where I was. My husband-to-be was employed in the veterinary hospital for that period.

We were married in 1947, and seven hours after our marriage my son left by steamer for America. He had had seven years of school—five years of elementary school and two years in a technical school.

I only had seven years of school myself. At age thirteen I left home for good because of the war. It was so terrible there on the border. I ran away to an uncle in Moldavia to get away from the shooting. My uncle promised to let me study but he didn't keep his promise. So I had to go to work in a tobacco factory and then come home and do the housework for my uncle's wife. She was miserly, even though he was a rich man. They treated me like a servant. It was a hard life. All that time I got no news from my family across the border. Then I met my first husband.

I got married very quickly and we left for Constanţa. After our divorce because of his drinking I lived with an aunt. My brother sent money from America to help support us from 1931 to 1936, when I found work.

In 1947, shortly after my second marriage, we sold our house. But it was exactly at the time of the money reforms in Romania, so we lost everything we had, everything we'd either of us saved.

My husband decided to retire from the job at the hospital and come back to Poiana Tapului in the Carpathian Mountains, where he had been born. There had been terrible bombardments in Constanţa, and parts of the city were in ruins. We had to leave without money.

Here in Poiana I was able to get a job as a maid in one of the government pension houses. Gheorghe found work, too. For a long time we were very poor. But gradually we were able to save a little, and then we put it all into some land up here on the hill, which we bought in 1952. By 1958 we started building our little house. Before that we lived always in a room supplied by the state. Luckily our health remained good during this hard period.

I worked for eighteen years, until retirement at the age of fifty-five: eight years as a maid, ten years in the hospital. My pension is five hundred eighty lei a month. I still work, of course, but now I take care of the house and gardens and in the summer an occasional guest. At that time we move in with the sheep in the shed for a roof over our heads.

In recent years I've given up eating meat. I feel strange inside when I eat any meat. For my kidney stones I take lemons. That seems to help. I was brought up to think of the cow as sacred, so how could I eat one?

Except for the fall I took from the ladder last autumn, when I broke two ribs while carrying some sacks of corn up into the attic, I have really nothing to complain of. I feel well, and I intend to live to my mother's ripe age.

But our worry is that there will be no one to look after us as she had if one of us goes first. My son I've never heard from again in all these years. We have a nephew nearby, but we can't really believe that he would care for us. My mother was with us until her death, in 1965, for the last fifteen years of her life. She was fortunate, I think.

The essential point for older people is having peace, a quiet life, and a set of necessary tasks that have to be done, like feeding the sheep or bringing in firewood for the stove.

George Alfred Lamport

Moorgreen Day Hospital, Southampton, England

Born 1887

Dr. Michael Hall, head of geriatrics at the hospital in Southampton, England and professor in the new field of gerontology, sent me to see one of the best geriatric facilities in England, Moorgreen Day Hospital. There I met Alfred Lamport, who came twice a week to Moorgreen since he was crippled with a severely ulcerated leg. His regular care at Moorgreen made it possible for Alfred to continue living with his wife on the edge of the common, in the council house that they had inhabited for the last seven years.

THOUGH I CAN'T walk and stand, the ambulance fetches me, you see.

I was born in Saint James' Road, Croydon, Surrey, and have a sister who will be eighty-seven next week. I was one of seven children; three sisters are still living, aged eighty-eight, eighty-seven, and eighty-three respectively. My wife was seventy-seven on the eighteenth June. I've been married fifty-three years in December. Married in 1920. It's been a fairly happy marriage. Every marriage has its ups and downs, you know. I find if you share and share alike and trust each other, it's alright. I always had a good character and that sort of thing. We never had no children, and it's not my fault neither. It was the wife's fault, of course.

I came out of the army in 1919. I was in the Garrison Artillery. I didn't want the army; I was just a wartime soldier, you know. I was very lucky never to have to go abroad. I was in the army four years, and we were married when I was thirty-three years old, just after I came out of the army.

My wife's health is still pretty fair, but she suffers terribly from hay fever. We live in the country and have to cut grass and things. The fact is she hasn't been out this year. I never go out neither now, but we have a neighbour who cuts the grass for us.

My wife helps me with my trousers and pants. I have very strong arms; that's why I do the pulley exercises, to make them strong.

I was a bad boy at school and I wouldn't learn. I didn't like school and I wouldn't do the work. My father took me out at thirteen years old, at the end of 1900, I suppose. I'm self-taught really. I was mad about horses and I worked with them for five years. I used to drive to the docks and get the sugar—I worked for a wholesale grocer—took the horses to the forge to be shoed, groomed them myself, and cleaned up the stables. My father was a salesman at a flour and cake merchant's. They had about sixty horses, I suppose. My father used to take me with him on his deliveries. The merchant sold everything: flour, bread, biscuits, sausages, and rice. Me dad taught me. Whatever he told me I did it. Of course, we obeyed our parents. I used to get a load out and take it to all the shops. One day a week, that was, because the other five days I would go to the docks to collect. You see, the ships brought the goods into the warehouse, travelers came round to the shops to get the orders, and I had to go to the docks to get the goods. Oh, I've done all sorts of things in me time. I've done laundry work. I also worked for a sweets firm. I used to deliver to different shops, always by horse.

My father was a workman. He brought us up, seven children, on thirty shillings a week. Of course, that was a long time ago. He's been dead since '32. Always poor, we were, but never hard up, if you understand. Always got what we wanted. Kept us tidy and gave us plenty to eat. But we was never rich. Brought up amongst the poor. I worked with him till I got married. Then I opened a newsagent's shop. I was twenty-two years in the same shop. Up at half past four every morning except Sunday, when it was five o'clock. I sold newspapers. It was my own shop. In 1946 I sold that and went on a holiday for a time. I bought another business in Brighton, which is down in Sussex, you know. I was sixty then, I suppose, and I sold up then. Coming away from there with two thousand five hundred pounds, a car, and a caravan. We lived in this caravan for fourteen years, but when it came the time as I couldn't walk, I asked the council to find me a little place. They found me a bungalow, where I am now. We didn't travel much in the caravan. We went down to Dover one day and stopped there fourteen weeks. It was lovely. We had a place on the Kings Down Cliff Estates, near Saint Margaret's Bay, where there is a lighthouse, you see.

I retired at sixty-five and my foot troubles began then. That's when I got me pension. Oh, I forget the amount, but it was small. It's getting better now, you know. I get more money now than I ever earned myself. We get thirteen pounds sixty pence each week. We only pay rent every fortnight—four pounds sixteen every fortnight. I get a rebate because of me age, because I am an old-age pensioner. We should pay about four pounds a week instead of two. I think it was about one ninety something—the rebate. So you can guess it would have been nearly four pounds a week.

After I retired I used to do some gardening. I like gardening. I'd walk around on a stick. Grow me own potatoes, cabbages, and runner beans, things like that. Of course, I can't do things like that now. It's three years since I lost the use of me leg. Anyway, I've been in the General [hospital] four times, you know—in 1968, '69, and twice in '71 for an ulcerated leg. It's still pretty bandaged up, you see. The leg's dry now, yes, but they got to keep it bandaged up so it won't swell since I don't walk about. The first operation was in 1932. Six weeks it was I was laid up and then I carried on again. Oh, yes, I pushed about. Managed to operate a car for about forty years after that. I've a clean license.

We have a lady who does the shopping for the wife on Monday, Wednesday, and Friday, so we are pretty lucky. We have a home help twice a week, an hour and a half, no charge. She comes under social security and will do what you ask her. She will clean windows or slip up to the shops for you.

I can't use the bathroom. That's why I come here to have me bath and me dressings. When I come on Friday I don't get me bath, I just get me dressings. They allow the wife to go to Harrington House once every two months to have her feet done. Fifteen pence, one-and-six, that is. I don't do anything here [occupational therapy] but I do some things at home, like polish the horse brasses, or I do little jobs for her, like open a packet of tea and put it in the caddy. But I can't do much because I can't stand, you see. We get on very well. I don't complain. I'm a cheerful sort of chap, you know. You ask for me and they all know me. If I want any beer there's an 'off-license', where you can order it and they bring it down. I was getting overweight so I've stopped it for a week or two. I'm supposed to be on a diet.

The heavy washing goes out once a fortnight. The wife washes all the small things, like my underpants and socks. We've got two or three friends who come up and see us every week. But my sisters are too old, you see. One is in Brighton, one in Peckham, and the other in Norwalk. My wife's family they all died off. She only has one brother about here, in Croydon, and another one in Canada. That's two brothers, and that's all she has left now. Her sister died a couple of years ago at about eighty-four. She has a niece and nephew, and we hear from them occasionally.

I enjoy coming here. I enjoy every minute of it. Well, look at all the people we can meet and talk to. You see, we have got some nice people here. Look at the girls, for instance, the nurses and that. They will do anything for you; you don't have to worry. At home I read the papers, and I don't wear glasses either. For the small print I use a spy glass. My wife she gets the catarrh. The doctor comes to the house once a month regularly. As for medicines, I take Lasix pills, two of them every morning; they are for the water. I have a painkiller for the pain in me leg. Then I have indigestion pills, because I don't have teeth. I threw my teeth away years ago. I tried three different dentures (and no one was there to pay for them in those days!). They come down when you go to eat, you see. Top plate won't stay up unless you buy some stuff to stick on it. I like a mince more than anything now. Anything that takes chewing I can't eat. We can't afford meat too often, but we have a chicken once a week. The wife resurrects it and makes a stew of it. We like fish—pilchards—which come out of a tin.

To get into bed, I slide off this thing [pointing to his wheelchair]. My wife helps me with me trousers and pants. I have very strong arms; that's why I do the pulley exercises here, to make them strong. Have a little arthritis in the shoulders. I worked all me life; I'm not a particularly lazy man and I don't mind doing a bit of 'that.' If I had my life to live over I would like to be a vet, but me father could not afford it. We've always had a dog and a cat. We got plenty of birds around the house; the wife feeds them. We face the common; our bungalow looks out right on it. Last year we had a carnival on the common, which was upsetting.

No, hard work never hurt anyone. Keep working; that's the secret, I think. I used to paint the caravan and clean the windows inside and outside; I used to build fences; got the palings, and cut 'em for me own garden. I used to chop wood and tie it up in bundles, and I laid crazy paving around the caravan. There's always something to do, you know.

After me father died I helped support my invalid brother. He'd never worked; I always had to hand him a copper or two. Finally, when I went into the army my brother joined the navy, but he fell down the ship's hold and died. [Tears welled up in his eyes.]

My wife and I, we're both members of the C of E [Church of England], but I never went much. Until I was fifteen I was made to go to Sunday school. We used to do as we were told, you see. They are saucy today. When you come in on a Sunday you washed your hands and had dinner, and always on time, too. But I don't think much about the past, except you come to ask me. It's morbid. What's the good of it?

We haven't got a telly. I'm in bed very often before seven o'clock. Get up about six or seven in the morning.

With strength and dexterity he wheeled himself across the doorjam from the printing room (which contained a small printing press) across the polished linoleum corridor; past open doors where nurses and a doctor were tending a woman with her leg up in a pulley; past an old man being taught to walk again in a mechanical walker, attended by a young man, the physical therapist. Lamport waved hello to a pretty young aide who was bringing the tea in on a cart and moved on to the physical therapy room. Here he wheeled the chair around and brought it to rest exactly in line with the two arm pulleys extending from the back wall. Energetically he went through his arm exercises—up, down, to the right, and to the left.

Symbolically, we eat half Japanese food and half American.

Thomas Oka

Oakland, California

Born Japan 1889

My friend Mal Wood, who had arranged the interview for me, offered to drive me over to Oakland where the Okas lived. We found the house, an older building of flats in a changing neighborhood, and there, on one of the higher floors, was the oasis that Mr. and Mrs. Oka's cheerful, bright apartment seemed to have become.

The profusion of healthy plants made it seem almost like a greenhouse. Everywhere on the walls hung Mrs. Oka's paintings, and on the shelves her intricate origami creations were displayed. She greeted us with warmth—a vivacious, pleasant woman. Her husband came in from one of the other rooms; he had the serious air of a scholar. Although he was quite Americanized and spoke excellent English, one still felt quite strongly that underlying and more formal structure of manners customary to the Orient of the past.

I HAVE BEEN in this country over fifty years. I am eighty-six now. I was born in Okayama, Japan, which is near Kobe. Mrs. Oka is from a small island. She went to high school in Japan and then came here with her parents. I had three brothers and two sisters; I am in the middle. My brothers all graduated from the University of Japan. My father used to be a samurai; he was adopted. In traditional Japanese society the first son always carried on the father's name and the second and third, when they married, took on the wife's family name. Now in Japan it is done in the American way. I graduated from Kobe Commercial School, which is a part of the University of Japan, and then went straight to the Mogi Company. They sent me to the United States in 1918. (Mogi was the greatest silk-importing company in the world at that time, but in 1920 it went bankrupt.)

I settled in San Francisco at first and opened a branch office there. Mogi Company controlled most of the silk production in Japan. They also owned two large banks, but they kept raising their prices and finally they had to shut down, so I was out of work.

I didn't want to go back to Japan, and a friend suggested I open a Japanese Insurance Company office, one which would serve the entire United States. I sold marine insurance, finally, because I couldn't get anyone to buy the Japanese Company policies.

My wife came over from Japan to study to be a dentist, but I could not support her, so she went to work in a dentist's office. We married in 1919 and have three children, five grandchildren, and one great grandchild. One of my granddaughters, Marianna Tcherkassky, is one of the principal dancers with the American Ballet Theatre. My daughter, who was also a dancer, traveled all over the world. She married a Russian prince. An interesting article about my granddaughter appeared in the *Saturday Review* of March 8, 1975. Princess Marianna Tcherkassky, my son-in-law's mother, was a renowned Russian soprano, and her son, also a musician of some stature, often appeared as baritone soloist with the Boston Symphony. So, you see, art runs in the family.

My daughter actually started playing classical piano as a girl, until some of her friends urged her to join them in ballet class. She began in Chicago, where we were living then, and later continued her studies at Madame Anderson's in New York City. She became manager of the Ballet Russe, and now she has two studios of her own.

My son joined the army and studied Japanese at the army school. He was with General MacArthur in the Philippines and then went with the American forces to Japan, where he served as interpreter. Now he is an engineer, mainly working in electrical engineering. He is working for the housing department. He used to come every weekend to visit us, but now he is just too busy. But still, we see him whenever we can get together.

My wife was a Christian when she was born in Japan. I became one when I was about ten years old. I wanted to learn English and I went to a Baptist missionary to learn the language. He took me along to church and I liked what I saw of the service. When I was in high school I did not go to church at all; in fact I never really started to go until we were living in Chicago. Around that time the war broke out. No other church except the Presbyterian one welcomed the Japanese into their fellowship at that time. Now we go to a Methodist church in Oakland.

We moved to Chicago in late '41 or early '42, when the American-Japanese war started, and we stayed there for twenty-seven years. I worked for McGraw and Company, which is a wholesale book house. I went into the book department. I retired from McGraw when I was seventy-two; then I visited my daughter in Kensington, Maryland; then off to New York for a visit and back again to Chicago. Finally we moved out here to Oakland.

I wrote for a Japanese-American newspaper—becoming correspondent for them in this country—and I did that until 1931. I now translate English to Japanese for the senior citizens' newsletter. Until I was eighty years old I could write articles easily and could remember everything about history and things, but since I passed eighty I forget everything.

After I retired I started thinking about religion—Buddhism. The Methodist Church doesn't teach the inner religion—just the outer. I read about both now. I would like to write, too, but I have no strength anymore.

I tried a number of other businesses—the insurance business, for instance, which I never gave up entirely. I finally quit in 1971, when I was eighty-two years old! In the thirties I had an automotive parts business, but times were bad then, in '33 and '34, and the business couldn't stay above water—it went bankrupt in 1934. I was penniless. My daughter was already dedicated to the ballet and it would have been a tragedy for her to have to quit, so Mr. Osoto sent my daughter off to ballet school (by then we had moved to Chicago). After two years of study only, she was sent to graduate classes in New York—a great honor.

When we first moved here, in '69, this was a quiet, residential neighborhood. You see, the building is a nice clean one and our apartment is bright and spacious enough—but the neighborhood is terrible! It is very dangerous here and we don't go out much at night. We go to the shopping center during the day because it is not too dangerous during the daytime. We still go to church every Sunday and to visit friends sometimes, but we don't go unless somebody comes to drive us.

Mrs. Oka teaches an exercise class every other Saturday at the senior center, and she exercises every day here at home. Also she learned how to paint at the senior center. She does a lot of it herself now and she only learned how four years ago. Now she is teaching origami at the center and also at the museum.

We carry Blue Cross and Blue Shield. We get social security and I have a retirement pension. We can manage on that.

When we came back from Chicago we went to study at the International Institute of Oakland, which is a social work institute that trains volunteer workers. No Japanese worked there at that time, so we asked to work among Japanese. We stayed there a little over three years. At first the state rejected the idea of starting a Japanese senior center—this was about six years ago. The Japanese Christian pastors asked them what they were planning to do, as there was a real need. Then they came to see me and gave me some money to start one at the Lake Park View Methodist Church, which is the one Japanese church in the area. The state says they have many senior citizens' centers in Oakland and in Berkeley, but the Japanese, Chinese, and other Orientals don't speak English, so they don't want to go there. The International Institute initially gave us twenty-five hundred dollars to open a Berkeley Senior Center for Japanese. It is located in the same building as the other senior center, and they just give us the space two days a month. The state gave funds to open centers in Hayworth, El Cerito, and Richmond because they didn't mention that they were founding specifically Japanese centers. But after one year, when they found out where the money was going, in the next fiscal year they cut off funds. Then the city gave us small tideover money. This October all funds expire and we have to go back to the cities again and ask for more. It's interesting work anyway.

I think we are different from most Japanese in this country because we associate with American people. For instance, my wife was invited to be secretary of the parent-teacher association and she had to learn to speak English to do it. We both feel American now. We are both happy we came over. We regret we have no more time, that we're too old to do some of the things which interest us. We are thankful for everything. Symbolically, we eat half Japanese food and half American.

Tivador and Juliska Pelzer

Budapest, Hungarian People's Republic

Born 1896 and 1889

Dressed in bathrobes and slippers, Tivador and Juliska Pelzer were walking slowly, arm in arm, down the long corridor of the hospital when I was introduced to them. The interview was made possible through the help of the Ministry of Health and a doctor, a friend of a friend, in Budapest.

The story of Tivador (born in Leva, Hungary in 1896) and his wife, Juliska (Szekszárd, 1889), interested me, as they were both patients in the same Budapest municipal hospital. This seemed a particularly humane and unbureaucratic solution to a dilemma, a solution to be emulated in the United States. In Hungary, it should be added, the population of those over sixty is now 18.2 percent (1974 statistic), one of the highest percentages of aged in the world.

The recovery of the Pelzers was progressing much more rapidly, one suspected, because of the arrangement. Although they didn't share a room, their rooms/wards were adjoining and all their social hours were spent together.

JULISKA SPENT FOUR months here with TB last year after our general practitioner discovered she had pneumonia and pleurisy. She was released cured. Then, six weeks ago I was brought into hospital, as my breathing was becoming very heavy and labored. I had had pleurisy seven times already until they finally performed some rather minor surgery in 1967, which helped me up to this time. The hospital and the authorities felt they couldn't leave Juliska all alone with her very high blood pressure, so they brought her along, too. Last year, when she was put into the hospital, I was all alone. I managed pretty well; I did the shopping and cooking, just like a woman. I learned well how to

We were put in the same hospital. Can you imagine how isolated we would feel otherwise?

cope when my first wife was bedridden for five years with arteriosclerosis.

Juliska and I were married in 1966, both of us for the second time. My first wife died in 1961, when she was seventy-one years old. She was a teacher, like myself. Juliska's husband was a bricklayer; he died in 1962, and they had been married for forty-two years. She has no children, but I have two sons. One is an engineer, who comes to visit us here every other Saturday. When we're at home he comes, too, though he lives more than fifty kilometers outside the city. My other son is manager of one of the railroad stores here in Budapest.

We live in Budapest in a flat which belonged to Juliska: one room and a kitchen. It's cramped. Before my wife died and while I was teaching, I lived in the country. I miss it. Too many people in the city! I was the director of a school in the village of Kunsziget until 1948. I had seven teachers under me. Oh, I loved my work. Before the war I taught everything. Later I specialized in math and physics for the ten- to fourteen-year-olds.

After my retirement I left the village because everyone I had grown up with, all my friends—even the local doctor and the pharmacist—had died. So I decided to move to the big city. I miss seeing the beauty of the landscape. One of my dreams is to be able to go back to Lake Balaton, but that takes money—more than we have. We both receive pensions: hers is eight hundred ninety florin a month, mine thirteen hundred. I've never been interested in acquiring money. As long as we can take care of ourselves we'll manage, but we have to calculate the money carefully. For instance, we can't afford to rent a television. That would be fifty florin a month extra, which is too much for us. But we have a radio. We like music, and reading. I couldn't survive without reading; I like novels, Hungarian ones especially (more than the foreign ones), but not modern novels. Juliska reads the papers. Our main regret is that we don't have enough money for cultural events. I've loved music ever since I had to study it for my teacher accreditation. Later I sang in a choir. I still like to dance, especially when they play gypsy music.

My father was also a teacher, but he taught in a religious school. Juliska's father was a carpenter. I had six brothers and sisters. Two of my sisters are still living back in the village and one sister lives in Riverhead, Long Island. A brother emigrated in 1945, but he died in America in 1956.

I fought in both wars. In World War One I got shrapnel in my back during the campaign in Poland and in the Ukraine. I was on medical leave for three months because my left hand became paralyzed; the shrapnel was pinching a nerve. Thank God, it could be operated on. I went back then to fight in Albania. There I caught malaria. In World War Two I was in charge of a food and arms depot. I was a lieutenant in the Hungarian Army.

Both my marriages have been good; we get along very well and I never get hit with the rolling pin! We are satisfied with our days. We do our little housework together, go to the food shops, then the library to get books. In the afternoon we go to the square for a walk. Then we eat and read and listen to music and go to bed.

The district nurse here is very kind—we're extremely lucky. After my wife was so sick and then when she came home, the nurse came to see after her and to check whether she was taking her medicine regularly. It was she who saw that we were put in the same hospital now. Can you imagine how isolated we would feel otherwise?

Here the regimen is very strict, as it would have to be. Rest every afternoon. But after the doctors' rounds in the morning and the treatments we are free, walking and talking, until lunch. Then, in the evening, we watch TV, and once a week there is a film. We are well satisfied to be here together, not to have to worry about the other. I believe it is a government policy and a most humane one.

I think one reason I've managed to live happily and in pretty satisfactory health all these years is that I've lived a sensible life. We never drank, except a glass or so on exceptional holidays, and we never overindulged in food.

I look back with satisfaction over my life. I am always happy I chose the profession I did. I saw my task as giving culture to youth, offering them resources for their entire life, which I found kept them away from the bars. I liked my work so much in fact that quite at my own expense and on my own time I gave a lecture once a month on history or art, using a slide projector. My old students used to come back to visit with me—and yes, sometimes vice versa. Our village is one hundred seventy kilometers away from Budapest, and when they came home, they touched base. It meant a great deal to me to see how they had developed.

Sister Aloisia

Salzburg, Austria

Born 1892

With the help of two young friends—Wilma Tanzler, an Air Canada stewardess, and Franz Weissenböck, formerly a seminarian, now a writer—I was able to visit with some Austrians. Wilma had a favorite teacher in her convent schooling years whose age was eighty-one (in 1973, the time of the interview). We drove from Vienna, through part of the Vienna Woods, into a district of the city called Rodaun. There we found the Convent of Saint Christiana. It was a handsome old building surrounded with gardens, standing next to the church, which had a baroque tower. We were received in the Mother Superior's reception room, a rich, rather Victorian chamber with delicate lace curtains, a large central table covered with a fine cloth, and several Biedermeier glass-door cabinets containing the convent treasures. On one wall hung an old, beautifully carved crucifix; on the other walls, portraits of various Mother Superiors and a painting of the saint herself.

The nuns greeted us and served us delicious Kaffee mit Schlag, *a special Viennese coffee with heaps of pure whipped cream. Then, after a few pleasantries, the Mother Superior retired, and we were left alone with Sister Aloisia. In the dimness of the room her kind face shone, and only the rim of the interior white cap and her cross stood out against the black habit.*

I WAS TWENTY years old when I entered the convent, but I had made up my mind about joining already when I was fifteen. At that time I was enrolled in the civil school (that is, *Buergerschule*), which in those days was also managed by nuns, in my case from the Saint Ursula Congregation. The nuns influenced my decision to join the convent. I remember walking up and down in the schoolyard with one of the sisters, and I thought to myself, I wish I could be like her. During that time I also belonged to the Holy Mary Congregation, a congregation for girls were responsible for their own religious

I never had privacy in my entire life. I was seventy years old when I got my room.

education and upbringing. I took this very seriously.

I don't know why I did not enter the convent from there, right into the Saint Ursula Congregation. God must had led me this way. One day I visited the Convent of Saint Christiana in Frohsdorf, a little village in Lower Austria, where I met Sister Eulogia, whom I liked very much. After talking to her at great length I decided that I would join the same order. And so I realized my girlhood dreams.

However, before I actually entered the cloistered life I decided to take some courses which would qualify me to become a sewing and needlework teacher and which would also enable me to teach some other handcraft courses that were required in those days. I only took these courses so that I would be able to do something useful for the convent after I joined. My first passion was becoming a missionary nun, but a doctor told me that because of my poor health I could never go into a mission and work there. He even felt that to work with children would be too hard for me. He suggested that I should work perhaps in the gardens or do some other less demanding work. Still, I always hoped to be able to go into a mission one day.

I was very weak and often ill. At the age of fourteen I even had to quit school for a while because I fainted so often. Nowadays these things are better understood and there might be cures. Perhaps I was anemic or suffering from hypoglycemia.

The first few years in the convent were very tough and difficult; that was during my probation years, which I spent in Metz, France, where our main convent is located. The reason it seemed especially hard was, of course, because of the strange language with which I had to struggle and the new foods I had to learn to eat. All this on top of the rigorous discipline of convent life. Before long I again became sick. I was so worried that the convent would not keep me, but the Mother Superior did not send me away. She said rather bluntly that I would not live long anyway. Ironically, there was another Austrian sister with me who was so full of life and health. She had a face like milk. Do you know, she died twenty years ago already and I am still alive. Strange. After I returned home to Vienna from Metz I recovered and overcame my physical weakness. I drank milk every day, three times a day, and that seems to have made me strong. Also the regular life-style of the convent has helped me, I think, all these years, and now, you see, I have become this old.

I continued my studies once I was in the convent, especially in music. I always loved music and I confess my greatest passion was to sing as a soloist with the church choir. That became my greatest joy and satisfaction.

Even though my hometown was Salzburg, as a girl I did not have many chances to go to concerts, but I always enjoyed playing music for myself. I still like especially Rachmaninoff, Beethoven, and Grieg; also, of course, our dear Mozart and Haydn and all the great classics. I learned to play a number of their compositions by heart on the piano. Now I mainly enjoy listening to music on the radio.

I taught here in the convent school until two years ago. My subjects were always French, *Handarbeit* [handcrafts], and religion. Alas, music I was only able to teach until 1938. After the war, when we reopened the convent in 1945, I was made head of the whole boarding school department and for some years had so much work to do for the school that I just did not have the time to teach music. I also had troubles with my eyes and could not read the notes very well. As a child I studied the piano but only got to the intermediate level; that means I studied for about three or four years. I never liked lessons in those days, but now I enjoy playing the piano very much. For three years I was even teaching the children here in the school, but this fumbling around on the piano got on my nerves.

When I was a little girl my mother told me that I used to go to church every Sunday. Then after church, on my way home, I had to pass a tavern where they played the accordian. Evidently I always stopped and listened to the music and then, of course, was late coming home for Sunday dinner. But scoldings didn't seem to help too much. I continued.

Later I studied the organ as well. Unfortunately, I was not able to practice it for very long, because I had learned to play on the old type of organ and never did master the newer kind. It was only during the time, when I was working in a parish, that I was able to play a beautiful old organ in the church to which I had been assigned. That was during the Second World War. The Nazis did not allow us to keep our school open, so we had to close down; the nuns were scattered about and had to work in different places and occupations. Most of us worked in parishes or hospitals, and the ones who stayed behind in the convent did some sewing in order to be able to survive.

I should tell you about my childhood. We were six children in our family, three girls and three boys. All the brothers are now dead. The first died during the First World War, in Dalmatia; he later was honored by the government. The second brother died in America quite unexpectedly of the flu, when he was at the height of his powers, at the age of forty-two. I lost my third brother two years ago, and then one sister died last year. Thank heavens, one sister is still alive. We were such a big family and now she and I are alone.

My parents were very busy with the six of us, which meant we often had to take care of each other. My father was working for the government; he was head of the registration office in our city. But my mother was always at home, a housewife, because with the six children she had enough work to do. Once a week she had a woman coming to help with the housework, but otherwise she did everything herself. She even made our clothes. We had a close and beautiful family life. That is why I almost think a child educates himself or herself—but within the strong protection of the family.

Now, in the convent I have a very good life, except for the little pains that bother me here and there. But one has always something to suffer; everyone does. I feel it is important to keep busy, to keep occupied, and not to think too much about the pain. And I do have a lot of work to do still. I practice and coach the acting with the children when we are giving our plays, and I also organize the exercise classes and the gymnastics.

In the morning, before the classes start, I go down to watch over the children in the classrooms because the outside teachers only arrive at eight o'clock sharp, and so I stay in the classrooms from seven thirty to eight. In these ways the time passes very fast for me. I take a good rest every day, and I enjoy life very much. If it is the will of God, I'll stay alive; if not, I'll go. In the convent we old nuns have many advantages over old people in the outside world. We always have some work to do without having to work full time. Whereas outside, once people retire, they have nothing to do. My sister, who comes for a visit sometimes, says that I have it much better in comparison to her life, because she saw that we are still really needed, we still have work to do, and there are always the children around. But I can't say that I understood all that already when I was young. I never thought about such matters.

Today it is sad; young people don't want to go into a convent anymore. It seems that they only desire superficial things: cinemas and pop records and constant entertainment. It is also very hard nowadays to discipline children. Years ago we were able to handle children much better. Now, even here in the convent the children are allowed to go home every weekend, and that makes it much more difficult for us; we don't have the influence we used to have. Today the child's mind is diverted too much—I'm speaking especially about the religious upbringing here. Before, in earlier years, the children were allowed to go home at Christmas, Easter, and the summer holidays—that was all. Then, later, they were allowed to go home once a month; and now, every weekend. Often I find the children think only about going home; they never get properly settled in. It makes it difficult for us. But I think it will be better one day. When these disruptive years are over I hope that people will be better again. The world has changed; youth has changed.

Today the young people have no more sense of shame it seems. For instance, when they have to change for the gymnastics classes the fifteen-year-old ones just undress, quite without thought, in front of the little ones, and this the children would never have done before. They used to hide in corners rather than let anyone see them when they were changing. Probably it all has something to do with the magazines the children read nowadays and the movies they see. Also, so many of the children, I find, don't have a proper family life. I really feel sorry for them; so often both parents are working and they seem always to be in a hurry. They have no real time for their children. There is no family atmosphere, no sense of togetherness. Only a few of the children are lucky enough to have their mothers at home during the entire day.

I don't blame the children for the situation now; it's really not their fault. They are brought up without belief, and though we try hard to teach them religion, if they don't have it at home it's just a waste of time for us to try to instill it in school. If they don't get a good example at home, they will never learn, will never accept it from us. But maybe not everything will be lost; hopefully some part of what we teach them will stay with them.

Many children come back to visit us after they quit school. Once a year the children have a reunion here. Those children who graduated before 1938 come each December eighth; those children from the period after 1945 come on the first Sunday in December. We are always very happy to see them again. It is then that we see that we have given them something of lasting importance.

I have never regretted joining the convent. I never had a reason to. Everybody has a "cross" to carry in life. There is always something which is particularly hard; in my case it was the illness, but I never regretted my vocation. If one has chosen the right profession, one cannot regret. In the convent we are very attached to God. Even in hard times I feel connected to God, and this happy feeling is always with me; it is that which keeps me young. Before I entered the convent I sometimes told people of my future plans, and they would say to me, "You are much too merry and happy to go into a convent." There are so many misconceptions about life in the convent!

Thank God, I don't have a husband, and children I have enough of! We devote ourselves to all the children—not like a mother, just to her own few. Even before I became a nun I never thought about a man. I was only fifteen, after all, when I made up my mind about this vocation. But even if I had loved a man, there is nothing wrong with that, and I would be able to tell you about it. But there never was a man in my life to whom I was close. My parents did not have anything against my plans either. Some sisters have difficulties with their parents when they enter a convent, but in my case my mother and father supported my decision.

My daily life is still very much organized. I get up every day at five fifteen and at five forty-five I go to pray in the chapel. Breakfast is at seven. Then I watch the children. When the children start their classes, I go back to pray in the chapel until nine, and then I go and clean my room. I go for a walk each day and pray the rosary. I still teach French; I have two students at the moment. Two or three times a week I spend the afternoon watching over the children when they are playing to make sure that they don't hurt each other. I have always liked the contact with the children; there is always something they need and they come to me for it. I go to bed around nine or nine thirty. I used to sleep with the children until ten years ago. Now I have my own room. But when I first got my room, I missed the children very much. In the evenings, when all the children were in bed and everything was quiet, sometimes a child would come up to me with some trouble or fear or sadness. Then I had the time to talk, and I was able to make a cross on their forehead; it was a beautiful and sacred time. I never had privacy in my entire life. I was seventy years old when I got my room. Most of the dormitory bedrooms had about twenty children in them. But I never minded having no privacy. I liked looking after the children and being with them, but now the younger sisters have taken over.

Once we were forty-four sisters here; now we are only twenty. Therefore, we have to hire people to do some of the work in the household, and we have also had to hire extra teachers. Our employees are good people, but it's very different now compared to the time when there were only the nuns. The employees do their jobs well, but they work exact hours and then go home. A sister works until the work is finished; she doesn't check the time. We are always here. But still it's better this way than not at all.

Because I always wanted to go into a mission and was never able to, I try now to work for the mission as much as I can, but of course from here. I collect clothes, which I clean, iron, and mend, and I make carpets from pieces of material and I sell lottery tickets and magazines to raise money. I'm a very dangerous person when it comes to that; people always have to buy something from me. It's so important for old people that they still have something to do. If people have no work to do, they are unhappy, bored, dissatisfied. I'm always happy the more I have to do. I don't have any friends left from my childhood days. They are all dead now; I'm the only one alive. But I think God wants me to stay alive a little longer. So I have my good sense of humor, and humor keeps me young and healthy.

See that drawer there; it's full of stories I've been writing. So the time passes.

Jenny Dunson

Miami Beach, Florida

Born 1890

I met Jenny at the Catalina Hotel in Miami Beach, introduced by a friend whose mother was also a resident of the hotel. They both came over as children from Russia, part of that great immigrant wave that landed, impoverished, on our shores after the pogroms in the late nineteenth century. Jenny lived alone (she died a year after the interview, I heard from my friend Florence Cohen) in a bright little efficiency room in an old residential hotel located a block or two from the ocean. She had her own icebox and bathroom and a small stove. The building was entirely occupied by retired people. There was no nurse on hand, nor were there any dining facilities. There was a small elevator and a front porch filled with rocking chairs.

I WAS BORN in Russia in 1890. We grew up around Kiev, where my father was a tailor. He manufactured army uniforms for the czar. My mother was a widow with four children when she married my father, also a widower, with four of his own. They managed to have ten more children together. We were very, very poor, as you can imagine. We came over in 1903, when I was thirteen.

I have been a Zionist all my life; in fact when I was married in Cincinnati, Golda Meir used to come by our house and also Ben Gurion and Ben Zvi. We had a lot of important visitors stopping by because my husband was an ardent Zionist. I used to wash their socks and underwear and consider it an honor.

I was never able to go to Israel; there was always something which interfered. So instead I did my work on this side, to help her [Golda Meir]. See my citation: "To Mother of the Year, for Generous and Continued Service to the Child Rescue Fund, Golda Meir, 1974." I have been living in Miami more than twenty years, and I have worked with them all along so I get, once in a while, all these little trinkets.

I was the youngest of the family and I always knew that I was not wanted.

My poor mother was fifty-two when she had me. Just keeping eighteen children in shoes and dressing the boys so that they could go to school cost more than my father could manage. Of course, in those days girls weren't expected to get an education—they just had to know how to cook so that they could get married. My father was a good orthodox Jew, but at the same time he wasn't a fanatic. I only had nine months of schooling in English when I came over here. In Russia I never went to school.

In winter I didn't know what shoes meant. One of my sisters would have to give me her shoes so I could go outside and get a little fresh air; I was as green as a cucumber, always lying about the house. Whatever my sisters outgrew or couldn't use I got—oh, I was rich in old clothes, Jenny was!

Mother worked hard to take care of us. She used to get up at four A.M. to bake. But I didn't know what personal love meant; I often felt I was in their way, always under their feet. That's the usual trouble with such large families—no time.

My father died two months after we arrived in this country. I think he couldn't stand the grief of being separated from his homeland. He used to sit in the window and say, "Look, even the garbageman who collects the garbage can speak the language, and here am I, who had an important job in Russia, and I can't even talk to anybody." He got so he wouldn't eat, he wouldn't drink; he was so discouraged. Of course, he was already close to eighty then.

When I came to America I went to work immediately. You see, my older sister opened a grocery store and I used to work for her. I got a dollar and a quarter a week, and my mother used that dollar and a quarter to get groceries. When I got a little older I began to work for the A & P chain, first as a clerk and then as assistant cashier, and finally, when I was fifteen, I was made manager of a store. My stock used to come out exactly at inventory time every six months, but it was hard work. It was hard on me: I was just a youngster and managing a store! First of all, I had to learn how to spell and how to write. If I wanted to live I had to go out and work. There at the A & P I advanced as high as eight dollars a week.

I don't think a psychiatrist could have done any better than my mother did with us eighteen children. Never once was it said, "your children" or "my children"; in fact, I never knew till I was grown up that my sister was my stepsister. We all stuck together even after we were married, and we continued to help each other. We were close, and that was every bit my mother's work. My father was a very fine man, too, an honest man, and I never heard them quarrel. Certainly not in front of the children. They had their own bedroom; perhaps there they had an occasional argument, but we children were unaware of it.

I tell you, when we came over here we almost had to charter a ship, because my sisters-in-law, when they found we were going to America, wanted to bring their parents over, too. There were over thirty of us who came all together.

I have only one daughter and three grandsons. The three boys are all in good professions: one is a surgeon, one an assistant professor at Brandeis, and the other a lawyer. I had only one child, because when she was five my husband had a severe heart attack and I had to go out to work. The doctor told me if I wanted to keep my husband alive he would have to be kept very quiet in the house and should never go back to work. He was well-nigh bedridden, and I had plenty of that for fifteen years. Working all day, rushing home and fixing dinner, cleaning the house, doing everything—and the more he stayed in, the more suspicious he became of me. If I was ten minutes late because of a jamup on the bus, he would ask me, "Where have you been? Who were you out with?" I would just turn around and say nothing. I guess I learned early on to become a doormat.

I went to work in Roamans, and I stayed there for twenty-two years, working in the stock department in the basement. When I retired they gave me a wonderful testimonial.

I wasn't young, in fact over twenty-four, when I married because I had to look after my mother. I was considered an old maid because I wasn't married at eighteen or nineteen years.

Toward the end my husband's mind was crippled from just lying there; he used to say a lot of things that got me discouraged. He used to punish me in subtle ways and, of course, we also had no sexual life. I was forty-eight when he died and I never got a new man because I was put off by that experience. I continued working until thirteen years ago.

After my husband's last heart attack we moved to Kentucky, and I bought a small village store. I had to do everything there—the buying and the selling. I was even the druggist. I had been told my daughter would get a better education in a small town, which was why I moved there. This was after I worked for Roamans. But I left Kentucky because the Ku Klux Klan became active, and though they didn't bother me, they were anti-Semitic. They were fighting each other with guns and I was afraid. Eventually, when I was sixty-two, I came down here to Miami with my sister, who had had to move here because of her bad heart and general ill health.

I went to Burdines, a store that caters to rich Jews, to look for work. However, they did not *hire* Jews in those days. I used to have to go in by the back door so that no one would observe me, and I was not used to that. I had to work in the dress department, which was quite different from linens, where I'd worked before. I had a boss, who, when I showed him my references, told me they didn't mean a thing. He said if you make your quotas all right you can tear up the testimonial. I thought to myself "All those years counting for nothing," and I couldn't understand it. I had a little money saved, and we were paying very high rent at that time, so when my brother-in-law said, "Just let me buy a lot and put up four walls. Everything else I can do later," we agreed. He bought a small piece of land. I managed to get my sister a job doing alterations at Burdines. With all three of us working we had enough money to buy wood and a few things for the house, though at first we had no windows or doors, just openings which we nailed shut at night.

My life wasn't a garden of roses. Nobody promised me that, and it wasn't, believe me. We lived in our house for quite a while; it was comfortable but small. I had to sleep on the living room couch.

It was hard living in the house at first, without windows or anything. Every penny we made went into the house. Then my sister had a stroke. I had to have oxygen near her bed, and night and day I was up—I could have fallen asleep on my feet I was so tired. Then my brother-in-law died suddenly, so I decided I'd have to try to get social security. My sister was getting only thirty-seven dollars a month and we couldn't make it on that. I retired from work as I had to look after her, but don't think looking after her was all I did. I was a baby-sitter for all the people on the court; I raised some of those children. My sister was as smart as she could be, but she couldn't move. She went on like that for about three years. While my sister was sick I also looked after the baby of one of my neighbors. She had to go into the hospital with breast cancer when the baby was three days old and I looked after it for eight months. I used to clean the house, give my sister her shots, and look after the baby.

But when my sister died this woman was very good to me. We are still friends now, and her children think of me as their aunt. When I first came here she moved me and even hung my clothes in the closet. She said, "Don't look back," because I was heartbroken about leaving the house. She offered to show it if anyone wanted to buy it.

I moved down here thirteen or fourteen years ago. First we had the big house to take care of and now, look, just one room is all I've got. I don't even clean, because there is a maid who comes once a week. But I am grateful because I get tired so easily now. There is no dining room here but across the street there are two nice restaurants; they are not kosher though. I have all my dishes here if I feel I want to do the cooking. I have to do something, so I buy a chicken and put it up.

I exercise—I do exercises *you* couldn't even do . . . my feet up over my head or I ride a bicycle. I have to do something active or I would end up like the women here who sit on their behind and do nothing. I don't go to senior citizens' meetings because I don't feel old enough. I don't like to just sit. Here I do a lot of reading, mostly Jewish newspapers.

I listen to programs that I enjoy. I don't like murder stories and things like that, but on Sundays we have a Jewish hour from half past nine to half past ten. Then we have *Face the Nation, Meet the Press,* and *Issues and Answers.* I like that. I like politicians, but I don't like dirty politicians. But I do listen to things that are worthwhile. I like to know what is going on in this world.

I often write, mostly fiction, but I don't do anything with the stories, except put them in the drawer. Sometimes when I can't sleep so good I sit over there by the desk and I write. I started this habit when my sister was sick and I had to be with her night and day. I had to do something to keep busy. I write about things I have heard about, things that happened to people.

I'm lucky; my daughter pays my rent here. I get two hundred and twenty dollars social security and Medicare. I pay twenty-five hundred dollars a year rent, but I get a maid and clean sheets and everything. I even have an air conditioner and it don't cost me nothing more.

I could feel better though. When you are eighty-three you get pains from getting old. About two and a half years ago I fell down three steps and broke my hip. I had to use a walker and still now need to use a cane.

With my bad foot I can't go dancing no more but my boyfriends like me just the same. Anyway what do I need with those old tockers anyway? Sex I can leave alone too. I never really had a boyfriend after my husband died. I was too busy looking after my daughter and later my sick sister. Who do I have to please? For what? For a home? To me *this* is a home. I don't have to worry about anything here. I have good friends around me and should I exchange this for washing some man's socks and cooking his meals?

You are looking at an old lady, but all the writers I still read—in Jewish, too—all the dramas. I go to the library, but I don't go to the *schul* because it is too far away, and since I am not a member, they make me go up another flight of stairs. That I can't do with my legs. So you know what I do instead? I can't cheat on God, so I read the Bible in two languages; I read it in Hebrew and I understand it in English.

I don't go out at night alone anymore, only when friends pick me up in their car. This place is pretty good, though; we sit around downstairs on the porch and tell jokes. I sit with the people when they are sick. When a person needs you, you have got to go to them. But that's the only time I go visiting in other rooms.

I cook for myself because I can't take salt. If I don't want to suffer with my high blood pressure I cook.

My life history, on the whole, is a sad one, but I never made it sad. What's the use of crying. I was tried so many times—as a child, with my husband, and then my sister—but I never told my daughter of my problems. Once I had a chance to get remarried, but I didn't do it because I didn't want my daughter to have a stepfather. Who knows what he would have been like? I think that is why she pays my rent now. A lot of what I experienced I could write about. See that drawer there; it's full of stories I've been writing. So the time passes.

John: *Since retirement I have paid a lot of attention to my inner self.*

Sooch: *I sense the possibility that some creativity may still exist in me.*

John and Sooch Rannells

Inverness, California

Born 1901 and 1900

John Rannells, an architect, and "Sooch" Rannells, a schoolteacher and social worker, are the parents of Malcolm and Betsy Wood, close friends of mine in California, who arranged the interview. John and Sooch are living in retirement in a beautiful modern house that John designed and, in part, built, located on the coast of northern California. It is hard to believe that they were born at the turn of the century; they seem to stand in the middle of life, deeply involved, and one would think that physically and spiritually they are perhaps in their fifties. At least half the interview took place while we walked through their favorite steep bit of forest, which led us down to the lonely rock-strewn shore of the bay. City-bred, they are obviously greatly enjoying their recent encounter with this wild and beautiful stretch of coast.

JOHN: I WAS born in Boise, Idaho and lived there until the age of nine. I had a brother nine years older and a sister six years older than myself. My father had been a mine superintendent in Guanajuato, Mexico before he got married, and then he was a farmer in Missouri, but when he moved to Idaho he went back into silver mining. He was a man of miscellaneous enterprises; in fact, he was in real estate in Oregon when he died. At his death I was eleven, and I was fifteen when my mother moved back to Ohio. Her family, an old, established land-holding family of Quakers, came from Springfield, Ohio.

I went to Ohio State University, where I studied civil engineering. After graduation I worked for Bethlehem Steel in bridge construction and then moved to New York, where I worked with the architectural consultant to the Regional Plan, financed by the Russell Sage Foundation. Then I had the opportunity to work on the George Washington Bridge for Cass Gilbert, a big architectural firm, where I stayed for nine years. I worked on the Supreme Court Building in Washington for several years on and off. After that I work for a colleague who won the design competition for the Oregon State Capitol. The job moved so fast we couldn't keep up with it by mail, so two of us were sent out for a week to tie up loose ends. It was a hair-raising trip through storms in an early, unpressurized plane, carrying only twelve passengers.

After twenty-odd years in architecture I went back to school and earned an M.S. in planning at Columbia University, where I was teaching graphics. Then I joined the research staff of Columbia's Institute for Urban Land Use and Housing Studies. My book *The Core of the City* was a study of changing land uses in central Philadelphia.

My next job in Philadelphia, under a new city charter, proved to be a great one. A crowd of well-placed Philadelphians decided to work with the Establishment while working for charter reform as the only way to get anything done, to produce any reforms. They created a planning operation and then went to Washington and got one of the key men at the National Resources Planning Board to run it. Incumbent politicians in the city government got all the credit for whatever was accomplished, and at the same time the charter reform movement was under way. All this was around the midforties.

My work in Philadelphia was for a one-year study of *all* transportation in the region, headed by Bob Mitchell, who had set up the planning operation ten years before and who was then head of the Department of City and Regional Planning at the university. There were two planners from New York, three graduate students, and a secretary on the team, and we did all the work. I am convinced that more gets done by small groups. We turned out an excellent job, which then became city policy. Much of it has since become national policy. This basic job of ours of establishing policy was then followed by work within the city administration, which began to put things actually on the ground. For example, we had studied how to subsidize fares on Philadelphia's commuter railroads, so as to avoid spending greater sums on highways.

From Philadelphia I went to Washington to work for the National Capital Transportation Agency as special assistant for planning. Our plans were controversial, but finally Congressional approval was given for a twenty-five-mile subway. After serving as planner, engineer, architect (I held Grade 15 civil service ratings for all three) I ended as director of architecture in charge of the design program, which was well along by the time I retired and is continuing successfully under the same outstanding architectural consultants—Harry Weese and Associates.

I wrote a technical column for *Progressive Architecture* for four years; that's where I learned to write. It was an awful chore, but it was fun. I also wrote a long piece for *Architectural Record;* the title is "Building in the Tropics." This is obviously an enormous topic and I got piles of reference material from the UN and also from progressive Britishers in Africa. The piece dealt with materials and design appropriate to building in the tropics; in essence, what it takes to exist in tropical countries. Immediately after the printing plates were destroyed the State Department requested one thousand reprints. A shame!

I am also a tough editor. My last job for the government was getting out reports, putting them in terms that can be read. I love design, but I am not sure whether it is worth writing about. The best books on it for the lay public are very simple. I may still get involved in producing something along these lines. I was making geodesic models long before Buckminster Fuller. Then I got into making molecular models. I sold some, but for lack of space I had to burn the rest.

The recent dreams of new cities and artificial environments do not please me. They don't allow for "what happens." A man I admire tremendously is the one who designed Brasília. I think it is as near perfect a design as you can get. What happened there, though, was quite unexpected: They built Brasília in the wilderness at the end of a very long highway with an army of workers, including the designers. All of them lived in temporary quarters. The funny thing was that these temporary quarters became the lively quarters, a lively slum. The planned city is beautiful but sterile.

I have been designing this house since long before it was built. There is still a lot of work here that can and should be done, but since I have a workshop downstairs it makes it easy for me. I'm particularly interested in doing more craft work.

Sooch and I have always loved the country, and we feel much better since we moved here. It's interesting that Sooch's people came from the land in Europe and mine did here. This is the perfect piece of land for us in our retirement—it's open. I don't think we could stand living in the woods. The woods are for walking in, not living in.

SOOCH: Since we came here I have started to enjoy hiking; in fact, we do a lot of walking. Retirement requires all sorts of adjustments. At first I was terribly lonely here; I missed my job and my friends.

JOHN: When we first moved here I volunteered to work on the Trails Committee established by the local environmental movement. Our work on it started about a year ago. It has involved a lot of tramping around but also working at headquarters discussing policies. There are problems when trails are shared by walkers and by equestrians, but there are places where separating them just does not make sense. It would be much too expensive to duplicate the trail system. Mainly we are interested in getting people to use the trails. You wouldn't believe what an extensive network of these trails there is passing through the most beautiful country.

The interview did not end here, but recently John Rannells told me that both he and Sooch were involved in quite new ventures so the earlier material was really no longer valid. The following paragraphs were sent to me as a substitute.

JOHN: Where am I now with myself, after all those years of retirement? I'm as busy as I care to be, mostly doing things I enjoy. When we moved out here from Washington I had a long list of things to do to the house and I have finished most of them, but there are always small improvements to be made. I like to design things that get built. I read quite a bit; I walk a lot in the beautiful national parklands near here.

For three years now my interest has been focused on a system for psychological self-appraisal called Trilog, invented by Arthur Rissman about seven years ago. My contribution is mainly in perfecting the graphic expression of this model of the mind's activities. As an engineer and architect I am accustomed to *thinking* in graphic terms. When we can get the diagrams to support and clarify the words, we've got something!

In my professional life I always seemed to be too busy to get in touch with my real feelings, too busy to realize how important feelings are to me. Since retirement I have paid a lot of attention to my own inner self and to my relations with others. Right now I feel fortunate to have had the time to get myself sorted out.

SOOCH: I suppose I should tell you a little about my earlier life, as John has done. I was born April 26, 1900 and was the youngest of five children. My parents came to this country from Austria—my mother was sixteen, my father in his early twenties. I know more about my mother's background. She lived on a flourishing farm. Her father was a scholar and an official in their small community. Her mother was very religious and planned her marriage to the son of a religious Jew. She refused to marry because she had fallen in love with someone else and after her lover emigrated and got a job here, he sent for her. He brought her home to a dingy basement flat in a New York slum. As she rode the elevated from Battery Park to her home, she wanted to know where the people lived. She thought the buildings were for storage.

While I was an infant my father became ill; he went to a hospital and never returned—TB. Mother, who had enjoyed a free and easy country childhood, went to work to support her four daughters and one son. My sisters and a cousin of my father looked after me. In comparison to her idyllic childhood, my mother's new life was hard—no sun coming into her home, struggling to earn a livelihood, while at the same time rearing her brood. But she set her sights for her children. Betty, the eldest, had a beautiful voice; Rose played piano; my brother and I the violin and the piano. Of the five children, three graduated from college and one from junior college.

When I was about twelve my mother thought I was too thin, too pale, and that I needed country life. She enrolled me in a settlement house camp and the next year succeeded in pitching two tents on the camp land. I grew tall that summer and flourished. I learned how to swim, to hike, to sleep out all night.

The high school I attended announced that violin lessons would be available for twenty-five cents a lesson. I enrolled. A couple of years later I joined a trio and we played at the Neighborhood Playhouse in New York's Lower East Side.

After graduation from Hunter College I taught in the New York public schools. I was very unhappy about the educational system. Children sat in their seats all day with no opportunity for freedom of thought, action, or feeling. I observed in two progressive schools—Walden and City-Country. I knew then that I had found my direction. I liked Walden and found a position there. I also was one of the first teachers at the Little Red School House.

In 1926 I married my husband, John Rannells, in Paris. For our honeymoon we bought bicycles and toured France. By marrying him I was introduced to his fascinating world, his incredible sensitivity to beauty, to form, to space, to the great natural world. On our return we walked in the country on weekends and on the New York streets during the week and saw the best of architecture—the bridges, the buildings—and I became aware of the force and energy expressed through the medium of architecture.

Two babies were born one and a half years apart. Watching their growth and development was continuously exciting to me, although periodically I felt uncertain of my role as parent. During the Depression I passed civil service exams to become a social investigator. In a couple of years I was supervising counselors in nursery schools. I retired in 1955, as John had an interesting job offer in Philadelphia, where I worked for Family Service of Philadelphia. When we moved to Washington for John's exciting work of planning the new subway, I worked for Family and Child Service of Washington and established a new program on family life education. I met with parents, teachers, students, and PTA groups and spoke with them about life and family problems. This work was instrumental in my own development. I was sixty-one when I went to Washington and retired in 1969. I felt now even more propelled toward an inner growth, one that I had been struggling with for most of my adult life. The meaning of separation to children, their growth toward independence and self-reliance, the important sources of energy in teen years, the need to break away, and the longing to hold on, the need for sexual gratification, parents' needs, the problem of couples who reach a plateau in their feelings and the struggle to survive in the relationship—these questions that were posed contributed immensely to my conscious understanding of my own growth and development.

When we moved to Inverness after our retirement I was restless at first and felt uncomfortable not having a regular job, although there was much to do to establish our new home. Nevertheless I yearned for friends, a circle of people. I joined the League of Women Voters, helped establish the first nursery school here, and was invited to be on the children's committee of the Mental Health Association of Marin. My early contribution was to encourage people trained in the field of mental health to work in the schools with teachers, parents, and children. After eight years I am still a member of that committee. I have taught a course in baby sitting to sixth-graders and have volunteered to meet with a group of young parents for a discussion of family life.

The mental health committee arranged to have Tom Harris, author of *I'm O.K., You're O.K.,* speak at Marin Junior College. I went with a friend and was so impressed with the theory of Transactional Analysis that I bought his book. John read it and suggested we go to his workshop in Sacramento. This lasted a week, and we were both stimulated and fascinated with the easy approach to self-analysis. John subsequently became a member, and we attended the annual meetings and a couple of workshops. One of the workshops was about a system called Trilog. John became very interested and involved and for the past three years has been working on a book with the founder of this system.

My daughter came to visit us with a friend who was working in a Sage group—Sage meaning senior actualization growth exploration. I attended a demonstration and was delighted with their approach to the aging. One year later I joined a group called Crossing Point #1, which was based on the Sage Process. Now once a week I travel forty-five miles in both directions to be with the group.

In February 1978 John and I went to Esalen Institute, at Big Sur, to attend a workshop called "Self-acceptance, the Freedom to Be." We were with people in their thirties and forties, and the exchange of life experiences were extraordinarily meaningful to all of us. I think everyone was both challenged and perhaps shocked at first when we said that we wanted to explore our feelings about death and separation. Later, the leaders of the group, a man and a woman, said, "It was a privilege to have you in our group." Old people need the stimulation of new experience as much as young people do. In fact, we need new friends, young friends, perhaps more even than the young do because often our older friends die or move away. One of the scary things about aging is that you know that one of you is going to be left. There is no solution. I think you can't ease the impact of mourning, nor should you, but you can talk about plans and that helps. But I don't think you can really prepare yourself.

In the Sage Process we concentrate on our breathing, a form of meditation, and we try to make acquaintance with our body: easy movement, unhurried, comfortable, enjoyable, no strenuous exercise that may damage small or large muscles. Gradually, we become acquainted with the way we use ourselves. Standing in a double circle we touch, and touching another human being is rewarding both in giving and in receiving. At some of the meetings we massage one another; our fingers dipped in warm oil, we sit opposite a partner and gently massage fingers. From this one-to-one contact intimacy develops; also compassion, tenderness, even anger and humor—a strange combination. At all sessions we get in touch with, discuss, our feelings. Sometimes we talk about new concepts or about Norman Cousins' article* and his philosophy of self-healing, for example. At some meetings we do spontaneous dancing to lively music. After a long period of neglect, these playful expressions of our free spirit in joyful movement are revitalizing to our bodies. Cousins tells us that joyous activity energizes our bodies.

Recently, at one of the Sage meetings, a discussion on anger brought out some interesting ideas: Is anger responsible for some of the accidents older people have? Should anger be suppressed? Or is it as normal a feeling as love or joy?

*"What I Learned from Three Thousand Doctors," *Saturday Review,* February 18,1978.

You may wonder why I needed this experience at nearly seventy-eight years of age. The purpose of my coming together with others in a group is to allay the sense of aloneness, to establish friendship with others on a deeper level, and to awaken my consciousness. Each of us in the group asks herself or himself, Who am I? What kind of body do I have? A new awareness now exists in me of the need to protect, to respect, and to value my body and my feelings. And I sense the possibility that some creativity may still exist in me.

Florida S. Maxwell, in her slim book *The Measure of My Days,** writes: "We who are old know that age is more than a disability. It is an intense and varied experience almost beyond our capacity at times, but something to be carried high. It is a long defeat, it is also a victory, meaningful for the initiates of time, if not for those who have come less far."

*New York: Knopf, 1968.

All my life I have loved the sea. I still have to go out on it to be happy.

Jakob Nilsen

Flekkerøy, Kristiansand, Norway

Born 1890

Dr. Jorge, head of the Kristiansand Hospital, Norway, arranged for one of his nursing staff, a young woman who spoke excellent English and who had lived in America, to act as my guide. We visited three nursing homes; a most impressive day center, with fine apartments for the aged built on the upper floors; and finally she took me to the island of Flekkerøy, where I was to interview an old fisherman—Jakob Nilsen.

The island is reachable first by a half-hour bus ride from the center of Kristiansand and then by a small ferryboat (no cars). It takes one over the lovely clear bay to the island. There is one taxi on the island. I had arranged for the driver to meet me and take me to Mr. Nilsen's house. On the island there is an international centre/school for young evangelists, a fish-packing plant, and the island store. Other than that it is an unspoiled, green, hilly place, rather reminiscent of Martha's Vineyard. The houses are neat, small clapboard structures built in much the same style as New England saltboxes. A narrow winding road leads to Mr. Nilsen's house, freshly painted and straddling a hill.

It was a two-minute walk, in felt bedroom slippers, for Mr. Nilsen to his fishing boat, anchored in a small inlet. As we walked down to the pier he pointed to an adjoining house where he had been born. Farther down the hill one could see the old schoolhouse he attended as a child. Inside, his house was neat and spruce, with clean white gauze curtains at the windows. The walls were covered with family pictures and mementoes. Mr. and Mrs. Nilsen sat in comfortable Victorian chairs at a round table where coffee and cookies were being served. A domestic oriental rug of a subdued, monochromatic pattern lay on the parlor floor, and through the passageway I could see an inviting, round, family dining table and to the side an old cupboard filled with rosebud-patterned china and a few pieces of silver.

I WAS BORN on the island in the house where my eldest brother still lives today. The house is located just down a little street from ours, where we have lived since our marriage in 1915. I had eight brothers and sisters, of which three brothers and four sisters are still living. All of my brothers became fishermen, all of our sons are fishermen, and my daughters are married to fishermen. One sister is in an old-age home on the mainland (she used to be the midwife in a village on the neighboring coast). My father survived to the age of ninety-five, my mother to ninety. My father was a fisherman, too. Of my siblings, the one who is eighty-five is the eldest; the youngest brother is seventy.

I became a sailor at fifteen and sailed around the world on sailing ships for one and a half years. My wages in those days were fifteen crowns a month; that was two dollars a month. But I left that life to become a fisherman. At first I worked on the crew of a neighbor's fishing boat. At twenty-one I was able to buy my own boat. Fishing is an up and down business. There were many lean years, years ago; it is better now because fish is more expensive today. We take the fish to the pier, and the city fishstand owners come to pick it up on our island pier and take it to the market. It is a good livelihood. There are fifteen hundred inhabitants on the island now; when I was born there were around a thousand. We had a school here which ran through the seventh grade supposedly, but actually it was divided into three sections: the little ones, the middle-sized ones, and the biggest.

We have some industry on the island: a fishnet yarn factory and a big freezing warehouse for fish, of course. And then the builders and carpenters. But we don't have a doctor on the island and no nurse.

We managed to fish during both wars, even with the mines. During the last war she [Mrs. Nilsen] had three sons and a husband going out to mine-infested seas, and each day she prayed they would return. In peacetime the South Norwegian fishermen primarily go out for mackerel, about fifteen nautical miles (five hundred kilometers) straight out into the North Sea. A mackerel run will last from six weeks to two months without letup.

A couple of times I have been caught in bad, bad storms. Once—I was about sixty years of age at that time—I was knocked unconscious by a huge wave, but luckily I came to in time! Another time I was knocked about so badly that I lost my memory temporarily, but somehow, operating by instinct, without consciousness, I was able to pull the lines and help my mates. Four of us men were trying to pull the lines taut, but we were afraid that they would get tangled in the propeller. We could not manage to free them, and so, as a result, the nets were drifting loose in the ocean. One huge mackerel hit the side of the boat—*smack*—so hard that it was thrown up into the air and landed topside. Thirty nets were ruined in that storm! And each one cost one hundred fifty crowns a piece (they buy the nets ready-made but weight them and cork them and put in the lines themselves). Another time our whole mast broke in half. This was when I was still on the sailing ship, in 1907, a long time ago!

Most of us married other islanders. We have stayed close to home. In

1915 I married; I have been married fifty-seven years. My wife is now eighty-two. She was twenty-five when we married. When I came along she was at home helping her mother; she was one of twelve children. Her father was a fisherman, too. We ourselves had five children, but one died.

The children are all here on the island. Only one son is married to a West Norwegian girl. He works on the mainland now. The rest live right here on the island, near our house. Our youngest son formerly had a boat of his own, but he couldn't find the necessary labor to operate it. So now he is a boat painter on the mainland. The two eldest sons share a fishing boat together. Our daughter lives around the corner here and comes every day to clean the house and help her mother. We are very lucky! We have thirteen grandchildren. As long as I am clear in the head I will stay in my own house. [I observed that both he and his wife had all their teeth, had good hearing, and seemed not to use glasses.] I'm feeling fine, too. Just a little bit stiff.

We are fussy when it comes to fish; we eat only the best. Every fish is alive until it drops into the pot! We eat mostly fish. Thank goodness, now there is a store on the island.

Once we went to Bergen on a plane, then six more hours by boat, and finally three more hours in a cab just to go to the wedding of one of our grandchildren. There was still snow up there in the mountains. Another time we went to the eastern part of Norway, also for a family wedding. I've often been to Oslo, of course. I've been inside all the big government buildings. In fact, I have shaken the hand of the crown prince! That was when I was foreman in the Fisherman's Association, our trade union. I was also secretary to our local Mackerel-Fishing Trade Union. I have been to see the "big ones," you see.

At sixty-two I retired and got my pension. But here's the hitch: you have to have fished for thirty-five years to get the fisherman's pension. A great number of us have fished for many years, but sometimes, in bad times, we were forced to change professions. Now, unfortunately, because of this some of my friends are not eligible for their pensions. At seventy the fisherman's pension stops and we get the government pension [old-age assistance]. We manage, but there's nothing for any extras. Our sons bring us mackerel and lobster. The only thing we grow are cherry trees. It's very dry here in summer, hard to grow produce.

My wife had seven years of school. After the first few years I went to the Coast Guard Captain's School to get the certificate for running my own boat and registering it. That was an eight-week course. Formerly I had a boat with a cabin which held six men—a sleeping cabin. But my wife never went out to sea with us. We used to go out for six weeks at a time, but we fished for mackerel only twice a year. At those times she was alone with the kids. We had salt barrels for keeping the mackerel and then sent the fish for export to America. It was salted right on the boat. The rest of the year we fished for herrings and some mackerel in the nearer waters. Sometimes, in winter, we were away for another two months, for herrings. That is besides the two mackerel runs. The children used to wait on top of the highest hill and when they could see one boat return, they knew the others would soon follow and all the fathers and brothers would be home. There were thirty boats total in our fleet.

I'd never been sick a day in my life. Then, one day I got a pain in my left side, which they diagnosed as angina pectoris. I had to go to the hospital for a couple of weeks. But I got it not from the sea, but from shoveling snow!

[Apparently in good weather he still goes out for day-fishing.] Today we went out for lobsters, my two sons and I. But I don't go along for the mackerel runs, not for six long weeks! That's too hard on my old bones.

All my life I have loved the sea. I still have to go out on it to be happy. I have had regrets only once in my life, and that was when the fishing was particularly bad. I was just newly married. At that time, I must admit, I thought a bit about working at a desk in the fishing plant and coming home at night to my wife.

It is clear that Jakob Nilsen and his wife have lived an unusually "centered" life here on this small island, with the security of having their family in close proximity. But generally throughout Norway one has the strong sense that the rest of the three million Norwegians in that huge, sparsely populated, still-wild land enjoy a similar sense of well-being. The social legislation is of such a caliber that it seems to throw a mantle of benevolent security over the shoulders of its citizens. Yet there is space enough for the sense of personal identity and freedom to remain intact. The people have not yet been niched, pinned, and identified, lifelessly, on the bureaucratic board.

Isaac Webster

Nottingham, England

Born 1898

Sir John Butterfield, an old friend in England, and now Regis professor of medicine at Cambridge, helped me arrange a number of the interviews, drawing on his international contacts.

At the time I wanted to interview an old miner, John and his wife, Isabel, were living in Nottingham, where he was vice chancellor at the university. He was able to arrange my visit with Isaac Webster, a retired miner. Throughout the interview Mr. Webster sat on the settee next to his old yellow Labrador bitch, reaching now and then to pat her on the head. His wife, in a steel walker, sat in the opposite corner.

I WORKED IN the mines until the age of sixty-five. Both me father and brothers were miners. Mind you, I was out of the mines for a long while. I was in the army for about seventeen years. I went into the mines at age fourteen. Before that I went to school (when I was three, I should think) and finished when I was thirteen. I worked in the potteries for one year. I didn't like it though. Five shillings a week they gave you, and when I went into the mines it was eighteen shillings. I was in the mines from 1912 to 1917, and then I was in the war—serving in France. 1919 I came out and was out for not quite two years when I enlisted again for twelve more years. I had twelve years in the cavalry. I didn't think at the time I enlisted that I would have to look after the horses. Oh yes, that was on your slate alright! Cleaning out the stalls!

First I was stationed at Orly, France, and then we was sent to Cairo—Egypt, I'm talking about! The scenery was alright but the flies were bad. Dry it was, and your face always burnt and sore from the sun. Give me the old English rain and mist! I was in Egypt for five years and then went to India. I was there, in a fort, for two years. Back here in 1929. That's when I made my mistake. I left the army when they mechanized the cavalry. I should have gone on for twenty-one years, because you get a good pension after twenty-one

When I'm in bed sometimes . . . it's galloping, then there's a break, it stops a bit. It's just as if it were an old clock. But I figure, while I'm breathing I'm alright.

years' service. The mining pension looks good on paper, but it doesn't go far nowadays. The pit pension is seven pounds a fortnight. That's three pounds ten a week. Anything extra you still have to pay for. She [pointing to his wife] had to pay for the home help when I collapsed and couldn't help her and had to be taken to hospital by ambulance. I had a heart attack. The home help cost me ten shillings a week, no, a pound, for two mornings for the home help and to have the fires made.

We've lived in this house now for three years, and we never had no luck since we come in it. Lived across the road forty-three years until they pulled it down. Loverly little house! I never thought I'd leave it.

I think they frightened me to death; this doctor's business with me heart. I used to drink a pint or two a day, but now I don't dare. Not since I got this heart thing. They told me not even to have a smoke. Mind you, it's a laugh [he says ruminatively, drawing on a well-worn briar pipe]. All this crawling-about business! You haven't to do 'this' or 'that'. Some days I feel as if I could jump to the moon, but other times it catches me. When I'm in bed sometimes it's bumping, it's galloping, then there's a break; it stops a bit. It's just as if it were an old clock. But I figure, while I'm breathing I'm alright.

She [pointing to his wife in her metal walker] had to have a special pair of shoes made this year. Mind you, I had to buy them. Cost me six pounds! You know them on public assistance, they don't pay for anything. That's the reward I get for working till I was sixty-five; we have to pay for everything. My wife worked until the old-age pension started. She was working for the home help until she got ill. She's all in steel on her back, you know. She's got degenerating disk of the spine, and she got injured on the home help spring cleaning for a woman. She was on the home help eight years (they compensate her now—hardship allowance), and she has been crippled about as long again, eight long years. Before retiring she was on war work, a machinist, and later she worked in the lace trade.

I was in the building trade for a while. If you was ever in a job that was a bit alright, they wouldn't keep you on for long. You see, these jobs used to keep you on only about a month, then the season would be over and they'd lay you off, and you would have to get another one. But I was never out of work long. Bitting and bobbing, that was the idea of it!

We were married seventeen years ago, I think it was—I can't remember. My wife here is seventy-three now. How old was you when we got married?

[She answers:] I've been married twice, I have. He hasn't! I was fifty when I took the plunge a second time, so that makes us married twenty-three years!

[He breaks in, with a gleam in his eye:] I couldn't get a decent woman, so I had to take one secondhand.

[Her answer is in kind:] Mind you, I could have married him before my first husband, but he wasn't good enough for me then!

[He continues:] The day of the heart attack I had the dog out for a run. Never knew there was anything wrong with me. I was to get the coal out of the coal house. I collapsed, couldn't breathe, didn't know what was wrong with me. I couldn't remember anything afterwards—going into the hospital or coming out, or how long I was there.

They told me I couldn't have no cigarettes or alcohol. I'm not allowed upstairs, you know, and me wife can't manage 'em either, so now we use the front room as a bedroom and just live on one floor. We pay two pound seventeen a fortnight for this house.

I had it easy when I was a bachelor. Lived with me mum till I was fifty. When she died I needed a wife. Came to live here as a lodger and we got together. I get the miners' pension and the old-age pension, of course, prorated. There's only one in my family still alive; but she has three sisters, only they live too far away for her to see 'em—they aren't well enough either to travel. She is the oldest of sixteen.

Mrs. Webster rises to a standing position in her walker and proceeds to roll past the old worn two-seater couch, through the narrow passage, past the sleeping old yellow Labrador, and into the tiny kitchen. The house is small and cozy. The "telly" in the corner, the old wooden wireless on a side table, a large striking clock with curved brass top over the mantlepiece, two geraniums sitting on the window sill, and the house painted in that indiscriminate beige-yellow-green, which could mean long worn paint or perhaps preference for a dim, neutral interior. She returns to the parlor, aluminum kettle in hand.

"Would you like a cup o' tea, luv, before I go off to the store? I like to pick me own bacon and cheese. That's me son, up there. [She points to a picture on the wall.] I got one son in Birmingham by my first marriage who works in a factory or something. We never had any children, him and me [pointing to her husband].

[He interjects:] I can't get a word in as it is! I don't know how we should go on if we had a kid. I shouldn't hear myself talk at all!

Isaac Webster settles himself back on the couch, one hand holding his pipe, the other encircling his dog, who had wiggled around his knees with expectation of a walk and/or a scratch on the rump.

Before this heart trouble I'd be going miles each day. Didn't know where I was going. Couldn't tell nobody in the morning; just tramping in the woods, anywhere. I used to go mad with that dog. Frightened to death now! Had some funny bouts! Makes you wonder at times. I don't want to go prowling round and collapse and lie a day or two before anyone can find me. Now these days I still get up at four o'clock, but after letting out the dog a minute I just sit and smoke and think. I only take her around the houses now for her walk, that's it! Then I come home. Or sometimes I do a bit of shopping for her [his wife] if she's got any. I was lucky I never got no lung trouble in the mines. Pneumoconiosis they call it. There's a lad just across the street who died of it just the other day. I always voted Labour, but they never did much neither. I've got naught for them all, to tell you the truth. I wouldn't care if the Pakistanis got in! They [the government] is always boasting what they are going to do for you—this, that, and the other. They give you a rise [in pension], but by the time you get it, six months later, prices have already gone up. It's not worth three halfpence! We have a social worker comes to the house. Oh, she's a good little woman she is, really. She potters in, and you feel better just to see her. She's a jolly sort of woman, but she doesn't come very often.

I don't regret my life. Nobody likes to go in the mines, but you've got to go or you've got no money and that's it. They are getting good money now, but what's crippling them is the taxes. And that's the reason there is so much absenteeism, because they've got to work three days for the tax man. So they would rather work less and have a little holiday. You're living in a house and your next-door neighbour is on public assistance and doing odd jobs; there's a lot like that. So you go in the pits these days, have a holiday, and go work somewhere else. It's the taxes killing everything.

The worst part of growing old . . . I think the worst thing is you know you are going to die. It's not that that bothers you—it's waiting for it that becomes so hard. You don't really feel any different, you know, when you're old. You're still you.

I shouldn't care tuppence whether I'm still around or not if only I could get some satisfaction from the doctors. All they do is tell you to take things steady. You mustn't get a bucket of coal, don't do this, don't do that. Trouble is I don't know how bad it is. Other friends get out of the pits and are scattered about for thirty or forty years, perfectly fine. But me . . . ! When I was in hospital they X-rayed me five or six times, and there was a spot on me film so they had to do it all over again, with the injections and all. There's only one thing that's keeping me from worrying too much (it's only when I get my pain I worry a bit). If it had been severe, then they'd have paid more attention to me. Otherwise they don't bother much. That's how I feel anyway.

I saw much injustice around me, and I became an activist.

Sarah Gastaud

Nice, France

Born 1906

The bright, modern apartment in Nice, France, where Sarah Gastaud, seventy-two, lives with her mother, Madame Leon Levy, includes an old dog and two cats. On the day of my visit, in June 1973, Veuve Isoard, Madame Gastaud's friend, who is also their cleaning lady, was present as well.

MY FATHER WAS killed at the front in World War One, when I was ten years old, and my mother, who had three children besides myself, had a hard time supporting us on a meager seamstress' salary. I was one of a set of fraternal twins, but I was never too close to my twin brother, because when we were born and our mother's milk supply proved insufficient, we were sent off to the mountains of Italy to the care of two separate wet nurses. I have kept in contact with my nursemaid, and she came to visit me several times during my childhood. Later, upon our return home, the school I attended was next door to our house. I loved school and was able to go until I was twelve years old, but at thirteen I had to start working and became a dressmaker's apprentice. One franc a day! Not even enough to keep my shoes heeled! I lived at home until I was twenty-one.

After my apprenticeship I started working for the Galleries Lafayette as a seamstress. I stayed there for seventeen years and only took off one year, at the age of twenty-two, for the birth of my baby. Later I had another son, who died of meningitis at four months of age.

My only son is now forty-five and is in the hospital with a virus. He has been there three months—very sick! One day he is suffering from paralysis in his legs; two days later he seems better or even fine; then back down again. The doctors tell me nothing. Nobody knows what is the matter with him. It's the first real sickness he has ever had. It's serious for him, you know, because he is a bus driver and now he won't be able to go on with his work. First the doctors think it's infectious rheumatism; others think it's a kind of male menopause. I don't know, but I'm very worried. He's married but hasn't any children, alas.

At seventeen, when I was working in the Galleries Lafayette, already I was known as "The Anarchist" because I wore a red scarf. But the title was accurate. I saw much injustice around me, and I became an activist. My first husband had also been in the Resistance during the war. He joined no party, but his heart was always in the right place. You know, communism was not well established in France in the thirties, so you might more rightly have called the movement anarchist or socialist in those days. Another girl and I spearheaded the big strike in the Galleries Lafayette. Oh, how I would love to be able to return to those days and live through it all again. It seemed to me people then listened to you much more attentively than nowadays.

The strike started in '36. We were earning only three hundred fifty francs per month. We occupied the factory for twelve days, never leaving. Food was smuggled into us by fellow workers on the outside, and we had managed to lay in some supplies. We won the strike and thereafter got the royal sum of one thousand francs per month.

My first marriage ended in divorce after seven years. I had a good lawyer, thank God. My husband left me to go and live with someone else in Marseille. While I was married to him he never really worked. I had to support him. He was always feeling tired, but otherwise he was a good man. As I was left alone I was forced to bring up the boy at my mother-in-law's. My son never really lived with me for long. He joined the Resistance during the war, straight from his grandmother's house. She died when he was sixteen years of age, and he went off to join the Maquis. Thank God, he was never caught! In 1944 many of the young men in the underground joined the regular army under General de Lattre, who liberated Strasbourg. Having been part of this force freed him from the obligation of serving in the army after the war. Subsequently he became a truck driver. You know, we are half Jewish, as my father was a Jew. My two brothers were arrested during the war; one by the Germans and the other by the Vichy French police. The first one managed to escape, but the other one was in a forced labor camp in Toulon. They were incredibly lucky and both survived.

Four years after my divorce I met my second husband. He was also divorced and was seventeen years older than I. He was a member of the Communist party and was a real activist. He had a piece of World War One shrapnel imbedded in his leg, which gave him such pain throughout his life that he was unable to continue working. He had to retire at fifty. Three times they operated on him! But nothing, neither the pain nor the operations, could keep him from his party work. Dating back to the time of his World War One service and the war injury, he earned a small government pension, which was augmented after his retirement by an equally small one from the tobacco company. We moved from Nice to a small town in the mountains where rents were low. I kept a big garden, so life was cheaper. We had gotten married in

1941 and by then both my son and his were already in the Resistance. They never really lived with us.

My husband organized a Communist party cell in the little town where we lived and in the two adjoining villages. During the war Tourette was first occupied by the Italians, then the Germans took over, and finally, after the peace, it was returned to French hands. We were often threatened as "known" Communists by each succeeding regime, but by some miracle we managed to stay on in the village, until five years ago when my husband became seriously ill. At that point we were forced to move down to Nice permanently to be near the doctors and better medical facilities. Before that we had always managed to come down South here for a few months during the coldest part of the winter. We used to rent a small apartment. The Nice climate was so much kinder to my husband's health. He died in 1971, in the hospital, of a lung congestion caused by a fall. He had been hospitalized three years. He couldn't speak at the time of his death and had to be fed intravenously. He was eighty-one years old when he died.

We had a happy marriage. Oh, we had fights sometimes like any couple, but we were very congenial together. Six months before my husband's death I was able to find this apartment. The one we had before wasn't close enough to the hospital nor to my son. I forgot to mention that we became very close, my son and I, after he grew up. In fact, I bought him an old house right near ours in the village of Tourette, so we were always together. Two years ago, when I became a widow, I took in my mother. It became necessary after my sister-in-law became so sick.

Of course, I have been sick myself over the last few years. I am still not well. I had four operations. I don't even rightly know what they all were as the doctors never tell you anything. I have had a breast removed, all my innards taken out (you know, a female operation), and then my stomach gave me much trouble. I have had two ulcers and two perforations. As a result, I have to be very quiet now. But I still manage to belong to my cell and to get to the important party meetings. I go down to headquarters each week and sometimes I do some work, like handing out flyleafs if it is an urgent matter. My last operation took place only last year. I was in hospital twenty-four days, then to a rest house to recuperate. My mother, meanwhile, went back to the house of my eldest brother. (I get along very well with my three brothers. Incidentally, they also vote communist.)

I only regret that I didn't get a chance to study while I was young. I would have liked to have been an historian. Even today I can add faster with my head than most people can with an adding machine.

I would like to be able to turn the clock back to my activist times in the thirties. I would be even more of a militant today! I still read the party paper, the journals, and the trade unionist papers and keep up with all the developments. And I maintain my friendship with those involved in the activist movement. There are a number of interesting youths in my cell, including two Black students.

Toward the end of my husband's life and after his death I used to visit an old militant friend who happened to live right next door to the hospital. For convenience sake I lived in his house in order to be near to the hospital and ended up doing a bit of work for him. He wanted me to stay on with his family, but I preferred to stay on my own. I can't ever thank him enough for what he did. He's been like a brother to me. He heads the district here.

My spirit or enthusiasm hasn't changed at all with age, but I would like to be ten years younger with more strength, also of an intellectual nature. I feel my powers waning and that makes me feel bitter. The party has no home for the aged, alas! To build one was part of the party platform, but we were defeated in the last elections. We are poor and that idea is now no more than a dream.

I would like to live a communal life. I feel "connected" with my comrades and I'm adaptable and sociable. I have sympathy for human beings and easily establish links with people. At the nursing home I felt surprisingly content. Now, of course, I have the worry about my mother. She complicates my life. I can't leave her alone and go out to see my friends. My brother's wife is crazy so he can't take her on, and my other two brothers have no space. That means the responsibility rests with me. My mother and I argue now and then, but in a way that also keeps affection alive. I wonder—when I reach her age—who will I have to stay with me? She is lucky to have her daughter to look after her! Both my son and daughter-in-law work. Anyway, I would prefer to be in a home than staying with them. My social welfare payments would meet the costs and I think I would be eligible. But it is not easy to find a good home and then to win a place in it. And, of course, when you go you forfeit your pension. All that remains to you is a little pocket money. You are free to come and go, but still it is not the same as your own four walls and your complete independence. I would not be able to keep the dog and the cats, and I would miss them.

My life now consists mostly of marketing, cooking, walking the dog, a little cleaning and washing the five days on which the cleaning lady doesn't come, and seeing to my mother. Not an exciting life, but the reading helps and the Party.

Matei Nastase

Otopeni, Bucharest, The Socialist Republic of Romania

Born 1897

I met Matei Nastase early one April morning on the cooperative farm (CAP) in Otopeni, just outside of Bucharest, Romania. A craggy, weathered old man, missing several of his front teeth, he was sitting on the ground on some old gunnysacks with five or six of his friends. With dexterity and economy of motion they were grafting various bushes and seemed to be preparing fruit tree cuttings.*

I was told he had retired eleven years ago but had been working as a skilled worker (this is possible in Romania) for half of each year on the large agricultural cooperative. He was receiving a salary plus his pension, which had been commensurately adjusted.

I WAS BORN in 1897 and have been married fifty-two years. My wife is seventy-five, and we have five children and four grandchildren. We live in our own home, right next to the house of our son, and have a garden where we grow vegetables and fruit trees. My main medicine, if I feel sick, is to drink a little homemade Tzoika [plum liqueur], but thank God, I've been lucky and my health has been good all my life. If I were really sick I could go to the co-op home for retirees.

In the summer I work from six thirty A.M. to five thirty at night, but if I feel a little tired I go to lie down underneath a tree and have a rest. My only real complaint is my teeth. I say work is the best therapy there is—I can't stay at home. I feel as though someone were pushing me to work each day.

I like my chief. We were comrades in the war together, first in Russia, then against the Nazis in forty-four. [He was decorated twice for heroism, I

*This interview and a thorough tour of facilities for the elderly in the twenty-fourth district of Bucharest were arranged for me by the Ministry of Foreign Affairs.

My main medicine, if I feel sick, is to drink a little homemade Tzoika [plum liqueur].

was told by the translator.] Another mate here was in the war with us as well. During World War One I was only seventeen years old.

I like the youth with whom I work here now and feel we work together well. Even though I can do maybe less hard work than I used to, I do more skilled work, so it balances out. The chief assigns us our tasks and checks our work output. I have found that we get paid more because of our longer experience. The managers of the co-op have discovered that we old tend to mobilize the young and give them a good example. For instance, I am always the first to come to work in the morning; that's because I feel a great responsibility toward my work and take pride in it.

Of course, we are lucky. The co-op has one hundred fifty of us old men working amongst the permanent staff of eight hundred (two thousand in summer). Some others of us are ill or are just living at home, retired. The ill are taken care of in the home of the co-op. There are three degrees of invalidism. Number one and number two groups have lost their work capacity completely. The third group have lost only a portion of their work output. A commission examines these matters and determines what is to be done about each individual worker. No blanket rules about retirement age. The third group, still able to work, receives a portion of their pension and a portion of their salary. This group has to work less than regular workers. I find it's better to be able to work. Even at home I'm outside in the garden a good part of the time, doing one chore or another, unless it's snowing.

My wife stayed at home all these years, looking after the children, baking, canning, cooking, washing. Our life is tied up here in the cooperative. In the evenings often we come over to see the films or go to meetings. If we are sick we know we can have care. We have a chorus, music, sports. We are believers—members of the orthodox church—both my wife and I. Yes, it's a good life. I'm satisfied; I can say that.

I prefer to concern myself with the broad operating principles behind the union movement.

Phillip Vera Cruz

Delano, California

Born 1905

The American Friends Service Committee put me in touch with AFL union headquarters in Bakersfield, California. They in turn led me to Phillip Vera Cruz, one of the leaders of the Filipino Farmworkers in the AFL and who was in 1975 a resident in the Agbayani Village, Delano, California. The village was set up by Cesar Chavez and the Farmworkers Union for retired members of the union, particularly for Filipino workers who had for years been prevented by the miscegenation laws in California from marrying out of the Filipino community. Because women immigrants were barred, marriage was impossible. Phillip Vera Cruz, still working actively for the union, had his office in the headquarters building in Delano, where we met.

I WAS BORN in the rural area of the Philippines, in Luzon. My folks were poor and never went to school, though someone taught my father to read and write. Even my mother knew how to read, though she never learned to write. Our family was of mixed blood—some Spanish. My father's mother was white. I think this may have influenced me to be fair toward people of all races. When I was a foreman in the fields in Elena I had Mexicans, Indians, a few Filipinos, and whites under my jurisdiction.

I am seventy years old. I came to the United States around 1919. My family had had some land in the Philippines, but by the time I left my father was already too sick to farm it.

I landed in Vancouver, though my final destination was the State of Washington. I was a junior in high school when I arrived. I had learned English in school in the Philippines. My first job in the States was in a box factory up North. Most of the workers were Greeks, Filipinos, or Japanese. I went to school during the day and worked at night, trying to send back money to help my mother since by then my father had died. I graduated from high school and managed college for one year, but I soon had to work full-time to be able to send any money home. I continued with college at night school, and I spent all my spare time reading in the public library. Once my sister finished high school she married, which meant I no longer had to help her. My brother passed his bar exams in 1944 and is now a practicing lawyer.

After leaving Spokane I moved to Chicago. I was making eighteen dollars a week. A Spokane friend and I leased a house and subletted rooms to others, so that in effect we were getting our rooms free.

It was '43 when I came to Delano. The wage for working in the fields was seventy cents an hour at that time. I came here to visit an army buddy and never went back, because the job back in the Middle West was no better than the one here. I belonged to an ethnic group who were not aliens but who were not nationals either. We were excluded from the citizenship laws. Whether you were smart or dumb, educated or illiterate, it didn't matter; you ended up in the fields. Even if you knew more than the owners you stayed in the orchards. They'd never ever promote you.

I joined the old AFL early on, though it wasn't until 1966 that Cesar Chavez joined forces with them. The big strike against the growers had started before Chavez joined. We all tried to cooperate with his leadership, although at that time he hadn't become a legend yet.

It's complicated. Cesar Chavez came from the CSO [Community Service Organization]. He dissolved his organization and then came in with the AFL. The old AFL leader, Al Green, had been very friendly with the Teamsters; now, after the merger, he was left out in the cold. Chavez' primary concern was always with the Mexicans, his own people. I supported the Filipino workers' merger with the new union forces. This was even before the strike, as early as '65.

I have been working here with the union ever since the beginning of the strike. The third day of the general strike in '65 I arrived at union headquarters in Delano. I was made a picket captain and had to lead some of the meetings. We ran a big hall where we used to feed the people. We had them sleeping there, too.

In '69 I was asked to represent the Farm Workers Union in London at the World Council of Churches conference. In the beginning the officers in our branch of the union had not been Filipino. We hadn't yet organized fully and were in a transitional period until we were given our own charter. But when we finally joined Chavez' union we had a membership of fifteen hundred Filipinos. I was elected second vice-president four years ago, in '69. In 1970 we finally signed the contract with the grapegrowers.

I wrote a piece called "Sour Grapes," which describes this period and particularly the Filipinos who work and live in the camps. It was published by the University of California Press.

The one thing I hated most working in the vineyards was the dust. When the grapes ripen and grow into full clusters, you have to clear off the leaves around them. They have to be sprayed with sulphur, and when you pull the leaves out the wind blows the chemical in your face. Lung infection results from this. You're apt to get asthma, and your eyes burn and water. But you only find out about the serious effects when you get older. I used to try to duck the blowing dust by standing on the other side of the rows, so the wind would blow it away from me. Many a worker's health would be saved if they were allowed to start working from one side of the rows, with the wind always at their backs. But the bosses' only concern is making more money. They let you drink from one dirty cup, so that if one gets sick the others do, too. You have to buy your own food. Since usually you have no transportation you have to be driven in by truck to the company store, where prices are higher. If you don't bring a cot, you sleep on the floor.

When I started in the fields we were not unionized, and there are orchards and fields still not organized today. But now I believe the bill will be passed and things will be better. There has been violence from the Teamsters but we are not afraid of them. [Since this interview took place California Governor Jerry Brown has signed the bill into law.]

When I was working in the fields there were always plenty of women available around the camps, but I didn't want them to interfere with my purposes. I am not a particularly unselfish man, but I felt from the start my responsibility was to my sister and brother. You see, after my father's death I was the eldest. I would rather shift the opportunity to them. I went through some emotional upheaval but I was able to control myself. Now I would like the comfort of having children and yet I don't regret the choices I made.

The theory behind this home for retired workers is good. Cesar founded it to a large extent for the old Filipino workers (none of whom have families because of the stringent miscegenation laws which were in effect for our people until World War Two). But it is hard to make old people adapt to new surroundings. You do your best to get along in the new conditions and you try to be practical in your interactions. It is very much the same with the unions: we have beautiful visions, but in practice things are resolved on a business level.

What is admirable here, though, is that people get involved in whatever work interests them. Anyone who was active in the union is eligible to live here. A Filipino member who used to do nursery work in Hawaii has become our expert gardener and planner. The lawns, the shrubs—everything—is his work. Another member built himself a darkroom and has taught himself to become our competent staff photographer. One of our women members is Chilean and is an Allende follower. She came to this country after a long career of teaching in Chile to become a VISTA worker. She met Chavez in New Mexico and has become an avid worker for the cause. She teaches Spanish to the young Anglos who come down here to work with Cesar and also does office work at headquarters.

I am not depressed about being old. Throughout my life I've always liked to be with people and that continues here, but I also like to be alone. When you are alone you can think better, more analytically. You are more able to keep your mind on the larger issues, you don't get as embroiled in petty matters. Even the farmworkers' movement only thinks of the here and now: "When can we get a new contract?" I prefer to concern myself with the broad operating principles behind the union movement.

I've tried to analyze the children who are working in the movement here now. They are the children of the affluent society. The children of the professionals. But their reactions are different than their parents'. I am an old guy, but my thinking is in line with theirs—they want decentralization of power. They want to carry it to the extreme and there I don't agree with them. But they have no love or respect for the Rockefellers of this world. More and more people feel that *nobody* has any business being that rich.

I often think the young would benefit if they would listen to the old. It would be a bridge from the past to the future. But unfortunately many of the old have not kept abreast of the times, and that makes the communication difficult in both directions.

I am not sorry that I came to the United States, because in the Philippines today I would be much more of a victim of the system. I came with the idea that I would start here at the bottom and make a successful life. I was caught by the slogans "Land of Opportunity" and "Equal Rights." But where is it better? The question is how do you work things out for people like us? I think the farm workers' union is becoming a true people's movement, and that is good.

My dream when I came here was that I would get an education. In the Philippines you have to have someone to back you, so lacking a patron I decided to come here. It didn't work out as I'd planned. I always wanted to go back home to help change conditions. But now the situation is even worse there, and I'll never get home.

Petronella Johanna Crommelin

Amsterdam, The Netherlands

Born 1892

Madame Crommelin, on the day of our interview, in Laren Gelderland, was sitting in the garden of her rented boorderij *(farmhouse) under a charming flowered umbrella. She was dressed in a white silk chemise dress, with a perfect pink rose at her lapel. An old mine diamond pin held it in place.*

MY HUSBAND, MAAN, died January '61. After his death I decided to stay on alone in the beautiful eighteenth-century parsonage, De Binnenhof, which we had restored after '45, when the occupation forces who had occupied it for five years during World War Two finally moved out. My two children thought I was quite mad to remain. I managed until '67, but it became progressively more difficult to find servants who would stay in such an isolated place. I sold the house in '68 and moved back to The Hague. The very contemplation of the move was sad for my old sheepdog and for me, too. I knew we would miss these country lanes along the fields, where we used to take long walks.

So now I come here for two months each summer. I rent this little brick farmhouse from the owner of the neighboring castle, a good friend, and look across the two grazing fields (aren't the horses charming, standing there in the misty morning light?) toward my former stand of woods. Being so close to De Binnenhof brings on bittersweet nostalgia but sometimes also unassuagable loss sweeps over me. It was such a beautiful house, surrounded by fine gardens: the greenhouse with my tomato plants and espaliered peach trees; the strawberry beds, rows of neat raspberry, currant, and gooseberry bushes; my little goslings quacking on the quiet canal and in its brown-black depths, reflections of stately beech trees with their sheaths of green moss on the gray trunks. I loved

I think that people have to assume responsibility for meaningful things, for beautiful old things.

bringing it all back to life, husbanding the land, watching it bloom again. The soldiers had nearly destroyed it.

Coming here is a nice break in the yearly routine. I go to the south of France and to Spain each year, but that is no problem since I have friends there with villas and I go with a student who drives me in my own car. If my old gentleman friend would make a proposition for me to accompany him on one of his voyages to America I would accept immediately. But otherwise I wouldn't risk it alone and at my age.

No one believes I am eighty-two. I think it has a lot to do with luck. I am one of the few who can sleep the moment my head touches the pillow. I've never needed a pill; in fact I react badly to almost all drugs. I can only tolerate homeopathic medicines and small doses even of those. But lately I have been plagued by a new torture: an excruciating itch which becomes especially bad in the small hours of the night. Awful! Last night it was so bad that I had to take something in order to sleep a few hours.

I celebrated my eightieth birthday by having a large reception with champagne and sandwiches in the distinguished old Johann de Witt House in The Hague. It is a seventeenth-century mansion, with lovely embossed ceilings and fine mantels, delicate old chandeliers, tapestries, and murals. It is beautifully and meticulously restored. The house is now used for weddings, receptions, dinners, and the like. One of my granddaughter Joy's friends is a talented floral arranger at the best florist shop in The Hague. She made breathtaking bouquets, just right for the house, in the style of one of those lovely still lifes by Jan Brueghel the elder. At first I was quite averse to the idea of the party, but my friends insisted: "You are eighty only once, and you simply *must* do it." So I invited eighty-five people for luncheon on the day of my birthday. The idea of luncheon was to enable the men to come, too.

I wanted to hear *real* gypsy music once more. I had always loved it since I was a girl. But to find a true gypsy troupe is no small matter these days! No one knew of any. They had evidently left the country or else had been absorbed in the general population pool of the Netherlands. Or perhaps, alas, Hitler had succeeded in eradicating them.

[A lovely, clear crystalline bell chimed the hour while she continued talking.] I cornered my dressmaker. He agreed to help. We finally found an old man who had come by caravan with his band of sons long before the war, from Austria-Hungary. We discovered the old man to be living in The Hague and asked him to reassemble the band just for this special occasion. He was delighted at the prospect and contacted his sons.

At the party they played in the large reception room and I received in the adjoining room. The next day a full portrait of me, surrounded by the musicians, appeared in the papers. After almost everyone had gone home the old man came up to me and asked whether now he would really be able to play for me. That hour, with just a few last friends standing there with me, was a sheer delight, a veritable orgy of sound. I think it was as satisfying to the musicians as to me!

In The Hague, besides my friends, I have a full life; more hectic than here. I drive my own car. I couldn't manage without a car. The public transportation services are terrible. Of course one can call a taxi from one's flat to go shopping, but the route back is the problem. Calling a cab is hopeless from a street corner, so there one stands, in a long queue, with one's arms full of bundles! So I take my car.

I watch only interesting programs on TV. In The Hague I have a marvelous telly with pushbutton controls. I watch the French films and some of the BBC programs like *Upstairs, Downstairs;* I simply loved *The Forsyte Saga* and *The Family Ashton,* the story of an ordinary British family during the war. Dutch television isn't too good.

I have my two chars who come twice a week from Scheveningen, a fishing and holiday town out on the coast. They still wear their traditional costumes. On Sundays they add their ancestral holiday capes made of a breathtaking shade of light blue. When they come to my door they remove their wooden shoes and don bright red *pantoufles.* Charming! Each has her own job. I learned long ago from my mother that you must never ask two women to do the same job; otherwise one will say the other has not done it right. Each week they clean the windows, air all the bedding, move the furniture out from the corners. The floors are waxed and polished, the furniture rubbed down with wax, and the cupboards and drawers are turned inside out. I like things done properly; I do them myself that way. I've been accused of caring too much about "things." But I think that people *have* to assume responsibility for meaningful things, for beautiful old things, especially if anything is to survive of the heritage of the past. Otherwise soon *everything* will be mass-produced and made out of plastic.

My daily routine starts as follows: I usually wheel my breakfast in on a cart, after my bath. I tackle the mail, the papers, and off I go on my round of errands to the post office and to the food shops. Nowadays nothing is delivered as it used to be. Another sad aspect of the times is the decline of taste or of any sense of intrinsic value. At the galleries, for the most ordinary nineteenth-century little romantic domestic scenes (sentimental kitsch!), they get thousands and thousands of dollars. That's why I hold on to my Jonghkinds and my Rembrandt etching. I sound like an elitist, but part of that is due not only to the sort of education I had, but really to a thorough exposure to serious works of art. I manage still to hear good music, to see theater, and of course I have an active social life (I play serious bridge) besides my work on the committee for Dutch Indonesian immigrants. The evenings I do go out, though, I always have a student come to drive me. I don't like night driving.

I still think the old farmers' way is the best solution for old age: Move in with your children when you can no longer manage on your own. On the farm that always meant your own quarters, the evening meal at least shared, a chance to help with the raising of the children, some work in the vegetable gardens, helping with the canning and the harvesting, and things of that nature. That way you continued to have some self-respect and you were not lonely or starving. Of course, this old system is built on the supposition that there is mutual love and a habit of respect, and maybe these qualities can no longer be counted on. I know I couldn't live with my children. I am too difficult; I must be in command of a situation. That is one reason I was always too demanding, too much a perfectionist and an autocrat to those who worked for or with me.

My children's lives are very different from mine. The war and the loss of Indonesia changed everything. My children live respectably in a tiny house, attached on both sides, with an even tinier backyard and a three-room flat. They have little money and no help, but they work and seem perhaps more satisfied and directed than my generation was.

My father seems to have been an advanced thinker for his time: a Victorian gentleman who believed in equal education for men and women. He allowed my eldest sister to study medicine, and she became one of the first woman doctors to graduate from the University of Leyden. My other sisters studied music in Dresden. One of them died of TB after she became an accomplished violist, playing with a recognized small quartet. My two brothers, the eldest and the youngest in the family, both studied engineering and did not follow in their father's or grandfather's banker's shoes.

My father may have had advanced ideas but he also had some odd ones. For instance, we were all forced to walk in the garden twenty minutes a day carrying heavy books on our heads to improve our posture. And we all had to learn to swim long before that became a fashionable young ladies' sport. We had a rather wild childhood. They must have been terrors, my brothers and sisters, traveling in large coaches to the watering places and the Kurhauses of Germany and of Switzerland, always accompanied by their entourage of nursemaids and truckfuls of white sailor suits and middy blouses to take care of the prescribed three changes of clothes a day!

I avoided a great deal of the excitement because I was born after my mother's near-fatal bout of typhoid and very much as an afterthought. My father is reported to have said to her after my birth, "The others you can get rid of, but this one I want for myself." I became his favorite and from then on his constant companion. He took me wherever he wanted to go. On Saturdays our routine was a tour of the antiques markets (I must have seen thousands of china-trade blue Delft cups as a child; that's why I know a good deal about antiques now!) and then through the back door of his office, through the garden, into the rear door of the synagogue, to which he had a key. Why we went to the synagogue I've never known. I know he had many friends there, but we weren't Jewish. Perhaps to understand this one has to have known Amsterdam in that time. It was certainly one of the great centers of Jewish life and culture in Europe. I still remember these sabbath visits with clarity. It must have made a great impression on me. We always sat upstairs in a curtained loge, where we could look down on the men in their hats and yarmulkas.

My brothers and sisters flirted with many of the ideas of that era. Two sisters became interested in Annie Besant and her theosophy and later became anthroposophists, that is, they followed the teachings of Rudolf Steiner. My husband and children were and are now members of the society.

My eldest brother emigrated to Argentina and was instrumental in starting the Argentine cattle industry with his imported Dutch Holstein cattle. But they were all dilettantes of sorts, my brothers and sisters, never sticking for long with anything, but all were bright and talented. I realize I suffered as well from the family malaise. I've even joined them in their esoteric inclinations, but I've never pursued these studies far enough to master the art of meditation, for instance. I know there are mysteries and hidden meanings behind experience, but I don't have the patience to pursue a disciplined study. I am intuitive and naturally talented in the occult sciences. I believe in the stars and I've had amazing experiences in this area. I throw myself into things often with passionate concern and energy. I drive myself too much.

You have no idea how I worked for the displaced Dutch people who came back from a lifetime spent in the East Indies, many married to Indonesians, and who were released from Japanese prison camps after the war, starved and often mutilated. They found themselves with no lives to come home to after the East Indies were declared independent and sovereign. No place was left for these homeless souls who had lived and worked all their lives in the Orient. My committee found shelter and jobs for them in Holland. We treated many sicknesses, including leprosy, and tried to help them to adjust to the hostile climate and the overcrowded miserable conditions. We gave them our clothes, our understanding, and our money. Or at least we raised money until the government finally began to see its responsibility. Of course, now our committee has been phased out.

This work had special appeal for me because of our connections, my husband's and mine, to the Indies. After all, he was head of the biggest Dutch shipping company to the Indies, The Rotterdamsche Lloyd, and we lived there for many years. It was a fascinating life and involved quite a bit of traveling, always with a certain style. I particularly loved Penang because I had a special penchant for the English style of things. We traveled on our inspection tours and took those marvelous slow boats, stopping at the teeming, pungent ports of the Orient en route home to staid little Holland. Life seemed gay out there, full of semimilitary and diplomatic protocol, with many servants and parties and trips deep into the jungles. I remember the colors, the shadows in the green opulence, and the juxtapositions of such disparate life-styles—native and colonial.

I've gotten ahead of myself though! When I was ten my father suffered a cerebral hemorrhage, and from that moment on he gradually sunk into slow death, four years later. Those years were spent by my mother and an accompanying nurse carefully bundling him up on trips to Menton or to the Italian lakes or to Interlaken, where it was hoped the benign climate or bracing air would initiate a cure. But he grew steadily worse. From then on I hardly ever saw him because he grew so remote, sitting in a chair or on his bed, not talking to me or anyone. He died finally, alone, in a nursing home. If only I manage to keep my wits about me till the end, that's all I care about. After my father's death my mother didn't know how to manage me. I suppose I had been spoiled by him. Early on I liked boys and the feeling was reciprocated. But oh, those friendships were innocent. In those days and with our upbringing you wouldn't dream of letting a boy kiss you! My mother never spoke to me openly about anything but she was suspicious about me. She thought my friendships awful! She had no way to handle me, and so she decided to remove me from temptation by sending me to a strict, I suppose fashionable, boarding school in the country. All nice young ladies from country places. But it was no real education and couldn't be compared to my challenging lycée in Amsterdam. I was always an A or B student, encouraged by my father, who had rewarded me with silver *kwartjes* (twenty-five-cent pieces) whenever I came home with a good report card. Now I found myself ahead of the country bumpkins in more ways than only academically. D'you know what outrageous solutions they found for my precocity? They put me behind a black screen at table, lest I converse with the other girls. Barbaric!

I could have been quite something else in my life if my mother hadn't made such inroads into my education. And she continued to do so after the Het Kopje school. I have the drive to do things well and the intelligence, and I should have studied like my sister Annie. I should have had a real vocation instead of doing charity work or planning gardens and renovations and fancy dinner parties and balls. Still, you have to make the best of the opportunities with which life presents you. Why did I work till twelve midnight five nights a week for twelve years for our Indonesian Dutch? Because I am driven to do something until it is accomplished. I suppose that is why the queen gave me her medal. Whether it was this work or something else more professionally based doesn't really make any difference as long as one uses one's capacities and energy.

After boarding school I did manage to go to a fine school in Geneva, Switzerland. Mother again called me back too soon, after only one year, to Amsterdam. It was a learning and, at the same time, a working arrangement. We did social work in the hospitals and prisons besides learning the usual subjects such as languages, history, and literature. It was a very worthwhile year I felt then, and I still look back on it with pleasure.

The next installment of my education was learning English. My mother sent me to Richmond to stay with a lugubrious family consisting of a mother and her two plain daughters. I remember them forever praying and reading the Bible before and after every meal. I suspect that my ticket fees also paid for their attendance at the opera, the ballet, and the theater. They were taking outrageous financial advantage of my mother! But in England at least I developed my lifelong passion for riding. D'you know that I was riding my own horse, sidesaddle, until I was seventy? I went out every day in Richmond Park, riding and jumping on big hunters. I still remember the awful squeaks and creaks and pinch of my boots and the clanging of my spurs as I had to kneel on the hard floor for prayers every morning before breakfast.

I can smell Richmond Park even today, with its huge trees and those wonderful woods and the deer that galloped with you and, in autumn, the bracken. A wonderful time, a simply horsey time! I had a huge straw hat from Fortnum and Masons and a lovely blanket coat, which was very much the fashion then. Funny how sometimes items of clothing come back into your memory. I hadn't thought of that favorite coat for years!

I returned to Holland after a year in England in time to have my eldest brother take me under his wing. He was quite worldly and decided I should be introduced to society—"come out," I think you call it. I was sent to an exclusive dance club and there I met my beautiful Maan. What a handsome man he was! And he remained that way all his life. A lovely time began—balls, dinners, parties, and riding, of course! When my father died I was made the ward of my uncle, Phillip Waller. Maan asked him for my hand and was told I was allowed to marry but only after a year. I was to spend the interim learning to cook and going to a household management school. Besides, he insisted, I must learn to manage my own financial affairs. Sound advice, I think. Once a week I had a man from the bank come to teach me accounting.

After our marriage Maan and I lived two years on the naval base, but then he was transferred as aide-de-camp to the governor general of the East Indies. I didn't want to leave Holland, and so to keep me happy he resigned his navy position.

Our children were born. I wasn't really a dedicated mother. Of course, I had a marvelous nanny, and I wasn't ready yet to give up my gay social life for domesticity. Maan was forebearing. He allowed me free rein and it was I who set the pace of our social life. He often went home at midnight, after the dancing but before the midnight supper, and I would go on alone. He preferred to go home to his poets and French philosophers. He was the intellectual of the family. Of course, I was physically much stronger than he. I rode and golfed and played tennis every day and then danced all night.

For a time we lived quite comfortably on my money. Maan had all sorts of opportunities—for instance, to go to America into coal production—but shipping attracted him most, I suppose, because of his navy training. So then we went to the Indies after all.

I had a headstrong, passionate, and, I suppose, self-indulgent nature. I was always more or less "falling in love" with this or that handsome officer. Nothing serious. I would have run Maan a wild goose chase if it hadn't been that he never objected to my behavior. He never said anything. Once our daughter asked him, years later, why he put up with it, and he answered, "Otherwise I would have lost her straight away, and for all the world I would never lose her." I had a completely different temperament, or perhaps it was simply a difference in vitality levels. Also our needs, I think, were different too, though I didn't realize it until much later on in life. Then you simply didn't talk about intimate things. Now it is actually quite easy to solve sexual problems if you can only be free to talk about them, of that I am convinced. Two babes in the woods we were. Sad! And in those days, of course, no one dared seek professional help; it would have been too embarrassing. Now that I am older I know what a tremendous effect sexual disharmony can have on one's entire life. Yet I know I loved my husband and he loved me, I think. He was an extraordinarily fine and evolved human being, and I am much more passionate but impulse-ridden.

Two doctors in Amsterdam just published a report on sex among the elderly, stating how right and normal it is and should be. But the children of the old frown on sex for their parents. It seems degrading or dirty or somehow immoral. We should have our minds directed toward our "future." Really, of course, it is a question of who will get the money. Why can't the old just be left alone to find solace in each other? Why is marriage even necessary?

After Maan's retirement he had to be careful because he had already suffered one heart attack. He had to have blood-thinning treatment at the hospital. Also he had trouble with his kidneys. But he wanted to stay in the country where, as he said, "I can walk on God's own earth, not on city pavements." He was very weak at the end. When he died I stayed in the country all alone. Several times I slipped and fell in the bathtub and there was no one to rescue me, so I was finally quite simply forced by circumstances to move to the city. Siekje, my dog, died just before the move, as though she knew there was no real place for her in the city. I am not at all religiously dogmatic, but I am absolutely sure that I am going on somewhere into another sphere where I will have to work out the mistakes I have made in my life. The older you get the more you see the things you have done wrong and you say to yourself, "How could I have done such a foolish thing?" I believe in Karma and I believe that you will come back into this world again to learn the things you still have to work out.

I can't see yet, for instance, what the most important moments of my life were. It seems it was more of a waterfall of events, one after the other. I only know that I always landed on my feet again, even when I thought, "Now, this will be the end of it all"; still, I would pick myself up and go on.

I think what was most important and formative in my life was the relationship between my mother and myself. We simply did not understand each other. She suspected me of evildoing with the boys, but it was totally unjust. I remember I simply attracted boys without trying to do so—even when I was eleven or twelve. I used to ride the train to my parents' country house each weekend and always, in the train compartment, I was surrounded by boys. One of them, eighteen years old (can you imagine?), wrote me love poems, which I still had till quite recently. I was eleven years old! But I loved another boy, also much older, who was in mourning. Roland Holst, the poet. He fell in love with me, too, that same summer. He used to fetch me and we would go off on bicycles into the woods. You wouldn't believe it, but we sat down on the moss under a tree and there we talked and talked and talked. We never, no, never, kissed! Or I would have thought it awful! They were always in sorrow, those boys. Either they had lost their mother or I don't know what, and then they came to me to pour out their hearts. I seem to have something which attracts men in trouble. I don't understand why. Roland wrote me four pages of beautiful poetry. I still see my little pink and white room and the cupboard where I hid the copybook in which he had written the poems, underneath my underclothes. If only my mother had understood, how different everything would have been. I was very much taken by all those sorrows and I tried to help him. The only thing I could do was sit there and listen to him. All he wanted was for me to come out at six o'clock in the morning to go to the woods with him to talk. But, of course, it would have been very dangerous if my mother had discovered it!

I don't ever think about my age. I don't feel it. I don't feel fifty, or sixty, or eighty. The days are too short for me, and I am never ready with all I intended to do. Sometimes I work till twelve midnight because then I am alone; the phone doesn't ring and nobody bothers me. It is at those times that I write letters and plan my life.

I only think it a pity that young people think me old. They know I am over eighty so they expect certain behavior from me, suitable for my age; but I don't feel old. Do you know what Maan always said I was in a former reincarnation? "Stable boy to Cleopatra!" That takes care of the horse passion and the love element in my life.

Strangely, you know, I still feel dynamic sexually. If I met a nice man who is sympathetic and available, of course I would be interested. The older man I see now and then I sense would like to get involved, but I don't love him.

I am so happy that at last I can talk about all these things to someone. It is a great relief! I've never really spoken to anyone except my great friend, the doctor. It seems so sad that a whole life should be lived somehow in a curtailed condition only because there were areas of life which one couldn't talk about.

I am what one calls in love now (though I know of course it is utterly foolish) with a much younger man. It's very sad. He is terribly nice to me and considers me with great respect. He is married and has a good and loving wife, but he likes my ambience, my culture. He has been wonderfully kind to me, and I have enjoyed every moment of our times together. He has poured out all sorts of things to me; we talk with great intimacy. He has had a difficult life and I have tried to help him with his sad situation.

Nobody has the slightest inkling that he exists. I don't know; I suppose it's extraordinary at my age! But perhaps if truth were known, it may not even be that rare an occurrence. I don't ever forget that he is so young and I am so old. Of course, it would be much easier for me to turn toward his youth with love than for him to turn toward such great age as mine. He has changed my whole life.

My dear doctor said to me: "Be happy that this comes your way!" and asked me was it a sexual affair. I said No. Yet it feels very important to me to have such a friend. And the friendship grows and deepens with each day. Often I question: "Should I allow myself these feelings? What will I destroy with them? the friendship itself? I have been living with it all since last October.

Should I feel guilty that such emotions still plague me?"

The old French clock had struck its clear, light, musical bell eleven times, and obviously it had become time for me to leave. I watched as Madame Crommelin rose to go into the dining room. She put out the blue cups for next morning's tea and the right, darker blue bowl for the garden strawberries. We had talked away the afternoon and the better part of the night.

I don't regret that I am an old man.

Oscar Forel

St. Prex, Switzerland

Born 1891

I met Dr. Forel in 1971 through Hal Coolidge, then head of IUCN, the research branch of the World Wildlife Fund, which is headquartered in Morges, Switzerland, on Lake Geneva. Hal brought us together because he thought that I might act as Dr. Forel's assistant on a photographic trip to Central America.

Since 1950, when he retired as head of Prangins, a large private psychiatric hospital he had founded on the shores of Lake Geneva, Forel has become renowned as a naturalist and a photographer. He did not give up his career, however, as a psychiatrist but continued through his teaching at the University of Geneva and in his writings. His second career has also brought him acclaim. Four books of magnificent color prints of what he calls his "Synchromies" have been issued in large editions and in several languages. These are close-up studies of tree bark as seen with Forel's extraordinarily sensitive eye for their immense richness of design and color. His work reminds me a bit of Ernst Haas' The Creation. *Exhibitions of Forel's works, enlarged to panel size, have traveled to Moscow, Bern, Zürich, Geneva, Paris, and Nuremberg, and the Smithsonian Institution arranged for a traveling show in the United States.*

It was agreed that I should meet Dr. Forel, after a direct flight from Paris, at the Miami airport. I expected a much older-seeming man; instead I saw him striding briskly toward me in heavy hiking boots—an unforgettable sight: Forel was wearing a safari hat and a khaki shirt; birdglasses and camera with telephoto lens hung from his neck; a heavy rucksack weighted down his shoulders; a tripod was tucked under one arm, and in the other he held his passport and a modest-sized overnight bag (which held all his clothes I was to learn). I seem to remember him wearing knickers, but that I am unsure of. I began to anticipate our projected trip with pleasure!

At the end of our photographic journey through Panama and Costa Rica he invited me to visit him at his twelfth-century house on Lake Geneva.

It was there I encountered some other aspects of the doctor.

Dr. Forel, in either setting—jungle or manor house—is a strikingly handsome man: slender, with snow-white hair and neatly trimmed beard. He is fluent in at least four languages, and his manner is intense but always gracious. One is soon made aware of his extensive learning and of the broad range of his interests. The tower of Le Manoir served as part of the town of St. Prex's fortifications in medieval days. Massive, two-foot-thick oak beams, which support the house on its ancient morass foundations, date back to this period as well. A venerable sycamore tree overshadows the walled gardens, which contain a great number of rare plants and trees. An aviary, built at the far wall of the carriage house, just inside a pair of ancient wooden gates, is filled with brightly hued songbirds. In the rear of the garden there are large cages for tropical birds, for guinea fowl, and for pheasants, which often strut about freely when the garden gate is closed.

At the top of the tower there is a room with windows clear around. It was the lookout in earlier days. On one side they look across the lake to the Alps and on the other to the vine-covered slopes of "The Alpes Vaudoise." This aerie of the doctor's has access only by way of a perpendicular stepladder, which Forel still uses with alacrity. "It is here that I come to meditate and write my aphorisms, two of which have been published privately. It is also the best place for listening to music. I come up here quite often and listen to my favorite composers, Bach and Mozart, because it's so quiet."

On the four walls of the tower room, just underneath the windows, hang a number of panels, woodcarvings of "Dances Macabres" that were done by one of the Forel ancestors. Throughout the house appear the varying motifs of his Synchromies in different color combinations: as draperies, bed canopies, even cloth wallcoverings and upholstery materials, all giving witness to the interest the Swiss textile industry has taken in his designs. I hear they have even been woven into rya-like rugs by a firm in Germany.

Forel's gallery, an area covering approximately fifty square feet of floor space and situated under the eaves of the attic, houses his collection of brilliant panel enlargements of the Synchromies, from which the various exhibitions are drawn.

I HAVE BEEN separated for thirty years or more from my wife, and except for my ailing daughter [she has since died of leukemia] who has shared the house with me this last year, my children are all living far from home. I manage to live here still in a manner rarely found possible in any country today. I am looked after by my devoted staff. I have a most marvelous secretary, Fraulein Issler, who helps me with everything—she truly thinks for me—then my excellent old cook, and my dear old waitress-chambermaid. Yes, I know how fortunate I am. I still drive my car throughout Switzerland with undoubted dexterity, but I'm afraid at high speeds, of which you wouldn't approve!

One daughter is married and lives in Finland. She is director of a hospital there. My son, who is also a doctor, has become a popular Communist Deputy in the Swiss National Council. I admire him greatly. It is his son who is my beloved young grandson. A brilliant and lovely boy. My third daughter, who is younger, is married and lives in Israel, where she is a nurse. She also has adorable small children. Le Manoir has belonged to the Forel family for the past two or three hundred years. I inherited it from my aunt and uncle; the latter was the mayor of Saint Prex. They were the founders of the Musée Forel in Morges, and it is their treasures, as well as the ones I have collected, which you see throughout the house.

During the years at Prangins I dealt with an extraordinary assortment of interesting personalities. One that stands out was a beautiful maharani who was desperately ill and for whom the only therapy which was finally able to restore her to her husband and children was the use of drastic shock treatments. You've no doubt read about Zelda Fitzgerald's sojourn at Prangins. A difficult woman!

I planted fourteen thousand rare trees on the grounds of Prangins during my tenure there, but I won't become known for that. My greatest recognition, ironically, still comes from being the son of August Forel. My father was a world famous entomologist; his speciality was ants. He was also an important neuropsychiatrist, the first researcher to do a cross section of the brain. Together with Breuer, Freud's early colleague, he made extensive use of hypnosis in his practice of psychiatry, and he wrote the earliest German tome on sex, *Die Sexuelle Frage.* Later I revised the second edition. I decided to follow in my father's footsteps because the study of psychopathology struck me as being one of the most humane and challenging fields. I count myself amongst the Monists, that is, Identity-Theoreticians, to whom it seems impossible to separate the psyche (the function of the brain) from the brain itself. If you ask me about the soul, that entity is built up gradually from the earliest years—and at death? Frequently the so-called soul separates from the body long before the actual death of the organism. May this misfortune be spared me! The medical profession should not continue a totally unfunctioning creature, fatally ill, who is no longer human and can only be kept alive by forced medication.

The third book of Synchromies has just been published in four languages, and fifteen thousand copies in this edition have been sold. But actually, I am more interested in my Aphorisms than in the Synchromies, perhaps because I detest big books. My own first "big" book was *The Psychology of Neurosis;* the second was rewriting and editing my father's *The Sexual Question.* I have done another book on the subject of rhythm; that's why I am so fond of music, because I am fascinated by the rhythms in all living organisms. But luckily I was sensible enough not to become a musician. Music, above all, lies above quarrels, philosophies, theories. Music is a language of feelings. I have always thought that the emotions are the real heart of human beings. I don't accept Freud's exaggerated theories but remain true to the cathartic method: "Reviving the trauma!" I have prided myself on treating patients no longer than six weeks. If a cure cannot be instigated in that length of time, the treatment will never be successful anyway.

My passion for photography started as did Lartigue's, when I was a young boy at boarding school, the Institute Glarisegg in Canton Thurgau. I had a marvelous professor of biology there who took us through the woods, the marshes, and into the mountains and taught us to observe nature firsthand. Sixty years later I called on him, bringing him some of my first Synchromies. He looked at me in wonder and asked, "Tell me, who taught you that?" I answered, "You; you were the teacher." Tears welled in his eyes; he was eighty years old at this point. My interest in trees had its inception during World War One. I was stationed as a first lieutenant in the high Alps, guarding the mountain passes. Each lunchtime, while my men ate their bread and cheese and drank their wine down in the valley, I climbed up to a high bluff where there stood a gnarled, weather-beaten old cypress tree. For days I meditated under that tree until I began to understand its language. Each knothole, twisted branch, and broken bough became a living history. This proclivity for a hermit-like existence, contemplating nature like a stylite, has remained a motif of my life. In fact, my autobiography, which won't be published except posthumously and then privately, is called *Bernard the Hermit.*

I suppose I am a bit of a "misogynist en herbe." Perhaps this comes from my childhood experiences. That much I'll give Freud. I had four sisters and an older brother. One beloved sister died young, at the age of nine, of encephalitis. Another sister died of stenosis mitral. She was a registered nurse from Canada, who went to the Belgian Congo and there built a missionary home for old missionaries. The third sister married a German psychiatrist, and my favorite sister, Inez, was the only one who survived to old age. She died in Canada last year. My father was thirty-six when he married my mother, aged seventeen. My eldest brother was born a year after the marriage and became not only my mother's favorite but seemed almost more like her lover than her son. They were very close. I never came to know my mother until this brother died tragically in his late twenties. He was brilliant and became a doctor like my father, with whom he was also very close. I felt somewhat like a foundling and was remote from the rest of the family. My father was constantly traveling to the far-off corners of the earth on one scientific expedition or another. He had little capacity for family intimacy and a poor sense of money. I developed a closer relationship to my aunt and uncle Forel than I did to my own family. In fact, a great many of my interests in art, history, the restoration of the ancient heritage of Switzerland, all this I get from my aunt. Last year, in fact, the city of Saint Prex, under my tutelage, won the Wakker prize for the best conservation of its history and monuments, and this year in January the street on which this house stands was renamed "rue de Forel." I have been largely responsible for the revival of interest in our ancient heritage here. We have recobble-stoned the street, found old street signs to hang at appropriate inns and shops; we have relighted the streets with old wrought iron lanterns and have cleaned and reactivated the beautiful village fountain in the piazza.

I am still finding time to read and observe. I am working on a book dealing with Alexis Carrel's *Man, the Unknown,* but I guess I would have to describe my philosophy as being negative. Science nowadays becomes more and more dependent on industry for its research funds. Medicine, therefore, becomes the tool of industry; pure science has become the slave of money—money directs politics and the result is more pollution. That's why I give more and more of my money to try to protect this perishable little biosphere. This process of decay has no end in sight. I envisage the suicide of humanity. Like lemmings, something drives us closer and closer to the cliff.

Paul Valerie said, *"Nous savons que les civilizations sont mortelles."* Yes, the evolution of humanity is irreversible. Therefore, I don't regret that I am an old man. I don't regret anything. I have been terribly spoiled. My pessimism sometimes makes me feel discouraged and guilty, but I can't change what I feel to be true about life. Sometimes I am ashamed to have been so lucky.

If only women would develop a bioconscience in their children, the children of the future would neither smoke nor drink nor make wars. Even the religions are bankrupt. They have had some two thousand years to prove what they can do, and it hasn't been much. I can't follow my father in his illusions about the perfectability of human beings; I couldn't follow him in his battles against alcohol, venereal disease, and such. I can't follow the hope of changing what can't be changed. I have traveled through many countries, but I tell you I can't bear to travel in countries where the children die of hunger and unattended maladies. *C'est étrange, l'humanité!*

It is easier to be old in a Muslim world.

Salim Issa Jeries Missleh

Jifna, West Bank, Israel

Born 1903

A political science student at Hebrew University brought me to the ancient Christian village of Jifna, where he'd grown up, and introduced me to Salim Missleh. Missleh and his wife live in an old stone house, vaulted, with thick masonry walls and stone floors set among terraced hills of olive trees. The town dates to biblical times. He was a poor farmer and owned a small grove of olive trees, a well-loved white Arabian stallion, and some doves. He still cultivated a small garden plot. A beautiful man, Salim wore an air of deep resignation.

MY NAME IS Issa Jeries Missleh. I am seventy years old and I have seven children—that is, five sons and two daughters. Four of them are married. One is in Ramallah, two are in Kuwait, and one daughter lives here in the village with us. I was twenty years old when I got married and my wife was seventeen. We have always lived here in this village. In fact, my father and my grandfather before him were all born here.

I look back with pride on a few things in my life: the trees I have planted and what I have built. I am a mason by trade. But now that I am handicapped by my age and am failing, I regret that I did not build more while I was able to. Sometimes when I think back on the things I was able to accomplish in one day in the past I am amazed. I used to work with heavy stones, cutting them from the quarry, doing as much work as six men from sunrise until long after sunset. Today I cannot; I have the will to work but I do not have the strength. Work on the land is a burden now. A pleasure, too, of course, but a burden all the same. But I know well enough that without it I would be unable to support my family, so I go on. Now I am just an old man without teeth. When my wife sits down she cannot get up; she has such arthritis. Thank God, our children are helping us (may God preserve them) as much as they are able. Especially my daughter here, who works with her mother in the house.

But my ambition is gone. In the past if I had a certain thought I would carry it out, but now I say to myself, "What is the use?" I am discouraged.

Two of our sons are far away in Kuwait, one is in Ramallah. The money I have left I must spend on our living here, not on transportation. Before the war, in 1967, they used to come home sometimes to visit, although one of them has not been back for fourteen years now.

I feel deeply distressed to think of my son who is unable to pay his rent. But what compensation is there in feeling distressed? I know I can do nothing to help him; I am powerless. One of my sons is a chauffeur, one in Kuwait works in a store, another is a laborer, and one works in Ramallah. And we, the old woman and I, and our daughter try as best we can to make as good a life as we are able. We go to church. What would it serve to be penniless and then on top of that not to go to church? At least there is prayer. And there are my friends. I have friends outside the village, too.

Our life has its joys, too. I feel happy when I see my grandchildren, when I see my friends. But our people have been poor for as far back as I can remember, and that colors our life. I would never have wished to become a leader, only to work hard and to support my family. My work was everything to me and now the joy in it is gone.

In spite of my old age, if there could be some way whereby one would be able to help and work in the interest of the village I would leave whatever of my own work I still have to spend all my time for the betterment of our village. For example, I have served on the village council, which worked on the water project, in fact, supervised the project from beginning to end. When new roads were opened I also worked on those. I always prayed for someone who would come to help us with the roads. There is still so much work to be done.

How can I be of help to others when I cannot even help myself? Sometimes I am even unable to rise after long periods of sitting. We are not people who have managed to save anything. Some help has come to us here in the village through the United Nations. Our health conditions are better. Another boon for us has been the establishment of a cooperative, where we can bring our olives to be pressed into oil. But generally, we have found that it is difficult to work on cooperative efforts; we ourselves need of help.

I told you that we are Christian Arabs, and that this town goes back to biblical times. But I must tell you that it is easier to be old in a Muslim world. Old age is more respected amongst them. The discouraging thing for us here is the sense of hopelessness in our situation. It will go on like this forever. Nobody cares. Our sons, the clever ones, are far away in other countries and we may never have the opportunity to see them again. We are poor with no possibility for change, and meanwhile my wife and I are growing old. Who, which one, of our far-flung sons will take care of us? And I don't want to burden unduly the two who live here close to us. The times are difficult for our people and always we see in neighboring villages across the West Bank more and more Israeli settlements going up on our ancestral lands and the soldiers everywhere, patrolling.

Yichyeh and Rivkah Kachzam

Ein Kerem, Jerusalem, Israel

Born 1904 and 1905

A friend in Jerusalem arranged an interview with Yemenite Rabbi Yichyeh Kachzam and his wife, Rivkah, who live in Ein Kerem, a former Arab village, which clings to a steep slope on the outskirts of Jerusalem.

Their house is a beautiful example of ancient Arabic design; the ceilings, high and vaulted, the triple-arched windows are cut into walls two and a half feet deep. The house sits on top of a hill reached by a winding, jagged footpath and alternating stairs. From its windows one has a view of the entire valley: its church towers, its red-tiled rooftops, the olive groves, and finally, in the distance, the remote hills that reach up to the sky.

YICHYEH: THE YEMENITE community here is small—thirty to forty families—and I serve as their rabbi. When I came to Israel I studied in a yeshiva for three months. We settled here, near Jerusalem, and a year later I was given this house by the Jewish agency in this small Arab town which had been overrun in the 1948 war. The house was a virtual ruin and I had to renovate it all by myself.

I am around sixty-eight years of age, my wife, Rivkah, a year younger. We neither of us remember our exact birth dates, but we came from Sanaa, the capital of Yemen, where we lived quite comfortably, born into well-to-do families.

I worked at the royal court of the king, the imam. I was one of the government minters, what we called a coin minter, and I held this position for twenty years, until the death of the king. It was after his death that the persecutions of the Jews commenced.

The immigration of the Yemenite Jews to Israel began after the pogroms of

Yichyeh: *Disasters are heaven-sent. No use fretting about them.*

Rivkah: *My husband, you know, is a learned featherweight, full of intellectual notions but with little practical sense.*

1949. This secret rescue operation of the Yemenite Jewish community was carried out by air, as land routes were blocked by the Egyptians. The hazardous project was not made public until more than thirty thousand Yemenite immigrants had already arrived in Israel.

As a youth I studied the Gemara [the second and supplementary part of the Talmud, which provides a commentary on the first part], the writings of the Rambam [Maimonides], and the rules of ritual slaughtering. I am very proud of my mastery of written Arabic. We Yemenite Jews give our sons a rabbinical education. My brothers and I were no exception. I only held a nonreligious occupation in Yemen in order to earn my livelihood.

Rivkah, the rabbi's wife, was an energetic woman and was the dominant figure in the family. Despite her illiteracy, she seemed to have a better memory than her husband; in fact, she appeared to know more than he about the family's past and present situation.

RIVKAH: I worked as a domestic help for twenty-two years, but at present my only job is looking after my own household. I grew up in a rich family, living in a village four hours' walking distance from the capital of Sanaa. My family lost its wealth on its departure from Yemen. The money, which couldn't be legally transferred, was distributed among other immigrants in the form of loans, but these were never repaid. We have been married for forty-three years. We got married in Yemen, where five of our children died in infancy. The other four now live in Israel. Now, in our retirement, we don't want to live together with our married children, although that would have been in line with the usual Yemenite tradition.

YICHYEH: We get a monthly welfare allowance of two hundred pounds and another fifty pounds from the Rabbanut (the chief rabbinate). We pay ten pounds a month for social insurance and sickness-fund fees. In spite of this, the government robs me of the little money I have. Our political affiliation is with the Mizrachi [religious party appealing mainly to Eastern Jews]. But we also belong to the Histadrut [Federation of Labor Unions]. [Yichyeh claims that he served in the army for six years, but his wife dismisses this as a lie and announces that he had actually been overcome with fear in the two previous wars and that he even fled from home during the 1956 war.]

RIVKAH: My work as a domestic for twenty-two years helped the family by augmenting our income both with my salary and also with the many gifts I received from my employers. Yichyeh took care of the children while I was away. Apart from studying the Bible, which is his major occupation, he was in charge of the shopping. I used to go to the mikvah [ritual bath], but now I usually go to have a bath at my daughter's house about once in two weeks.

The Kachzams' living conditions are poor. The WC is in the backyard. There is no hot water, and washing is done outside in the yard with a hose.

My husband, you know, is a learned featherweight, full of intellectual notions but with little practical sense. If it hadn't been for me, the family would have come to grief long ago! [One senses that Rivkah's role as primary family breadwinner has given her the dominant position.]

We do not have any serious complaints. Thank God, we have enough food and all of us have jobs, and we have certainly never considered going back to Yemen. Disasters are heaven-sent. No use fretting about them. We love the country of Israel with all our hearts, and our only wish and prayer is to remain peaceful and healthy.

[The rabbi interrupted:] I spend most of my time in my two favorite occupations: sleeping and reading. I am convinced that women are the best medication for men, but my wife gets angry when I say that. Our marital life is a happy one.

[But, his wife argues,] If you had come later in the night you would have witnessed our quarreling! But we enjoy our battles.

[Puffing on his huge standing hookah, Yichyeh begins a discursive description of marriage, Yemenite style.]

YICHYEH: In Yemen when a boy approaches the age of eighteen he becomes eligible for marriage, and the quest for a bride is undertaken by his parents. The couple is usually not acquainted before the matchmaking has taken place. The woman has no say whatsoever in the making of the choice, which involves the parents on both sides and the rabbi as go-between. Great importance is attached to the ancestry of the groom. The bargaining position of the bride's family is better when the groom shows interest in the bride. Upon marriage the girl leaves her parents' home and joins her husband's family. She is virtually at the mercy of her husband's parents. During the engagement period the bride and groom are not allowed to see each other. The same custom applied in our case. A year elapsed between our first meeting, which also became our engagement, and the wedding. During this time we were not allowed to see each other.

[She broke in:] The life of a girl in Yemen is difficult in many respects. Early childhood is passed in the usual way, in play and songs, but at the age of seven the girl is expected to start helping with the household chores. Although Yemenite women get some religious education, most of this education has to do with female obligations. Our sense of inferiority and resentment is reflected in some of our women's songs. We were not allowed to leave our house and were expected to play only with girlfriends. Life in the village was even harder than in the cities in that it was more physically demanding—for instance, wood-chopping and water-pumping. It is no wonder, then, that we Yemenite women associate immigration to Israel with improvement of our lot. We soon learned that the Israeli woman is taught how to read and write. Really, immigration has changed and revolutionized our lives! The Yemenite woman's adjustment to life in the new country has been relatively easy and happy due to this improvement in her condition. Thank God for being in Israel! And you can be sure that I have never felt any longing to return to Yemen. I provided my daughters with the same education as that of their brothers. I am certain that their choice of a husband was better than mine!

[He interjects:] Matchmaking, in any case, is in the hands of God. [And adds a humorous afterthought:] Had I been given a second choice I would most certainly not have chosen such a Yenta.

RIVKAH: As a woman here I have had ample chance to leave my house, although my occupation of domestic helper is not highly regarded in this country. My husband looked after the children while I was away at work. The traditional parental roles were reversed. I only go to the synagogue on Jewish holidays. He claims that he doesn't mind that women go to the synagogue, but at the same time he doesn't ask me to go. I have four brothers, all living in Rosh-Haayin, and they all still take care of me as if I were the unmarried younger sister. It's very nice.

[Rivkah went to the refrigerator and brought out a pitcher of grapefruit pop. She poured us each a glass.] We enjoy the privacy we have here. We have only one son living at home and he is out working all day. In the evenings he goes to the café with his cronies, so we don't see much of him. He came as an afterthought, when I was already forty-three. In Yemen we had to live in one room, my husband and I and all the children. My husband was off at the mint all day, and then at night he was with his brothers, reading and praying, but I had all those children to contend with. And always we lived under his father's and then later his older brother's control. Finally, when both of them died, thank God, my husband became the head of the household. He inherited his father's room, but I had to stay back in the old quarters with the nine children! That's why we have no intention of moving in with our children, now that we are near to retirement.

Our girls have received their elementary education just like the boys, except our firstborn, who never studied and got married at fourteen. I was married at nineteen! The eldest boy did not like studying; he ran away from school at an early age. We decided not to press him in this respect. You can only lead a horse to water. The children see each other often. Our sons all hold either agricultural or industrial [manual] jobs. They show care for us, I'm glad to say, and come to visit us frequently. On the holidays they come to stay with us, although the girls do so much less often, as they traditionally must follow their husbands. Recently I fell ill. My daughter took me in and looked after me. I stayed with her on the moshav [cooperative farm] for two months. Their lives are quite different from ours, and I think it is an improvement. One of our daughters uses contraceptives and only has two children. That's much better than the slavery of bringing up nine children with no money. But my eldest daughter, the one who married at fourteen, followed in my footsteps; she has eight children. We never used contraceptives ourselves. After my period we used to abstain from intercourse for fifteen days; when the abstinence period was over I had to go to the mikvah in order to bathe. Intercourse was only allowed after this ritual purification. [Both volunteered the information that Yemenite Jews do not believe that sexual intercourse should be restricted solely to the reproductive function, but rather that it is clearly also intended for pleasure.] We still have a good sex life, just as before the menopause. [The rabbi puffed contemplatively on his hookah and now and then ran his fingers through his neatly coiled sidecurls, watching us with penetrating and shrewdly appraising black eyes.]

We do not have many friends here, although our house is always overrun by his visitors seeking advice. He'll tell you such bits of wisdom as "Eat cabbage when your stomach is upset." My husband has absolutely no interest in politics, although he is forever carrying on his grudge against the rabbinate, the government, and the Histadrut.

YICHYEH: Well, all of them rob me of my money!

Rivkah offered me a large platter of tangerines. Rabbi Yichyeh raised himself from the sofa, hookah in hand. A black-clad, impressive man, hatted, and with a long beard, he walked slowly over the stone floor and passed through the ancient, arched, four-foot high wooden door into the next room. Here was his world. Four beds flanked both walls; they were covered in old, faded tapestry. At the far end of the room stood a cupboard, which contained his raiments. In front of the casement window he had set up his desk: a small, rectangular table covered with the Talmud and other holy texts. He sat himself down and, quite oblivious to our presence, he began to pray. A single, bare forty-watt bulb, hanging on a long brown wire, dangled over his head. As we exited from the room into the courtyard, we heard the repetitive murmur of his prayer.

Chickens crisscrossed the small, paved area outside the house. Rivkah, who had come out with me, reached for a rusty tin can that was standing on the outdoor pantry shelf and threw them some grain. A two-burner butane cooker stood on a wooden ledge and a water hose lay coiled on the ground. I waved good-bye to her. She stood there, paisley handkerchief tied around her head, apron on, a strong, sturdy woman, with a crafty intelligence.

John James Haran

New York City, New York

Born 1906

A social worker friend who worked with the elderly in New York City suggested that I talk with James Haran. He thought Mr. Haran's stories about the Irish community here around the turn of the century would be fascinating. He warned me that Mr. Haran was quite ill with heart trouble and emphysema but added that he thought he was lonely and would enjoy talking, which turned out to be the case.

I was asked to come in midafternoon, when Mr. Washington, his home help, would be there to open the door. The apartment was small and dingy, and at first Mr. Haran was very hard to understand because of his hacking breathing difficulties. But his Irish charm overcame the obstacles. We established an enjoyable rapport.

I WAS BORN in 1906, right here in New York on Fifty-seventh Street and Ninth Avenue. Both my mother and father came over from Ireland. There were fourteen children—eight boys and six girls—but only five of us are left today. My mother was thirty-five when I was born, and I was about the seventh or eighth child. She had one girl, then eight boys, and then five more girls. She prayed for girls.

My mother came over as a seamstress to work for the Bingham family; he was Carnegie's partner. Later she became a fashionable dressmaker for a number of society women such as the Astors and the Vanderbilts. She was a high-powered woman and was very well connected on the political scene. She was friendly with Mrs. Al Smith, Jimmy Walker, and a Mrs. Meenan, who owned the Good Humor Company.

My family owned a saloon. It was located on Fifty-sixth Street and Ninth Avenue and was called the Makaraun, after the Makaraun River in Ireland, which runs through the toughest section of County Sligo. My father took that name because our bar was right in the middle of the toughest section of Hell's Kitchen.

Yes, I say that I am happy in my old age—as happy as you can be when you've got heart trouble and emphysema and are alone.

My father was tough, too; my size, but strong. He was a handsome man. I was the only one of the boys who wasn't a fullback. I always weighed about one hundred twenty pounds. There's a picture of my parents. My mother was a beautiful woman, don't you think? Bright and witty. You can see it in her face.

As the bar made money they bought property—profitable furnished-room houses. During Prohibition the saloon was turned into a speakeasy, and the money started pouring in. Later my mother used to speculate in real estate.

I was twelve or thirteen years old in 1919, when the Volstead Act was passed. I used to have to fetch two hundred gallons of alcohol from the wholesaler. They had it packed in forty-gallon cans. The price of raw alcohol was three seventy-five a gallon, but the stuff was so bad that we paid nine seventy-five to get United States Pharmaceutical quality. The jobber would bring out two hundred gallons. They were giving us rotgut and charging for the good. The only one who had a sensitive enough nose and could tell the difference was me. I would go and smell it, and if they were giving us the wrong stuff I would put a big X on the can and they would never say a word. Usually, out of the forty cans they would have about ten wrong. Before USP we used to bring it up to a chemist to test. I can smell anything to this day. I also used to make whiskey when I was twelve years old. I know it sounds like bragging, but nobody could do it quite like I could.

We had a chauffeur, who regularly made the whiskey, but he also used to sweep the sidewalk, take care of the furnace, and of course drive. Whenever the guy didn't show up in the cellar, I would have to go down to mix the liquor. We were making twelve thousand dollars a month in our heyday. There was a little opening in the cellar ceiling, and the bartender would shout down "three fives, two twos," things like that, and I would pass up the stuff. One variety was forty cents and the other seventy-five cents a glass. It only cost us a few pennies to make. Still, it was better whiskey than they get today.

My mother had the five girls to dress. She would go down to the finest stores and bring home three or four model dresses at one hundred eighty dollars a dress (in those days that was a lot of money). Then that night she would cut all the threads, lay out the pieces, and cut copies from them. Then she would sew the originals back up again and send the dresses, probably better than new, back to the store.

My father belonged to all the Irish organizations. He was secretary of Curry's Club—an honorary position. We all went to the church on Fifty-ninth Street and Ninth Avenue; that's where I was baptized and married, too. The Church of the Paulist Fathers. It's one of the most beautiful churches in New York, I think, with fourteen altars inside. The church is verging on bankruptcy now—a deteriorating neighborhood, you know.

My father, he wanted to give everything away. One time he fell and broke his hip (around 1919, I think it was). He was laid up three or four months, so the bartenders got in the habit of taking the money up to my mother. But she'd say, "Oh, no, pay the bills first. You've got to pay the bills." My father'd answer, "The bills are paid." But turned out they weren't. When he died he left thirty thousand dollars worth of notes.

By the time my father recovered from his broken hip, Prohibition was in full swing. He was scared to death selling illegal liquor, afraid he'd go to jail. And sure enough, he was one of the first ones to be arrested under the Volstead Act.

My mother, she didn't give a damn. After his arrest she just gave him seventy-five dollars a week spending money and took over the whole shooting match. She bought three houses with the money she made in the speakeasy. He wouldn't move in because there was a mortgage on them. He was very strict, a real old-world Irishman. It meant that she had to sell one house to pay the mortgage on the other. She paid thirty-nine thousand dollars and sold it for one hundred sixty-five thousand dollars—that was in the good times, 1925. They were large houses. For instance, the one we lived in on Fifty-seventh Street and Ninth Avenue had twenty-one rooms. Of course, we needed the room: fourteen children, a chauffeur, a cook, and a maid. Fifty-seventh Street was a nice neighborhood in those days.

Though I did go to a Catholic school for a while, I started out in a public school and ended up at Dwight Prep, which was one of the more exclusive private schools in those days, at Seventy-two Park Avenue. First I was put into a commercial course. Then when the money came in they could afford to switch me to the college preparatory section, so I had to go through the whole thing again. I was glad though, because I was accepted as a special student at Saint Viators in Kankakee, Illinois. (Fulton Sheen went there, too.) I was at Saint Viators a year and a half, until I developed some pretty serious eye trouble and nearly went blind. For a time I couldn't see at all, and for eight weeks I was kept in a darkened room.

When I left Illinois I came back to New York and shifted to real estate and insurance school. I went into that field for about ten years and took care of the family property because my mother needed help with managing her real estate. I started out driving for her, and then gradually I got into managing the office and collecting rents.

The crash came suddenly, and my mother lost seven houses in one year. We thought she would go insane, but it didn't bother her at all. She was over seventy when she lost her money—over two million dollars! Most people would find it very hard to adjust to such a change in their old age.

Being Irish, I've always been a Democrat. I remember a funny little incident with Jimmy Walker. When my mother and father took a trip around the world he came to see them off. My mother lined us up against the rail, and we were introduced to him, upon which he said, "Mary, I see twelve vacations right there," because every time she had a vacation she had a baby.

I stayed on in the real estate and insurance business, working for her while it was going good (1927 to 1932), but then, like I said, the bottom dropped out of the market. I was still living with my mother then and managing her property, because I didn't get married till I was thirty-four.

As business got worse and I could see my mother was milking the properties, I decided to go into partnership, out on Long Island. My partner was brilliant but turned out to be a crook. He opened fifty drugstores in a stretch from Hudson, New York down to Madison Square Garden. In three months he managed to own our whole business, even though he'd put nothing in it, and I'd invested all my savings: fifty-one hundred dollars! When I realized what had happened I got a lawyer.

I never got a nickel back. He'd cleaned me out of everything. There were three partners in the business. We bought a garage and two gas stations, a lunch wagon, a tire stall, and all sorts of automotive equipment; just in Valley Stream alone we had managed to get seventy-five thousand dollars credit. We had the best corner site (Carvel built there afterwards). Yes, he was a smart man, but the wind was up and I could have gone to jail—fraud, you know. Stuff wasn't paid for. As treasurer of the corporation I wrote a check for twelve hundred dollars, but it bounced. So I went to the police and somebody there told me they had been chasing him for years.

My mother wouldn't help to bail out the business, though she did pay the lawyer, but that was all. They sent him to jail for three and a half years, but that didn't do me a bit of good. I had lost my fifty-one hundred dollars. Later my mother did give my brother and me two thousand dollars so we could open a Chesterfield's on Broadway and Forty-second Street. But about then my brother started drinking (about two quarts a day) and he went down the hole. We got him to a hospital. He was up there for three years and they dried him out. Later he used to curse me for just having a glass of beer. He died twelve years ago with emphysema.

My mother moved in over the bar and grill, with the five girls. I had to sell my insurance to make ends meet. I got a check back for eighteen hundred dollars. My mother, who was used to spending money—a lot of money—got hold of the check, forged my name, and cashed it. What are you going to do, sue your mother? I could have called the police or the Metropolitan Insurance, but I would have felt like a jerk. I couldn't do a thing about it. I knew I was finished, kaput, nothing more I could do. I'd gone down to about one hundred five pounds by then.

When I lost that grill, see, I had no references, 'cause I'd been working for myself all that time. I was thirty-four years old and I wanted a job, but I couldn't find one because I'd never worked anywhere except for my mother or myself. So I had to take a job as a dishwasher in Bickford's for twelve dollars a week. Luckily I knew the treasurer at Bickford's, otherwise they never would have hired me, thirty-four years old, to be a dishwasher.

I was there about two weeks, I think it was, when the boss came over and said to me, "Did you own Chesterfield's?" When I said Yes, he said, "What are you doing as a dishwasher? Come out and work on the counter." I was promoted to third assistant manager, a position which they had at that time.

Finally, I went right up to the top, but they couldn't give me an advance on nineteen dollars a week. Imagine, thirty-six people under me and I made nineteen dollars a week.

In 1940 or '41 I met this girl and I took her home. My mother disapproved and kicked me out of the house. She never had much use for the boys, except for Charlie, who looked the spitting image of my father. I don't spend much time thinking about things, but I do like to talk about the past. That girl became my wife, Nancy. When I met her she was working as the head teletypist for Crowell and Collier (they were still publishing.).

When we got married, in 1941, I wanted her to quit work pretty near from the beginning. See, I was working nights as a bartender and she was working days. I'd be off Wednesdays and she was off Saturdays and Sundays. It was no marriage. I'd leave her notes—that was all. I didn't want to wake her up at four, when I'd come in, so we hardly saw each other. Later she'd only work when I was laid off, for three or four months at a time. Then when I got rehired, she'd quit again. When she wasn't working she used to come down to the bus to meet me at two in the morning and we'd go have a drink. She'd cook me anything I wanted at all hours of the night. We were married thirty-six years—well, thirty-three really—'cause she died three years ago. We got along very good, a real honeymoon for all those years.

Only trouble was my work. I could have got back into some restaurant business of my own, for say five thousand dollars, and made a lot of money, but my wife just didn't want me to. She wanted me to be a bartender. It seemed safer. She didn't want me seeing any girls in the back office. But, believe me, when you are working twenty hours a day you are not looking for women. I don't know to this day what it was about her, but I adored her. Still, it's too bad I put up with her fears, because I should have opened a place of my own again. About three or four years ago, before she died, she said, "I'm sorry, John, I was so jealous. You really should have had your own business." My personality would have fitted in with it, you know.

I was working for a while in one of the biggest convention hotels in Brooklyn—The Bernardo, owned by Frank Costello. I'd seat as many as thirty-five hundred people at one time, eleven weddings per day. So you can see, I had no time for girls. I mean, you couldn't even think. I used to make out the checks, too; something no other bartender ever did—at least no banquet bartender ever did. They trusted me.

I had a knack for math, which is why I was surprised when I did the bank balance wrong last December. It hurt me; I really thought I was becoming senile. It's the lousy system they have with the bank book, though I know I was also at fault. Cost me thirty bucks—that's what hurt me more than anything else—'cause thirty dollars out of less than two hundred fifty dollars is a lot of money. I don't even get a full two hundred fifty dollars; it's a little less than that [$224 from social security and $21 from supplemental security income]. I was telling the lawyers from the church yesterday that out of just fifty-one dollars a week I really manage pretty well: I pay the rent, the gas, the light, union dues, and the telephone plus buy a bottle or two. Laundry, too, and some things you need to buy like a pair of pliers or a toothbrush.

I never could save any money. Even today all the rest of my family is rich but me; I'm the only poor one. But none of them seem to be any happier than I am. Yes, I say I am happy in my old age—as happy as you can be when you've got heart trouble and emphysema and are alone. No regrets on reflection, except that I didn't save more money when I was younger. Trouble is, my wife and I always had two homes—and that ate up the money. Not that they were so fancy! A place on the beach in the Rockaways and an apartment in the city. We lived in this one for twenty-seven years and were down in the Rockaways since the year we were married. Money went quickly, especially in the last few years since I got sick and could only work two or three days a week. In the last years of work, bartending at night, I'd even have to take a cab home to the Rockaways because I felt too sick to make it on the bus at that hour of the morning.

I first developed emphysema about nine, maybe ten, years ago; that's just about when I stopped smoking cigarettes. (I still smoke a cigar, though.) I was still able to work full-time then. It became more serious gradually. The whole trouble was I was working too hard (Far Rockaway *and* here) seven days a week. I adored my wife, really, because she was a doll, but she was also on the selfish side. She knew what she wanted and my trouble was I wanted to give it to her. But you just can't work one hundred hours a week and stay healthy. And I just worked and worked until finally I collapsed.

Murphy, my oldest friend, is a successful lawyer. His father and mine started saloons in the same year—1892—and were good friends until my father's death, in 1924. I worked for Murphy from around 1969 to 1971, I think it was—for about two and a half years. I completely lost sight in one eye while I was working there. It happened while I was putting a customer out during a fight. The insurance company claimed it wasn't accidental unless you had a bruise to show. I had none, so no fifteen hundred dollars. I was operated on but they weren't able to save my sight in that eye. Fortunately, the other eye seems to have gained strength since then. I also developed a prostate problem round about that time and had to have those two operations within a month. As I wasn't old enough then to qualify for Medicare, the union paid for it. I was very lucky in that.

I am seventy now. I took my retirement around sixty-two because my wife wanted me to. She was worried about me and she also wanted the money. Nevertheless, I went on working part-time, about two days a week, at Murphy's. Nobody else would have put up with my breathing troubles, but he was a good friend and knew I needed the extra money. That was my last job. You're allowed to do a certain amount of part-time work and still collect social security.

Nancy was great. Before she got ill she used to take me out every day in the wheelchair. She'd bring along a little bottle of scotch in case I had a bad spell. She'd take me out in the park. There's a beautiful little park right in the next street (I think Rockefeller or somebody like that built it). Well, she'd take me there, but first she'd get me a container of black coffee. Then off she'd go to do her shopping or to the library. Meanwhile, I'd be sittin' out enjoying the sun for two or three hours. She'd come back for me and we'd go home. I couldn't walk anywhere by myself in those days. Now at least you can see I can get up and down a little. Still, I don't want to overdo it, though the doctors tell me to keep moving, that it's important for the circulation.

My wife died of cancer three years ago. It really came as a terrible shock, a real shame. She was sick for a year, and they wouldn't tell me 'cause my condition was so bad—the emphysema, you know; they thought the news would kill me.

Nancy's nephew worked in the dialysis unit at Elmhurst Hospital, and as they suspected kidney trouble, he arranged to have her admitted there. But it turned out not to be her kidneys. They performed surgery, though I didn't know anything about it until my brother-in-law called up and said, "John, they operated on Nancy and when they opened her up she was so full of cancer they just closed her right up again. She won't be alive more than three weeks." And it was true, almost to the day. She was sick right here in the house. We took her to the hospital at the end; she was only there six days. The doctor told her in July 1972 that I had only eighteen months to live. In December 1973, exactly eighteen months later, she was dead. Nobody can believe it about Nancy's death; she was the healthiest looking girl you'd ever seen.

It's been lonely without her. But now that Mr. Washington comes weekdays to help me it's a little better. At least I have somebody to talk to. He even promised me, now that spring is coming, he'd take me out a bit in the afternoons when it's nice; I look forward to that. Social Services hired Washington to help me a couple of hours a day. They pay him three dollars an hour. I guess they've finally realized that it's cheaper to keep someone like me at home with homemaker care than in a home or institution. He makes me breakfast, but he never gets here till one or two, so it's really lunch; usually eggs and bacon, juice, milk, and toast. Then before he leaves he gives me some more milk and juice and canned fruit plus a sandwich for my supper. He does a bit of cleaning, makes the bed and changes it when necessary, takes me to the hospital when I go for my checkup, cashes my social security check, does my shopping, et cetera. I suffer from emphysema and a heart condition (they tell me the right side of my heart is just about nonfunctioning), and I am troubled by severe shortness of breath, so that I need an oxygen tent by my bed. I use it about five or six times a week.

Though Washington comes five days a week, I'm now really trying to get additional help Saturday and Sunday, since you can see I just can't manage alone. But the policy is home help five days a week, not more, or else placement in a nursing home. So it's not likely I'll get it. Efforts have been made to get me into a home, but I've fought it. Since Mr. Washington came, about eight months ago, it seems to be less likely they'll move me. When Medicaid funds first became available a whole lot of people were moved to homes, at least those who were no longer able to look after themselves, but then came all the scandals and funds were cut.

I know I'm lucky that I'm on the ground floor here as there's no elevator. Otherwise I would be gone long ago. It does have its disadvantages, too. There's a wild bunch of kids in the neighborhood. It's just a matter of time before they pry open my door. I hear them working on it and fiddling with the lock. They're on the stoop drinking, smoking grass, and yelling till all hours of the night. I used to have a good bolt lock, but I gave it away so that I wouldn't lock myself in. Washington and my neighbor have keys to get in. This apartment is rent-controlled at eighty-seven dollars a month. The woman upstairs, who just moved here, pays three hundred dollars for the same thing I've got; only difference, really, is new paint. Can you believe it? I paid sixty-one dollars when I moved in twenty-seven years ago.

Oh, I'll live. Not long, but I'll live. Every time I go anyplace now, they say, "You son of a gun, you should be dead!" I was operated on four times in the last three years. The prostate operation turned out to be benign, except there are repercussions, you know; it's not completely perfect. Then came the operation for a mass in my breast—in a woman they call it a mastectomy—which turned out to be OK, too. There's nothing I can do about it all now, between the old age and the heart. On top of all that I have polyps in my rectum. For a while there I had to have an examination every two weeks to check them. I was sent down to Bellevue for barium tests. Luckily, they aren't cancerous either.

I'm not entirely alone in the building here because the girl across the hall has the key, and she brings me the papers every day and occasionally cigars or a cake or a piece of pie. But she hasn't got time to sit and chew the fat because she works eleven hours a day. Murphy comes by about once a week and has a drink and spends an hour or two.

This winter I had a bad virus. It was over George Washington's birthday. I sat alone and immobilized in this chair for four days. I was totally paralyzed; just couldn't move. Mr. Washington was off because of the holiday, and I just couldn't get myself over to the phone or to the bed or to the bathroom. I had nothing to eat either. I was sick for a whole week.

If I went to a good home like the Mary Manning, something like that wouldn't happen. I realize that and I wouldn't mind going in lots of ways. But on the other hand, I'd be in other kinds of trouble. No freedom. First when you enter they take all your money, then they dole out twenty-five dollars a month to you. That just isn't enough; not for presents, stationery, union dues, telephone calls, and so on. Like this week, for instance; I spent twenty dollars on liquor, but that has to last me the month, naturally. They do have a bar there, but I don't know what they charge per drink.

You know, it would cost the government four or five times as much to keep me in a home as here. They'd get the two hundred twenty-four dollars from my social security per month, but they'd have to make up the rest.

I'm still living. And I'm cheerful. I'm not morbid, not too depressed. See, I have the church come. Last night they came: two lawyers from the church. They spent about two hours with me. I tell the people about Jimmy Walker, about the old times, and they can't believe New York was like that seventy years ago. The priest comes the first Friday of each month and says Mass.

I'm not allowed to go to church anymore. I went for the last time two years ago, to the Anniversary Mass for my wife, but I only got within a block of the church. It's the stairs, and then, even if I'm in a wheelchair, somebody has to carry me up the stairs, and that's an imposition. The only time I go out now is for the hospital visit.

I'm alright once I get my books. See, I'm selfish, but I think old people generally are. I read in bed mostly. Reading takes my mind off things. I'll read anything: biographies, detective stores, travel books, novels. My mind, thank God, is as clear as it ever was.

Of my family my sister Mary is the only one who still comes to see me. Another sister won't talk to me; don't ask me why. She's the one, my "twin," with whom I was so close as a child; in fact she used to go to sleep in my arms when she was little. Two other sisters moved to Florida. I never see them and can't afford to call 'em.

My doctor is a very lovely gentleman, but it doesn't do me much good to talk to him. I ask him, How am I doing? and he answers, "Oh, you're doing just fine," but I know that isn't the truth! I wish they would talk to you more honestly. He always tells me not to drink; he is very much against liquor. What he doesn't realize is that, see, I can't get my breath. Just the least little bit of effort and I lose my breath completely. You've heard me, that awful rattle in my throat. Now the alcohol helps me. That's all I know. I take a drink and my breath comes right back. I went to see the doctor last Thursday in the clinic. I had to have three drinks before I left just to get outside the door. When I used to go to the park, I'd have a nip at every block and sit down to rest just to get through those three blocks. I can't dress myself in the morning. I have no energy at all. Everything wears me out.

I started going down to Bellevue, to the geriatric clinic (oh, they were marvelous—thirteen doctors—and they gave me every kind of test!), when I had a spell in the park a couple of years ago and they had to call an ambulance. It was pretty funny. One of the doctors asked me where I lived, and I said, "Central Park. A nice neighborhood, you know." I think they thought I was a bum. So I told them I had a four-room apartment a block from the Waldorf and they thought I was crazy; didn't believe me. I said, "I don't care whether you believe me," but they wouldn't release me because they really still thought I lived like a vagrant, in Central Park. Certainly this is not a gracious apartment or beautiful, but it is *my* apartment.

It doesn't matter to me anymore whether I live or not. If God were to call me I wouldn't mind. Let God's will be done—it's not that much of a pleasure anymore, you know what I mean? Having you here, it's a pleasure, but when you go I am alone until one o'clock tomorrow afternoon.

Ragnhild Balchen

Kristiansand, Norway

Born 1901

Kristiansand is the southernmost city of Norway, lying at the tip end of the long Scandinavian peninsula that dips down into the North Sea. It is a small city of about 59,000 inhabitants, and therefore I felt it would be a typically representative town as regards its population of elderly and their care and condition. I spoke to the head social worker dealing with the elderly at the Kristiansand department of social services, and there I was told about the fine local day center. A visit was arranged, and I was able to spend a day there.

Ragnhild Balchen greeted me at the entrance to the center, where she teaches a weekly literature course. One immediately sensed her to be a woman of intelligence and power, not in the least burdened by her seventy-three years. Her eyes were of an intense beautiful blue, almost gentian. They were set in a matrix of fine creases and crinkles, the result, I suspect, of a life-long readiness to laughter. Her cheeks, rosy and pleasantly plump, reminded me of an Irish girl I once saw standing by a road in a sunlit rain who had such rare coloring.

The center is located on the ground floor of an attractive new building, which contains as well three floors of small modern flats (one room for singles, two for couples); these are built specifically for the elderly and are supplied with special toilets with handles and with seats in the shower stalls. A nurse comes in daily in case there are any health problems, and the occupants have the downstairs facilities of the day center at their disposal. There, five days a week, they may have a hot noon meal, and there is a meeting place for games of bridge, Scrabble, or just talk. For the ambitious, a wide spectrum of courses is offered in areas ranging from metalwork, stained-glass work, mosaic, rug- or jewelry-making to active classes in folk dancing and gymnastics; a literary discussion group is available as well.

I WAS BORN in Kristiansand in 1901, the eldest child and only daughter. I

The world around me interests me, and I'm grateful that I've been seemingly blessed with unusual energy to do, . . . to enjoy living.

was only seven years old when my mother, at twenty-seven, was left a widow with five other small children to care for besides. She had married at eighteen years of age. My father left her his combination gunsmith shop and bicycle sales and repair business and more debts than assets. Mother sold the business and instead opened a sweets, fruit, and tobacco shop, which she felt to be a more manageable business for a woman alone. I, being the eldest, had to help after school each day, first in the shop, then at home, and especially with putting the younger children to bed.

A closeness developed between my mother and me which lasts, in spirit, to this day. Soon the small shop offered her too little challenge, and she became the local census taker, or *Volks Register,* for which work she was later decorated by the king. She lived to be eighty-six years old. At her death she had great, great grandchildren. When the king decorated her and found out that she had grown children, he said, "You must have started very young." She answered, "Yes, I did, but if I had life to live over, I know I wouldn't do it again. Not five children in a row by the time I was twenty-five." Over her lifetime she had become an independent woman, a precursor of our new women.

I was able to attend eight years of elementary school. Then I went on to the Handel School, which you in America would call business school. Around the age of eighteen I took my first office job, but of course, all my earnings had to go to help support the younger children in the family. I managed to escape further responsibility to the family when, at age twenty-one, I married.

Our life became easier when my mother took on her new duties as *Volks Register.* She made still another career change a few years later; she became a social worker and ended up finally as the chief of social workers in the city of Kristiansand.

My husband is a businessman. He deals mainly in margarine. But by avocation he is a musician—a fine musician. He plays the violin and for many years conducted the orchestra in Kristiansand. Before the advent of sound in the movies he even played accompaniments for the silent films. Many years ago, of course. Happily we have been able to share our love of music. For instance, I've been singing in the local women's chorus for more than twenty years (in fact, I founded it).

Like my mother, I have been interested in social work, though necessity, in her case, dictated that she work for pay, whereas I volunteered my services. I've headed an active housewives' association for a good part of my life. I remember, just before the war, in 1939, I was chosen as the Norwegian representative to a large international conference of women held in Finland. Luckily my husband, who was willing to look after the children in my absence, didn't share my political passions and so didn't mind staying home. I still recall the excitement of that trip—finding so many strangers who shared common goals and feelings.

Politics has been an enduring fascination of mine. I've served as foreman for the leftist party here for fifteen years, from age forty-five to sixty, after my children were grown. Now I work here at the Center for the Elderly. We have accomplished a great deal over the years in augmenting and improving the social services of Kristiansand. Here in Norway, as everywhere, these services have not always been as good as they are now; we are rapidly catching up with Sweden and Denmark, and I think it is safe to say our standards of care are superior to those you'd find in most other Western countries, except perhaps Holland. When I was leader of the women's group, we began to organize visits to the elderly. At first the headquarters for this was my own home; later the municipality took it over. It is now quite professionally run.

When the war started, my husband and I took the children, my mother, and his mother and fled to the woods. We stayed there, foraging for more than three weeks, until my husband and mother went forth as a sort of patrol to see whether we could go back to our homes. We were able to return but had to "lay low," always hoping to make ourselves as unnoticeable as possible to the Nazis. Life was pared down to its barest essentials. No organizations met. We managed, always on bicycle, by smuggling food now and then from the farmers or, clandestinely, from the fishermen whose catch was, of course, ordered to go to the occupation forces but who saved a good part of it for the local people. The house where my mother worked many years as *Volks Register* was turned into the headquarters of the infamous SS. Here they tortured patriots.

During the war Russian prisoners of war were encamped in Kristiansand. Our youngest son passed the camp each day on his walk to school. The prisoners' misery and hunger affected him profoundly, and he took it upon himself to become their courier. He brought them food and other necessities. It was most dangerous but I couldn't bring myself to stop him. Many years later some of the Russians came back to ask for him. He had only been nine years old at the time. It took courage! And in gratitude they remembered him over all those years.

After the war, and reaching middle age, I began to have a growing feeling that I must do something with greater scope than look after my children or garden and house. I became restless, having no professional outlets and a great deal of energy. It became hard for me to sleep nights and I was often irritable and nervous. If I had been able to go to the university (as I certainly would have done had I been of a later generation), I would have had a profession, but as it was, I took on what I knew well: I became the hardworking volunteer director of the household school in Kristiansand. I served in this capacity for twenty years, retiring at age seventy. Today, of course, the same position is a paid one demanding a respectable salary.

While serving as director of the school I became involved in other community work. For instance, I headed the visiting home nurses. These practical nurses were not RN's; they performed light nursing and some homemaker care. Then I served on the consumers' council, which was an interesting experience. (There were two men and myself serving at the same time.) Finally, I was elected for the term of eight years to serve on the city board, our town parliament. There are sixteen representatives sitting on the board at a time, each for an eight-year term.

Now I am enjoying teaching a literature course here at the old people's center. While I was serving on the board I had to get in the habit of reading quickly, since each day on my desk I would find accumulated piles of official documents. I had to plow through them, but now I am reaping the benefit of that training. It makes the preparation for my course no hardship.

At the center I recently joined the folk-dancing class and I love it. But that is all; I take no other classes. Everyday I swim with my grandchildren. The coastline around Kristiansand is beautiful, with rocky promontories and sheltered coves and islands. It's a joy to explore, and we often go on outings. In winter I try to go swimming once a week at the swimming club. Of course, Norwegians are great bicyclers and walkers. Everyone takes to the woods on weekends to bike, sail or swim, or ski in the winter. It was only ten years ago that my husband and I were still taking our yearly bicycle trek across the country to Bergen on the west coast; that is quite a distance you know. I still love to travel but not by bicycle any longer. We Norwegians come from strong stock—fishermen and farmers—who have lived all their lives in an unfriendly northern climate. Perhaps that is why we are hardy. We have had, up to a year ago, the oldest retirement age—seventy—in the West; I think perhaps we live longer. My husband, as an example, is one of twelve children, and up to now only one has died.

This center for old people was founded in '53 by a number of local organizations. Members of these groups volunteered their services; in fact they still do. However, nowadays the city government pays for the facility: a million krone this year alone. Recently we have had a paid director, trained in geriatric work, running the place.

You ask me and I often ask myself what I have done to retain my sense of youthfulness. People notice it, so it must be a fact. Well, I think it is my sense of humor which has never deserted me. I've managed to keep a certain freshness, I guess, because I'm not easily bored. The world around me interests me, and I'm grateful that I've been seemingly blessed with unusual energy to *do,* to involve myself, to enjoy living. I love to be with my grandchildren, to make things for them, like knitting sweaters or crocheting. Keeping my great garden in order is quite a chore, though I enjoy it, and there is challenge in teaching my course. I have to keep ahead with the reading. The chorus rehearsal, held each week, has always remained sheer pleasure.

I have no regrets about my life. I have had a fine and loving husband and that has made the difference, although at the moment I am worried about him. He is feeling a little poorly. But for me, I am fine and I look forward to more productive years.

I feel so blessed because I have my wife and children still with me.

N.J. Bell

Alabama

Born 1896

Jim Bell and his wife greeted me graciously, standing on the white clapboard porch of their house in a small rural town in Alabama. Their faces bore an inscrutable air of peace, inner tranquility, and regality that reminded me of some Ethiopian prince and his consort. Then again, their bearing evoked the image of a Black Grant Wood. I could not tear my eyes from the lineaments of those two faces. What else was one reminded of? some Chinese ancestor painting? a Thai buddha? Jim Bell's voice was so delicate as to become almost inaudible on tape.

I WAS BORN in Mount Willey in 1896, so I am seventy-nine years old. We moved here when I was sixty-five. Came from Briggs, Alabama, which is about fifteen miles away. I was renting my farm from white folks there until they threw us off the land when we was registering to vote in '64. Sometimes I think it was a good thing, because I planned to quit anyway and that gave me the push to come here. You know, I built this house myself. I didn't get no help either—none—except from my son.

My dad was a farmer. There were seven of us in my family, and when I was a child I had to work in the fields with him because I was the oldest one. I only went to school three or four months a year. You know, you can learn more when you teach yourself if you are smart, but I missed going to school. I love to read, so I read anything I can get a hold of. I'll give you an idea: I learnt about insects from government pamphlets and that helped me a lot in my farming. Bad thing is my eyes are giving me trouble now, so I can't read so much. Funny, but I can read better at night now than during the day.

All my brothers and sisters is dead except me. I don't know whether they didn't take care of theirselves, but they all dead. My oldest sister died when she was sixty, but the rest was young when they died. All except one was young when they died.

When I was a boy my grandfather used to tell me about slavery. He came from Virginia. His master's son wanted to come and raise cotton down here, so my grandfather came along with him even though he was free by then. After a time, that white man went away from here and he never did come back again, but my grandfather stayed on in the house. Fact, they tore that house down only about ten years ago. The colored man always had the white man's name in slave days, and if the white man sold him he had to take the new owner's name. They used to sell them just like we sold cattle. My grandfather was sold when he was a baby, with his mother.

He was a Clayborn. In his time there be about three hundred Clayborns. He was over one hundred when he died, and he worked right up till the end. After he got a certain age he came and visited his different children, and he was out there helping us all. He made over sixty thousand shingles for the different houses. When he was staying with me he used to walk over two miles to work at daybreak. My grandmother didn't live as long as him. They had been married while he was still a slave. They were Baptists like us.

My father was coming on ninety-one when he died. He held up good. He topped a tree just before he died, and he used to fish some right up to the last. We is used to work. Now we buy things, but then, except for sugar and flour, we used to grow most everything else. My granddaddy had a water mill and he could grind the wheat himself.

My wife came from the same place as me; we went to the same school even. I reckon I always had my eyes on her. Our families belonged to the same church. My wife was working at picking cotton when I married her. Her mother helped her when she had the babies—we had eleven of them. She was sick most of the time when she was carrying them and had to go to the doctor's a lot. She feels pretty good now she's over with the children.

But she used to work with me on the farm, too. We'd make our own butter, which she would churn; I have did it myself. We had so much milk—we had thirty-five cows—that sometimes we would give it away and sometimes we would give it to the hogs. Made 'em fat. We let the cows out during the day and penned them at night. My wife would bake our own bread, but she doesn't do it anymore; it's too much for her.

We still belong to the church down in Briggs. I probably wouldn't have had to move if I had jest told them I hadn't registered. I knew alright I would have to move at once if I told them the truth that I registered, so I plain didn't say. A lot of people were too scared to register. The bosses wanted you to vote their way, and they wouldn't let you go to vote unless you did.

I was with the last white man three years when he threw us off the land. He'd bought the place from my former boss, on whose land I had worked for many years. He'd been alright. A lot of people moved away from here then because they couldn't find no land to buy. Lucky I had a son here who found me a piece. I have five acres of land now and I sold five other acres to three of my boys, so there were ten altogether. I had a few cows when I first came. I don't have any sons who are farming. One son works in a store in

Birmingham and my baby boy works in a bakery in Montgomery. He's the first colored fellow to work where he at, and they tell me he's a real good baker. He used to live with us until he built his own house around here. He don't like the big town.

When I was young I always worked with my father and for nothing; that is, until I went to the army and got married, when I was twenty-two. My wife and I have been married since 1919—fifty-six years—and I have been farming all those years. The first time round I stayed on one place eight years, then I moved. Then the next place I stayed in from 1926 to 1965. I never have moved too many times. I farmed in the same way as my father. I watched him carefully. I started with forty-five or fifty acres. Always had syrup which I used to sell. I raised hogs, too, but could only do that as long as I could raise the feed. Round here we called the dark land crawfish land because you stayed with it a long time. I had better corn land where I moved from.

I had a cultivator pulled by horse, and some mules, too. My sons helped me farm until they got growed. At eighteen they went off. Then I had to do most everything myself, 'cept I would send them to sell the cotton for me.

Since I have been growed I have hunted, though I ain't hunted none since the first year I moved up here. I gave it up when I got badly lost one time just moving round and round in that marsh. Couldn't find me way nohow. That put the fear in me. At the old place I knew every tree and fence line.

I kept right on working when I moved here ten years ago; I never did retire. I still have a smokehouse where I used to cure the hogs. I was raising the feed till last year, but I don't have no more hogs now. Lately I can't walk right. First off, the doctor told me it was my nerves which was bothering my legs, but I wonder. It's age, I guess.

In World War One, when they discharged me from the army, I was real sick, but I didn't take a dose of medicine for all those years since then. I was the first one they let home from this area after the war, in 1918. When I got here my stepmother wouldn't let me take the medicines they gave me at the infirmary—she used her home remedies. I didn't start getting scared until a lot of people died with the flu; that's what I had. It was a terrible epidemic. I must have been a healthy man to get over it. A few years later I had yellow jaundice, but the doctor didn't know it at first. I was bad for five months. My poor wife. My sons were all small then, so my brothers had to help with the crops. The doctor telled me my heart ain't bad now. All that is wrong with me is old age.

I feel so blessed because I have my wife and children still with me. My grandson is living with me here. We are a real close family. Sometimes on Sundays we have a yard full of cars out there. We kill a chicken or two, have a big dinner, and we are all together. We have some chickens, but we don't raise them to sell. They lay eggs most of the time, but certain times they stop. We let them run free in the yard—eggs taste better that way.

We have been lucky; we haven't had a bad storm since the first year we moved here. Lucky it didn't touch the house though. We were out on the wagon when it hit. We tried to find shelter in a house, but the lady wouldn't let us in; she was that scared. Our church blew down, down yonder. We used to have floods, too, round about here. Sometimes it ruined the corn by covering the stalks. The river used to get quite a quarter of a mile wide when it was flooded, and normally it was just a little creek.

I tell you, things sure is better now for us than during the Depression. I was doing pretty good after World War One. Cotton was fetching a pretty good price then. You could raise something to eat, but trouble was you couldn't get no money for it. Corn sold for twenty-five cents a bushel. They used to store the cotton and then make mattresses out of it. Lots of mattresses. Sometimes I worry about the world now. Some ways it seems to be a worse place. People robbing each other. Even in this place here.

We never started to vote till '64. You know, some of them white folks are still building private schools. My daughter went to Alabama State College, and she is now teaching in a white school. One of my daughters marched on Selma. If I am made to feel welcome I'll go to a white man's house.

Of an evening now I watch the news and I know what's going on. I keep up with it. Every time there is an election I go to vote. Our sheriff has done fine—first Black sheriff elected in the county. People like him 'cause he's fair. Used to be a white sheriff around here beat up people for no cause. You know, he's a deacon in the church now.

I am a deacon myself at our church, but I never have preached. Most every morning I listen to a preaching program on the local radio station. Then I read the Bible often. Fact, I study it; that's right. Me memory is going a bit, though and I can't remember the verses. My eyes skip around and it's hard to try and stay on the line. But I have no regrets about my life. I think it's wrong to say a life was wasted. I even thank the Lord for the hard times, because anyways you can't be happy all the time, and I don't worry too much.

Helen Antonova All

Queens, New York

Born 1904

I met Helen Antonova All at a Living History class at the Sunnyside Center, in Queens. This course was part of about fourteen such classes that have been given throughout different parts of New York by the Brookdale Center on Aging of Hunter College and have been funded by a grant from the New York Council for the Humanities. I came to Sunnyside to photograph the participants at one of their final meetings.

I was struck by Mrs. All's face—a sensitive, somehow passionate, mobile, sad face, framed by that beautiful old-fashioned hairdo that was called Schnecken *when I was a child in Switzerland (in her case, two little, still somewhat titian-colored, braided buns, one on the back of each ear). I spoke to her briefly, and she told me how much the course had meant to her. It so happened that that day Karen Kearns, the historian who was conducting the class, was handing out Xeroxed copies of autobiographical pieces that had been written by various members of the class. Upon reading Mrs. All's, I knew I had to do an interview with her.*

A few weeks later I called her and we agreed to meet at the Russian Orthodox Church of the Savior, where she worships. In the dark, rich, incense-laden interior of the small church I sought her out among other members of the congregation, while the sonorous priests' voices and choir's responses sounded unfamiliarly in my ear. I looked up into the small dome, with its delicate hexagonal cupola, from which light was pouring, and watched the reflections from the golden cross behind the altar screen and the many lights of flickering candles. I felt I had been transported to the Russia of prerevolutionary days.

MY FATHER WAS a political prisoner, exiled to the island of Sakhalin on the Pacific coast. He was a member of the social democratic movement in Russia, in the early years of the century. My mother was a grammar school

I told him, "Sorry, but I don't want to be a movie actress. I want to be a mining engineer."

teacher on the island, and that is how they met. My mother was a cripple; her hip joints were paralyzed after she had had scarlet fever as a child, and as a result she was unable to stand up straight. Her father was mayor of the capital of Siberia, Irkutsk. My mother was the eldest of seven, and she was only fourteen when both of her parents died. My mother felt responsible to educate the other children, and to do so she went asking for help to all sorts of organizations, czarist and otherwise. She had a very difficult life. Almost all her siblings died shortly after they graduated, except for two sisters, one of whom became a chemist and the other an artist. Her mother and the other children died of TB. She herself graduated from high school and then taught the little ones; her youngest sister was only one and a half when their parents died. Her grandmother helped as much as she could with finances.

She struggled with her crippling disabilities as best as she was able, until, at age thirty-three, she decided to see one of the great orthopedic specialists in Saint Petersburg. He said she should undergo an operation to rebuild her hip socket—an operation never before performed. She was a year and nine months in hospital; they chopped off one of her legs with a chisel and constructed an artificial joint made out of her own bones (they are using plastic for that now). Then, after nine months, they did the other leg. Only chloroform was used as an anesthetic at that time, and four or five doctors had to hold her down while the head doctor was polishing her joint. It was excruciatingly painful, and she cried out, "Why are you torturing me so much?" He answered, "Because I want to be godfather to your children." And he was, too.

After all kinds of therapies and treatments she could stand straight. She had often wanted to die during her youth because it was impossible to walk without being able to straighten up. She used crutches. The doctor told her when he finished the operation, in 1899, that she would be able to walk again but only for a little while at a time. Then she would have to sit down and rest because there would be no natural lubrication left in the joint. She was also told she wouldn't be able to have children because of the operation; that if she became pregnant she would have to go to the hospital and have a Caesarean delivery, because her bones were not pliable enough for her to give birth naturally.

You know, people are strange. They wouldn't employ her because she was a cripple, except on that island, where no one else wanted to work. In Siberia she would sit and cry for days on end when everything was snowed in. My father was a teacher there also. He had no profession because he had been only a medical student when he was exiled in 1902 or 1903 for taking part in the uprisings.

I was born in 1904. My mother was on her way to Saint Petersburg on the Trans-Siberian railroad for the operation when she went into labor, a month early. The conductor put ice on her belly in order to try to delay the birth and a midwife was called. She took my mother off the train and placed her in her own little room, located right near the railroad tracks. When the midwife realized about the doctor's concerns—after it was too late already and I had just been born—she said, "I would never have tried to deliver you if I had known." When my mother reached Saint Petersburg a few days later, my father was already there; the Czarevitch had also just been born, and all political prisoners were given amnesty by the Czar. I think I have always had trouble with my nerves due to that premature birth.

My parents stayed in Saint Petersburg for three years, and then, because of what was probably political dissension, my mother wanted to go back to Siberia. My father did not want to go because he was again becoming active on the political scene. My mother, who was much more conservative than my father, felt loyalty toward the Czar, who had helped her in raising her brothers and sisters, I imagine. She never spoke of it. So my father remained in Saint Petersburg and she took me and left. He died shortly thereafter, and all I remember now is laughing wildly while being carried on his shoulders, and pulling his curly hair. Since then I have always been attracted to men with curly hair.

My mother took a job as tutor to a rich family in Zeya, Siberia. The trip was arduous. In Blagoveshchensk we had to transfer to a small paddleboat and proceed up the tributary of the Amur River, the Zeya River, six hundred miles north to the small town of Zeya. It served as a harbor for several of the gold mines located in the hills, up the river. In this little town I spent my childhood. It was almost the coldest place in Siberia, but I remember the mountains purple with azaleas in the spring.

My mother had to prepare the two youngest children in a well-to-do merchant's family—with five sons and a daughter—for entrance into high school. That family had—besides the big house—warehouses, a store, several bungalows, a large vegetable and flower garden, steam baths, stables, stalls for cows, pigs, dogs, and a chicken coop with a pigeon roost situated underneath the roof. My favorite place as a child was the open stable, where I used to visit with the horses. I developed my life-long enthusiasm for riding there and learned to drive the carriage as well.

When the children in the family had gone off to high school, my mother found a job as principal in a state grammar school. One always hears that in Czarist days they never cared about educating the people, but in Zeya, which had a population of six thousand people, we had six grammar schools and one high school, which seems to indicate that quite the opposite was true. I myself never went to grammar school. I learned mostly by listening to my mother while she was teaching others. In fact, when I was three I could read. People used to say, "Why is she holding the book in her hand like this and moving her finger?" And my mother would answer, "She's reading." Even after we left our "family" we stayed in close contact with them and used to spend all our holidays there.

Mrs. Ivanoff, my mother's former student in Djilinda village, had one day brought her little boy, Kolya, to play with me. "Here's a playmate for you," she said to him. "I don't play with girls," he answered, with disdain. "I can be a boy," I said, and with that I ran to my room, put on a pair of pants, and then came back out. He liked that, and we became fast friends.

I used to travel a lot with my mother, and people were always asking me, "Well, what do you want to be when you grow up?" And even when I was three the answer was always the same: "A mining engineer." That was because the town of Zeya was the last town into which they could ship the provisions and technical equipment needed for mining. I remember seeing the caravans of camels and horses bringing the goods in during winter. In summer the steamboats provided the transportation. In the winter the miners, who, of course, couldn't work in the deep snow and ice, would come into town to celebrate. I remember they would show off by bringing large kegs of vodka on the carriages or sleds, and then, to impress the people, they would hire other sleds and put empty barrels on them to imply how much money they had earned. I always liked the atmosphere of those men coming in from the mines, though of course they would often get quite drunk.

We never had an apartment of our own. Mother just rented rooms, until I had learned so many bad words from the other children in the house that Mother moved us into a priest's house, which was alright until the priest's wife started having babies and needed the room. So then Mother asked whether we couldn't have a room right in the school. The warden of schools provided us then with a space at the end of the schoolroom, only separated by a partition. We lived there until I developed scarlet fever and diptheria and had to move away.

I was fifteen when I graduated from high school in Blagoveshchensk. My mother had been teaching school when the revolution broke out, in 1917. In 1919 Communist authorities said to her, "We can't pay you the hundred rubles a month you were paid before. You will get fifty, and the janitress of the school will get the hundred." So my mother said, "Then let her teach the classes. I resign." At that she went back to one of the families and taught their four grandchildren just for room and board, so at least we weren't starving. I had gotten a job after I graduated, in 1921, as an actress on the stage. I was giving a show every night for Communist soldiers, but the pay was only some dry tea, oil, herring, and things like that. But on Sundays we performed for ordinary people, and they paid money, which was divided between the actors that were in the group. So I didn't earn very much, and mostly we did Communist propaganda plays. I played the role of "Liberty" twenty-one times. I loved the stage very much, but my nerves would not let me go on. Still now, every little change makes me nervous, and of course, stage work is always full of ups and downs. The actors had to be married either to a Red Army soldier or to a member of the party, or be members themselves. I was on the blacklist already in my last year of high school, because they knew my mother came from an old bourgeois family and my father was a social democrat, so I was known to be an anti-Communist. As a consequence I lost my job on the stage.

We went to the authorities and told them I wanted to go to Vladivostok to continue my education, and the man said, "Alright, but you can't go now. You will have to wait, because there is civil war going on." This was in 1922. He gave us a pass to go but said, "Do not take any books, silver, or gold with you —nothing." In order to be able to survive en route, we sewed the gold pieces we still had left under the buttons of our coats, even under the pocket buttons. We had a beautiful little old box with a false bottom, and into that we carefully packed our few pieces of silver and jewelry that we wanted to take. I wore this ring. Fortunately, they did not search us too carefully.

Then we sold whatever we had to Chinese people—a little furniture and this and that—even though we were in the Communist sector. Earlier there had been a regiment of Japanese who had occupied Zeya for a couple of years, even the school where my mother had been teaching. And so I had learned Japanese. I was always good at languages.

Finally we left for Vladivostok, only to find out that there was also fighting going on between Harbin and Vladivostok, so we couldn't get there after all and ended up in Harbin, Manchuria.

In Harbin there were many escaped Russians, all of them without money and nowhere near enough jobs. The family of the old woman I mentioned earlier was as good to us as they could be, but they were also having financial difficulties. Occasionally we would be invited for a good meal at one of the houses of the wealthier families, in the richer part of town, and then we would have to go back to our own quarters in the lowland marsh district, where we could get a room for five dollars a month; it was the worst part of Harbin. I used to scavenge for food in the rear area outside one of the food stores, looking for scraps that had been thrown away. We finally found a job working at the racetrack on weekends. Both my mother and I manned ticket booths, but it didn't last long; when the rains came in August there was no longer a job, for the horses only ran in summer, when the weather was clear.

I was lucky that I had learned Japanese, because that's how we were able to get away from Harbin. A Japanese man who had opened a café in Tokyo called the Café Russie, wanted to find a waitress who spoke Japanese and Russian, and he came to Harbin for this purpose. He was immediately ready to hire me but refused to take my mother along. I was equally stubborn about bringing her, and finally he agreed to bring us two tickets for Tokyo the next day. I worked in his café for about one year. We lived on the second floor of a typical Japanese house, with mats on the floor for beds. Rats ran through the house and over the paper-thin roof at night. When I first started working, my arm got paralyzed and I couldn't do anything. That was pretty difficult, as I had come to work as a waitress. A Communist doctor stopped by and checked me; he gave me a bromide—a whole big bottle. It had been given to me for my nerves since early childhood, and I have recently heard that it affects memory. I never have had a very good memory, and now I forget everything.

After we had been in Japan for a year we started to think about where I should go for my further education. I had never given up on that idea. We were making one hundred yen a month at that time, seventy-five for me and twenty-five for my mother, who was looking after the café owner's lovely little boy. I wanted most to go to France. I had learned French in high school and had made translations of French poetry into Russian. German I'd given up on the minute the war started, for patriotic reasons. But we couldn't get a permit to go to France, and although we put all our money away in the bank for the trip, it proved too expensive to go to Europe. So we decided on America. We bought our tickets and had our passports ready. Our departure date was set—September 2, 1923.

We were still in Japan at the time of the great earthquake. I remember that terrible day vividly; it was the first of September, 1923. Friends of mine from Russia, who had gone over to America on a boat only to be turned back because the quota figure had been met, came back to Japan and were visiting us the very day of the earthquake. It happened just as I was showing my friend a little bottle of delicious perfume that I had gotten. Later, after the earthquake, she was wandering around dazed, with the little bottle still in her hand, open.

I had just been to the public baths. The first time I had gone there with one of the other waitresses, I said, "But there are men there!" She answered, "They are not men but *banta-san,* meaning the attendants who scrub your back and hand you the towels. I got used to it after a while, but it was hard at first. There are mirrors all around the walls, and all the women sit around the mirrors, putting on that white makeup and putting their hair up with those elaborate combs. The Japanese always said, "Everybody has a body; some bodies are more beautiful than others, but everybody has a body. So why hide it from each other? What you have to hide are bad thoughts, bad deeds."

Suddenly the second floor of the house in which we were living began to heave toward me. Soon it was totally knocked over and just hanging across the electric wires. I ran into the kitchen of the house and called my mother. All the boxes of sugar and tea were falling down on her as she stood there in the kitchen, and the cook was pouring cold water onto the stove because he was afraid the fire from the stove would spread. He called to my mother, "It's alright; just stand still." Then we carried my mother out of the house to the canal and waited. The earthquake seemed to be quieting down.

We decided finally to go back to the café, trying to retrieve some of our things, our tickets to America and our passports, and whatever money we still had with us. (We had intended going to the bank that very day to take out the one thousand yen which I had saved over the year, but that was all lost it turned out, in the great fire after the quake.) My mother remembered that all our documents and tickets were in her skirt pocket, upstairs in our room. I was scared the stairs would collapse, but I ran up anyway and got the skirt and two rings—this one amongst them—also our precious little box with the false bottom that we had brought from Russia. Then I reached for a chair and took down our two icons. There was besides a beautiful big silver one, but I thought, "What will I do with that? How will I carry it?" It was such a miraculous icon anyway and had brought us such good fortune already that I was somehow convinced it would survive, even if I left it on the wall. The flames were beginning to lick through the second-floor window and the fire was already spreading throughout the city.

I ran out of the house, and I remember falling down on the ground and feeling absolutely paralyzed. That had happened to me before and I was told it was nerves [shock would be more likely]. A kind German we knew came over and put a pillow under my head. He said his place was already in flames just a few blocks away. The owner of a restaurant came over with his two children and a nursemaid. They warned us we must flee the city and told us we should walk about ten miles to his brother's house. "We'll keep the older children with us so we can clear out the valuables from our house, and you take the little ones, together with the nursemaid."

So we started to go toward a big plaza filled with people and their possessions. Mother said, "Go, save yourself; I just can't walk any further," but I refused to leave her. I sent the nursemaid ahead with the children and my friend Mary. At that moment there came a little Japanese man who said, "I want to help you." And I said, "But what about your wife and children?" He answered, "We are in our homeland, but you are guests here and we must save you." And so he led us out of the plaza and onto the road, crowded with refugees and their carts with baggage. Later we heard that most of those people in the plaza were burned and their possessions, too.

That evening we couldn't walk any farther. My feet were bleeding because I had not put my stockings back on after the bath, and my shoes were cutting deep into my feet. Finally we came to a park and collapsed onto the ground. A few hours later my mother woke me. "Helen, Helen, wake up. The trees over there are catching fire already." So we got up quickly, but first we looked all over for our Japanese friend. He had vanished; probably gone to rescue his own family, we thought. Just then he reappeared. "God forgive me for stealing," he said and therewith pushed a pallet-litter cart with two handles toward us, onto which we loaded my mother. He and I pushed her, each one taking one handle, and so we slowly but indefatigably moved throughout the night.

Toward early dawn we reached the suburbs of Tokyo, where the café owner's brother lived. We collapsed onto the crowded floor of the main room and fell into a deep sleep. The next morning we looked for our savior, our little Japanese friend, but he had left just as mysteriously as he had appeared, and we had never even been able to repay him a yen for his kindness. I truly believe the Japanese people are the most kind people on earth.

For two or three days we felt new and ominous tremors, and each time we ran out into the open. When the fires finally subsided, a number of days later, we ventured back into the city. There was nothing left of the house or the café, not even the icon. The bank had been burned down with every cent in it we had saved. The only thing left standing was the Imperial Hotel, where the Red Cross was headquartered, and they were handing out food and medical supplies and clothing. Then we learned that the ship we were to have taken on the day after the quake had departed, but they told us we would probably be able to take one from Kobe. Two weeks later we were taken from Tokyo via Yokohama to Kobe. Yokohama had been totally razed. My friend

Mary's husband was lost during the quake, but they were reunited when we reached Kobe. He had been in Yokohama at the time and miraculously survived by swimming out from the burning city to a boat. At Kobe we were put into an overcrowded refugee ship, with no money except the one hundred fifty yen we had had with us and our tickets, which read San Francisco, even though we were headed toward Seattle, for which we had to pay fifty yen extra.

On board ship one of my feet developed an infection from the long walk and I had to visit the ship's doctor. He cleaned and dressed it and then suddenly his hand reached up toward my bare thigh (I no longer owned any stockings!). I slapped him hard and he spit out at me angrily, "You'll pay for this!"

When we got to America we were separated from the other refugees and herded into the deportation dock. There I was told someone had issued a report that I was a prostitute and so we would have to be sent back. But, thank God, after ten days of agonized waiting, Miss French, a kind woman from the Young Women's Christian Association, took pity on me and said she would bond for me. So we entered the States. We all had to show fifty dollars on entering. After I'd passed through and mother had, we agreed to lend fifty dollars to another woman, who would return it immediately she'd gone through the line. But we never saw her again, and so we had only fifty dollars left to our name.

It was hard trying to earn a living if you didn't speak the language. I was a housekeeper for one month for a family with three kids, but that was such dreadfully hard work that I quit. The pay was one dollar a day. It was tough; we were living in a five-dollar-a-month room without a kitchen. After many frustrating false starts I finally got a job from a nice Greek café owner which paid two dollars a day. I worked for him and his partners throughout the next few years. Later, when I was in college, I worked there holidays and weekends. It was hard in those years. I became so nervous worrying about the high gas bills we had to pay—twelve dollars a month when I was only earning twenty dollars. But I liked working there; they were kind and often sent home food for my mother and me.

In a year I saved enough money to enter the university. From the second year on the Russian Students' Fund paid my tuition and thirty-five dollars a month (which I repaid in its entirety later). I began my studies toward the degree in engineering. The dean who admitted me told me that as a woman I would never get hired, but I told him I only wanted to stay in the United States for five years and then go back to my own country to work.

For the first two years the course was in general engineering, after which we began specializing in mining engineering. At first I did not do very well, of course, because I did not have any knowledge of English. But I finally graduated in 1928, after doing my practical training in the laboratory of a mine in Idaho, where my mother and I had to live in a small shack near the mine shaft. In this lab I was given the job of assaying the ore, that is, getting the metal extracted and analyzing it after the ore has been crushed.

Yes, I worked all my life; no man ever supported me. I loved my work and had no other thought but to do it well, but because I had striking looks it was often difficult. I used to make myself deliberately ugly, but still I could see it in the eyes of the men with whom I was working.

After my summer's work and with the prospect of graduating very soon, I felt that I had done so well with the work that I dared approach the mill superintendent with a question about future employment, but he said, "No, I just thank the Lord you're leaving! These last months have been hell at home. My wife is consumed with jealousy and all she does all day is sit by the window of our house checking to see whether you are going into my office or whether I am going to the laboratory." Ironically, he was a most correct man, an older man.

It is funny; when I was in college in Seattle I had a friend who desperately wanted to become a movie star. One day when a talent scout came around she said, "Let's go and see him," and so, to accommodate my friend, I went with her and we met him. She was a very beautiful girl but the joke is he didn't pay any attention to her and said to *me,* "You are exactly what we are looking for and so photogenic." He tried to sign me up for Hollywood. I told him, "Sorry, but I don't want to be a movie actress. I want to be a mining engineer."

While I was at the university, working constantly in the labs, I developed silicosis of the lungs from the excessive dust; I was quite sick for several months. Finally it was the doctor who suggested I try smoking "because the nicotine will form a film over the lungs," and it did help. I am still smoking and have no silicosis.

I was run-down by years of hard work without rest, but as graduation loomed I was glad to be free of the unfriendly atmosphere of the male students who made my hardships even harder. This all-male world was rejecting of a foreigner, and especially of a woman! I had to refuse the scholarship offered me to continue my studies for the master's degree because we needed money. I had no choice but to go to work.

The dean of the School of Mining, who had originally told me that "No one will ever hire a woman," helped me to find work. He told me that a large jewelry firm needed a metallurgist to make and to analyze gold, silver, and platinum. There had been one other graduate at that time, a man, who was offered the position first, but he proved to be unsatisfactory so I was given a chance. Suddenly I was making one hundred dollars a month instead of five dollars a week; for the first time we could move from our five-dollar-a-month room to a small apartment with a kitchen.

After a year of work we went on vacation to Salt Lake City, where I hoped to find work in one of the mines. But it was 1929 and no one was about to hire a woman mining engineer, especially in Mormon country. The crash came during our Utah vacation. I returned to find my job gone; the factory had closed. Finding another job proved very difficult. It was accident almost that we ended up in a small mine in Funter Bay, Alaska.

There were almost no women in Alaska, so the expectation was that I would marry there almost immediately. Also, there were a number of Russian bachelors working in the large gold mines in Juneau. Some had come over illegally, in rowboats, from Siberia.

I was hired by a Funter Bay mine owner, but in the preliminary transactions he had wondered why a man should have a woman's name—soon he learned. His wife wrote, telling us to bring a firewood stove, pots and pans, a washtub and pail, dishes, and so forth. She sent snapshots of the shack we were to inhabit. It was unbelievably primitive and you could buy nothing there. In winter we stuffed rags and paper into the cracks to protect ourselves from the winds and snows.

On our arrival in Alaska we had to stay a few days in Juneau, waiting for the small steamer to take us on its weekly trip to Funter Bay. My mother, in her crippled state, couldn't climb down into the little steamer, so one of the Russians seeing us off lowered her down in a crane. That same man became my first husband. After he had met me, he made many proposals to me and I refused him and refused him. He was a very attractive man and had been an officer in the Russian artillery, until the revolution. He finally came to see me in Funter Bay.

At the mine we took our power and water from a waterfall, and in winter, of course, it froze, so the mill and all work had to stop. My boss was going to New York to raise money for further expansion, and during that time I decided to go to Juneau to see the priest. My boss had made some awkward advances to me, which I repulsed, but it was a difficult situation in such a close and small mining town; he was married. I really think I began to think about my own marriage as one possible solution to this problem. So I stayed there, and right in the priest's house my friend proposed to me again, and though I said No, No, No all night long, I was thinking, Shall I or shan't I? Even his friends came over and asked me, telling me, "He's so unhappy and depressed. Please marry him," so I thought I would. Next day, when we went to the courthouse, they asked, "What's your profession?" and I said, "Engineer." They said, "No jokes here; you are under oath to tell the truth." But I said, "I *am* an engineer." The judge married us and we never had a religious service at all.

That first evening we went to dinner with some friends. He got so jealous that I was smiling at his friends and so mad at me that he threw a plate and grabbed my ring, which he also threw across the room. I thought, My God, what have I done? Right away, I knew it was a mistake. He had to remain working in Juneau and I went back to Funter Bay to work. I found it hard to tell my mother. It was a big blow to her that I had gotten married. Despite my early intuitions about the marriage, I decided to try to make him happy.

I got sick there during the time I was married, perhaps from standing in the icy waters so much, surveying. I began to have female problems. The owner of the mine brought over a nurse by boat from the cannery across the bay, and she brought some ergot. I think perhaps it was a miscarriage, because after the ergot I began to menstruate again.

My husband was an extraordinarily passionate and attractive man, and I was very much drawn to him, though at first we didn't see each other much, he still in Juneau and I in Funter Bay. So I asked my boss to give him a job. At the end of April he was given a job at the site and then it really started! Oh, yes, he became jealous of everybody and he was very rude. In the morning if the workmen said "Good morning" to me and I smiled back at them, the next thing I knew he had thrown a hatchet at me. Then he decided he couldn't be there just as a worker and have his wife above him: "I want to be an engineer, too. I'm going to the University of Washington to get a degree." So I was forced to leave my job and go to Seattle with him, all the while getting frantic telegrams from my job saying, "Come back, come back."

My mother, of course, had to come with us, and we had a big fight over that, because I wanted to be in the same cabin with my mother on the boat. But he said, "No, you are going to be in the same cabin with *me.*" I was frightened of him. He was a violent man, especially if he had been drinking. It was difficult for my mother to live separately from me because she always needed help dressing and undressing—she couldn't bend down, you see. He was at the university for two terms, and in the meantime I was looking for a job.

I got a job at the counter in the marketplace, and then a "mining" company wanted me to do the analysis of gold and silver. The hours were from eleven at night until four in the morning. I worked for a few weeks but was never able to collect for it because that fake company disappeared and I could not find a trace of them.

It was impossible to find a decent job in Seattle, so while my husband was still at the university I took my mother and went to Coeur d'Alene, the mining district in Idaho, where I, with recommendations from my former boss in Alaska stating that I could do everything, landed a job as an accountant in one of the mining concerns. At the end of a month I got food poisoning and was sent back to Seattle. I was paid for two months, so I was able to pay for my husband's fare back to Juneau. I moved, with my mother, to California, where I found a position as a research engineer for several mines. It was very hard work, and I couldn't move the big sacks of ore, so the supervisor said to one of the men, "Why don't you help her." He said, "Because she is getting just as much pay as we are and she can do the same work."

In San Francisco there was an annual ball for the benefit of the Russian war veterans from the First World War and from earlier wars in Russia. For four years I was elected Princess of the Ball. I also used to sing at various occasions there. Once, at a big party where I sang, an old man came up to me and introduced himself: "I'm Professor Rienzi. You have a beautiful, natural voice and you know how to use it very expressively. But your voice is not *'set'* yet." I told him I couldn't afford to pay, and he said, "That's alright. It would be my pleasure and would give me honor if you would study with me." I took about ten lessons. He told me, "No smoking, no drinking, no singing outside of the lessons." He also told me I would have to cut out "carousing." Well, I couldn't keep that up.

After a while I told him, "Look, I don't want to make a career in singing; I am a working engineer. Thank you, but I don't really want any more of your lessons." I was singing gypsy songs and popular hit songs of the times. I had a contralto voice. One of my friends used to introduce me at some of the gatherings where I was singing with the following words: "Listen to this phenomenon of nature—the woman basso!"

In a few months my husband came back from Alaska. We lived together for a little while longer, but at the end he used to sleep with a loaded revolver at my head. Finally I was so frightened I went to the police station and said, "Protect me somehow." They said, "We can't put a policeman by your bed, but we *can* help you get a divorce." Because he had caused me to lose my job and I couldn't support him and his drinking, he went back to Juneau and I started the divorce proceedings. We had been married sixteen months.

When he left he took all the papers I had written earlier in college for my first-year English course requirements. I had read all the classics and then started to write my life story for the composition classes. My teacher had then said, "I can't put it down; I'm so fascinated. But when I reread the work I start to tear my hair because every word is a mistake." Of course, I had never taken any English, and therefore I didn't know any grammar.

My next husband I didn't marry. It was a common law arrangement, which was legally acceptable in those days. After my first experience with marriage I was wary. It lasted six years, but we did not live together all that time because, like all men, he couldn't stand his wife being smarter or more educated than he was, so he also decided he had to go to the university. I was living and working in Berkeley then. At the weekends we were together, but we didn't live at home then because my mother and I had only a room and a kitchen. He was a Russian, too, and at the university he also studied mining and petroleum engineering. He was a nice man, but I didn't love him. The doctor had told me that in order to cure my nervousness I needed a man, that not getting normal sex was destroying my system. So I told my friend that and we got together. He always begged me to marry him those six years, but I said, "No, I don't want to." Finally he got a job in Ventura, and I saw him only occasionally.

Then I fell in love with a man who proposed to me, but on condition that I quit work. He was the man I truly loved. He said to me, "I am an engineer of good standing, and I want a wife who stays at home and with whom I can be in society, raise children, and not someone who works with men all the time." I used to meet him often, but I always took mother along, even for our weekends. Then very suddenly he got married and never told me anything. I heard it quite casually from a friend. I was terribly hurt and angry.

I loved that man very deeply, but I couldn't have given up my work for him, which was my passion, nor deserted my mother, with whom I had shared all my life and who was my dearest friend. I knew that she needed me. I always prayed to God that I could be like my mother. She never judged and forgave me everything. She was a wonderful woman. She was a very clever woman and she helped me all throughout my life.

I remained very close to my mother always. That's why I suffered such terrible loneliness after she died, in 1939. We had moved to New York City by then. In fact, that's why I got married right after her death: I couldn't stand being alone. She just died one night as we were playing cards—my husband-to-be—Nicholas All, the writer—another friend, my mother, and I. She collapsed at the table and we called the doctor. He could have helped her by giving her mouth-to-mouth resuscitation, but instead he asked, "How old is she?" I told him, "Seventy," to which he answered, "What do you want to torture an old woman for." And he left. I tried to revive her myself; I could still hear her heart beating, but her breathing had stopped and the heart became fainter and fainter, until it stopped.

I was terribly nervous and quite distraught after her death, so I suggested to Nicholas that perhaps we should get married, but he didn't want to at first. He told me he had a wife back in China, but I reminded him he hadn't seen her for years. "Look," he said, "I'm not a marrying man. I can't live in a cage." But I told him I really felt as though I were going crazy, so he agreed and we got married a few months later, in 1940.

You know, the interesting thing about my husband is that I already knew him from my Seattle days. One night I had gone to the movies with a friend, who couldn't take me home because he had to go to work. As he saw Nicholas approaching on the street he thought perhaps *he* would do it. Nicholas said, "Yes, but you'll have to walk. I never take the trolley." So we spent literally most of the night walking, the most circuitous route, through parks and a graveyard, all the way home. It was about seven miles, and we talked all the way about poetry and life and Russia and work. Then I never saw him again until 1939, when the man living next door to our apartment in New York City said, "All is here, you know." So I decided to look him up. He died in March 1977, and I still can't touch his things without crying. I wrote two poems about him after his death. They were published in a Russian-language newspaper.

I published one book of poems in 1944 called *Reflections,* and quite a number of other poems have been published since, in our paper. My husband and I both belonged to a group called The Circle of Poets, who were located here around New York, all Russian émigrés. An anthology of the fourteen poets was published, with ten pages for each poet, appearing alphabetically; the first ten pages of that book were All's. Now there are only three of us left. I started when I was six years old reading poetry. I remember someone asking me, "How do you write poetry?" and I said, "That's easy. Just read Pushkin, then you'll know." I started writing very young, when I first started to rhyme words, at six years of age.

Nicholas had been a member of the Czar's honorary guard, which was a position open only to the sons of prominent families; you had to have your own horse. He was a superb rider, and when we were first married we used to go to some of the Western ranches together, whenever we were able. He had also been in the Russian navy, trained at the academy. Later, after his arrival in America, in 1923, at first he appeared in vaudeville acts as a balalaika player and also as a Russian and gypsy dancer. He finally became one of the most respected and well-known journalists on the Russian newspaper. He had a column in which he interviewed many of the celebrities who came to this country, both Soviet and White Russian.

I worked in Pennsylvania for a time, where I was working when the war started, in 1941, in a big smeltery. I almost went blind there; the chemical fumes poisoned my eyes. Also I was exhausted from overworking. Most of the men had been drafted, and so I was working sixty hours or more a week for only twenty-five dollars. I was trying to do their work and mine as well. A government inspector came to the plant to see the working conditions and told the boss he should pay me overtime. His retort was, "She was contracted to receive twenty-five dollars a week. I don't pay overtime." Eventually he raised me to thirty-five dollars. I was very lucky; after I left the smeltery my sight improved.

We bought some land in 1941, in Lakewood, New Jersey, and together we built our own little house in the woods. Although we planned to move there altogether in 1973, after we retired, somehow it never happened. We only stayed there weekends and summers. He really wanted to live there, but I was nervous about the isolation and the winter snows. I have been too lonely and afraid to go there by myself since his death. When I can, I rent it.

The last fifteen years, while I was working in New York City, we lived in a house in Mount Vernon. For a time I was employed by Anaconda. I had to make a beautiful scale model and then paint it, just like a piece of delicate sculpture. It was a model of an open-pit mine in Chile and was to indicate the layers and the percentages of ore there.

A man from the Brooklyn Navy Yard offered me a job at one hundred thirty-eight dollars a month, but I said, "No, because I am already earning a hundred sixty-five working for Anaconda." His answer was, "This is a government job I am offering you. You are a woman, and you'll get paid a hundred thirty-eight whatever you do and wherever you do it and no more." In some ways I suppose I was foolish, because I would have gotten a good pension from the government. Instead, all I have is social security. I owned some stock, in lieu of pay, in one of the companies for which I worked, but they went broke and I lost it all. No, I have never gotten rich from my work but it has been an interesting life. Mostly I have made about one hundred dollars a month, when you average it out. It's hard to believe how badly we were paid for many years. The last job I did lasted about fifteen years; it was designing bridges and highways. For a time I worked in New Rochelle, designing the New England Thruway which was being built there.

For our vacations my husband and I traveled every year—four times to the Holy Land, once as tourists and three times as pilgrims. I felt that it was my spiritual homeland, although I almost died there of virus pneumonia. I was nursed back by Arab doctors and nurses. Then we also went to Africa on a safari, to Egypt, and to all the countries of Europe, but we never got back to Russia. I would love to go again, but I am afraid to, as I don't have my citizenship papers. All I have is a green card. Don't forget I was born on a train, so I love to travel!

Since my husband's death I am even more terribly nervous. Once, when I had had a bad attack of nerves, in California, a long time ago, a psychiatrist I visited told me, after prescribing a bromide: "You'll never go crazy, though, because you are interested in too many things." I guess it still holds true; as long as I can go out I am alright. I go to the Russian Orthodox Church of Christ the Savior on East Seventy-first Street, then I go two or three times a week to the center [Sunnyside Center in Queens], where I take some classes or just go to eat and talk. I started to write again recently at one of the courses offered by the center—a personal history course, which was very stimulating. We all worked on our life stories. I find, though, that I get tired very easily, especially in the morning. This tiredness is obviously related to my depression.

I do my best work at night because that's when I feel best. I don't go to bed until two o'clock in the morning. I write letters and read. At the moment I am reading Madame Tolstoy's fascinating, ongoing memoirs of her father, which are appearing in the paper each day. The telephone rings without cease all evening, but in the morning, when I am so lonely that I am losing my mind, nobody thinks of calling. All tranquilizers make me sleepy, and since this is the main thing I have to fight, the sleepiness, I don't want to take any. The doctor at the center prescribed two kinds of tranquilizers already, but they were both impossible; I just couldn't take them. I feel sleepy most of the time, even in church, which I love so much. Perhaps it's the standing [in the Russian Orthodox Church the congregation stands throughout the service, except for a few chairs brought in for the elderly]. We have lived in this same little three-room apartment for the last seven years.

My health has always given me problems, especially my nervousness, which has stood in the way of many opportunities in my life, even from the early days of my acting. I think that was also why I was never able to carry a child. I had three miscarriages. Of course, working so hard also played its part in that. While we lived in Mount Vernon I was plagued by terrible stomach pains, at least that is what they thought it was, until the doctor, with the help of X-rays, diagnosed it as back trouble. They discovered my spine had cracks in it, which were due to osteoporosis. I have had to do exercises for my back ever since, and the osteoporosis has caused me great troubles. I break bones so easily because they are so fragile. Last year it was my wrist and my hip which broke when I fell while hailing a bus. I have to be terribly careful all the time now; it's a nuisance.

In the mornings, when I wake up, the nervousness becomes almost unbearable; I can't stand to get up. Sometimes I feel almost senile then. I can't seem to remember. I take vitamins and am careful with my diet, so it isn't that.

I think it is the terrible loneliness, yet I don't want to go—I simply dread—going to a home. I wish I could find a sympathetic man, but it's too difficult at my age. I long for a human touch; at the church they "respect" me too much for any closeness to develop.

I never got a pension, though I received my plaque for fifty years service to the profession from the American Institute of Mining and Metallurgical Engineers. I became a member of their Legion of Honor at which time they gave me this little gold lapel pin. I didn't work for most of the companies long enough to be eligible for a pension. All I get is social security and that's how I manage.

My great sorrow now is that they are changing our Slavonic service in the church to the English one, phasing out the language gradually. But the language is part of the religion, and the service, as it is spoken and sung in Russian, has been part of me since earliest childhood. I remember so well driving to church in a carriage as a child, with the old woman, and hearing that wonderful deep singing and seeing the glow of the candles on the icons. It is simply not the same in English; it loses some of its meaning, not only for me, in the translation. I see it as a tragedy, and I almost decided not to go back to church any longer. I think the American members think I don't like them, but that is not it at all. They are fine people. Yes, my life has been an interesting one but a hard one.

We must each journey to our own centers, and wake old gods.

Frank Waters

Taos, New Mexico

Born 1902

After I had done the interview with Dorothy Brett, her friend and neighbor, John Manchester, suggested that I might want to talk to Frank Waters, the writer, who lived just a ways up the road. A phone call was made and an interview arranged. I turned up the dirt road at the foot of Taos Mountain and found the pleasant adobe house where Waters lived.

A friendly, slim, and straight-standing man greeted me at the door. He spoke with an easy Western colloquialism and an unassuming manner, whether we were discussing horse pastures or Tibetan Buddhism. Since the day of the interview, in May 1975, I have had two or three Frank Waters books as constant bedside companions, and I often find myself reading a chapter or so, wanting somehow to stay in contact with this mind, hoping thereby gradually to familiarize myself with the immense store of wisdom and knowledge he offers us about the American Indian heritage.*

I WAS BORN and grew up in Colorado Springs. My grandfather owned some mines in Cripple Creek and my father worked up there, helping to develop the mines. Of course they went broke. As a matter of fact, when I was young I lived for a time with my father on the Navaho reservation; he was part Indian, you know. He came from a different people, a Cheyenne tribe, in the Great Plains, but he spoke their language and had many Indian characteristics, so he fitted in pretty well there. Ironically, on another side of the family, I stem from an old Southern family from South Carolina.

In those days people didn't identify with their Indian blood because people in the West regarded Indians as the Southerners regarded Black people. They looked down their noses at them, thought of them as trash. In Colorado

**Book of the Hopi* (New York: Viking Press, 1963); *Mexico Mystique, The Coming Sixth World of Consciousness* (Chicago: Swallow Press, 1975); *The Masked Gods, Navaho and Pueblo Ceremonialism* (Chicago: Swallow Press, 1950).

Springs, when I was a boy, the Ute tribe used to be allowed to come back to Colorado Springs, to that land on the mesa just below the foot of Pike's Peak, their old homeland, and put up their tepees and camp there all summer. I used to go out with my father, who was a close friend of Buckskin Charlie, chief of the Utes. He knew them well, but our visits were looked down upon by the white people in the town. There was nothing very romantic about it, but it was interesting. I guess my father felt some affinity or he wouldn't have gone. I guess I have been around Indians for some reason or other almost all my life. When I moved here, to the Southwest, in the late thirties it was natural to keep up my contact with them. I tell you, it's a fad now for everyone who is interested in Indians to make a claim of Indian blood; they say, "I am part Cherokee." But there must be millions of people who make that claim and most of them are phony. So I never make a point of it, but I feel a deep connection.

I went to Colorado College and took an engineering course; I was there three years. I could tell then I wasn't cut out for an engineer, and I left school and went to Los Angeles. You know, life has a way of catching up with you. I got a job as an engineer with the telephone company down in the Imperial Valley, on the Mexican border. I was down there a year when they sent me back up to the Los Angeles main office, where I worked for a while. Then I decided I had better start writing, and I quit and became a writer.

All through college taking engineering I never had a course in English or literature at all. I think all us engineers in the class, when we finished, were unable to write a letter applying for a job without copying a form letter from a textbook. When I was in seventh grade I had a very fine teacher, but that was all—just a great school teacher. I suppose she may have influenced me.

Except for a job in Washington as consultant to one of the war agencies, and a couple of stints as scriptwriter in Hollywood, some consulting at Los Alamos, and serving as director to the New Mexico Arts Commission, I have been right here, living in Arroyo Seco [outside of Taos, New Mexico], since '46. I had been living in a little old Spanish town on the other side of the mountains—Mora—for about a year. That's where I wrote *People of the Valley.* Of course, I would occasionally come over here—it's only thirty-seven miles—before I came to Arroyo Seco for good.

The first of my novels was a Colorado mining trilogy. It came out and then went out of print very early; this was in the thirties. Then just recently—oh, in about 1970 I guess it was—I combined all three volumes in one volume and called it *Pike's Peak.* It's part autobiographical; I used a lot about my own family, so this relationship of whites to Indians we spoke of earlier is pretty well dealt with. It's been republished by Swallow Press.

All my books seem to take a long time to write, usually about two years. I used to work at night, but my eyes got bad as I got older and I was too tired, so I switched to a morning person, when I am fresh. I think if you want to write you have got to keep doing it regularly. You shouldn't write unless you have to write.

I have done several books on Indians: *The Man Who Killed the Deer* is an Indian novel; *The Masked Gods* is the first big nonfiction work I did. Then I did this big book on Hopi ceremonialism. I lived there on the reservation over two and a half years. After that I did *Pumpkin Seed Point,* which is personal, dealing with things that happened to me while doing the Hopi book. It was difficult at the start, when I lived on the reservation, but I was always working with an interpreter and translator, who helped me to make contact. The book was actually written by about thirty old Hopi elders. Their name, their clan affiliation, and their village are all stated in the book. They were very happy to talk in Hopi on a tape recorder. Those tapes are now a permanent record so that no one can say it is Waters' wild imagination; they were given to the museum of Northern Arizona. They were glad to talk without payment, so that their children would know what their fathers believed. They were not paid as anthropological informers are. We did one or two at a time, then we would get other people to work on another ceremony—like that. It was a great experience for me. Gradually there have been several books built up on these subjects in this way.

I think all Pueblos are very much alike, and I have found during the research for this last book, *Mexico Mystique,* that there are similarities and parallels without end with the pre-Colombian peoples in Mexico: Aztecs, Toltecs, and Mayans. It is all one context of belief and it is all Indian America. They share this tradition or myth of the four or five successive worlds. The ancient Greeks had similar beliefs. You find them in innumerable cultures. Of course when you go back two thousand five hundred years you don't know exactly, but I would suppose that it was the priesthood in those early societies which developed and retained this esoteric learning. How much the average poor people knew of the mysteries I don't know; but our only record of it is through the early writings. There are correspondences and a very full development of this whole idea to be found in Tibetan Buddhism. Through my interest in trying to find the meaning of all these Southwest Indian ceremonies, I encountered these beliefs which run through so many cultures. Nobody had taken any interest in the ceremonies before. They had always just been looked upon as something amusing, a nice colorful dance. But I was interested in what they really meant, and in trying to delve into this I read W.Y. Evans-Wentz, whose four volumes on Tibetan Buddhism are primary sourcebooks. We were friends for seventeen years, until his death. We were both struck by the similarities and parallels between American Indian and Tibetan Buddhist religious beliefs and rituals. Dr. Evans-Wentz was working on a book on the sacred mountains of the world, which included these beliefs common to Indian America and Asia.* He was a very fine man and he is one of the people who sensed so clearly that Taos Mountain is one of the high energy places in the world. I've always felt myself this was a place of very high vibration. Strange how the mountains in all parts of the world breed mystics, people who are in

*Frank Waters has advised me that he is now editing and annotating this posthumous book for publication.

touch with their intuition, with the collective unconscious.

There is greater interest now than ever before in Indian ceremony and belief; undoubtedly because we are beginning to see where our blind pursuit of the rational, scientific, and materialistic values has led us—into ecological disaster. *The Masked Gods, Book of the Hopi,* and *Man Who Killed the Deer* are being used as texts in I don't know how many colleges and universities and high schools. There is a course on my books being given in the English department of the University of New Mexico and also at the University of Nevada at Las Vegas. I gave a series of lectures at Colorado State University in 1966, but that was not on Indians, but Western literature.

I haven't been away from here except for six months, when I was on a Rockefeller Foundation grant in Mexico and in Guatemala doing research for *Mexico Mystique.* I got my main information from visiting all the archeological sites for which the government had given me permission. Then I did a lot of research in the famous National Museum of Anthropology's library in Mexico City.

My wife was still alive at the time we settled here in Arroyo Seco, where we were the only Anglos in this Spanish village. In fact, this used to be one of the headquarters of the Penitente sect here. Mora was another. One time I was invited to witness one of the Penitente Easter ceremonies over at Mora. Of course they had blocked off all the roads and they were carrying rifles to keep people away. I knew it was off limits, but I was walking down the middle of the road one time anyway, when an old man sidled up to me and said, "Would you like to meet me under the old cottonwood two miles south of town tomorrow at noon?" and I said Yes. So I had a woman friend of mine prepare a dish of sprouted wheat and two-dollar bills tied with red yarn. I went down there and stood underneath this tree, and then down the canyon came this whole file of Penitentes that surrounded me. They motioned to me to get into the file going to the Morada, or the Penitente church, for the ceremonies. After the rites the Cristo carried the cross up the canyon, where he was placed on the erected cross. They tied him on by the arms and ankles, with ropes in this case, thank goodness. Nevertheless, it was very dangerous because of the strain on the heart; he could have died. They only left him up just long enough for them to be able to say their chants. It is considered a great honor to be chosen, and they always volunteer to be the crucified one.

The ceremony becomes a self-expiation of all transgressions made during the year, and it comes at Easter so it's a great release, a great rebirth, just as spring is in nature—casting off all the cold of winter. The Penitente sect (or Penitent Brothers), which was indigenous in New Mexico, was an offshoot of the early Franciscans prevalent here. Formerly anybody known to be a Penitente was excommunicated from the church proper. So it was not generally known who belonged to the sect. I used to go swimming with some of the young fellows, and I noticed that a lot of them would leave on their shorts and undershirts at first when they went in the water, but later they relaxed when they found out I was alright. I would notice the marks of the whipping on their backs. The Penitentes developed as a great political force in the state, and due to this, more than any other reason, the policy of the Catholic church finally changed. They no longer outlawed them but just accepted them. Then, with new roads coming in and opening up these remote areas, it all died out. I found them to be a very fine people, despite what used to be said about them.

When we first moved here this old dirt road was absolutely impassable six months of the year. My neighbors, Jose Maria Quintana and his family, looked after me very well all these years, feeding the horses and looking after the house whenever I had to leave. My other closest neighbors, Salome Duran and his wife, were equally helpful.

Some of the Eastern religions have interested me as they did Evans-Wentz. I think they are probably all good, especially when you are young, because they teach you self-discipline. These yoga systems that developed three thousand years ago in the East were valuable because people then needed the discipline, but I think our consciousness has developed and changed, so that we don't need quite the same tight strictures.

I like the story of an old Eastern sage whose student asked him, "Now, when I do meditation, what posture is best? Should I have a tigerskin to sit on? And just how should my legs be?" (You know, the three yoga postures.) And the old sage answered, "The right posture is in the mind."

I will be seventy-three in July, and my life hasn't been too smooth as a writer, so I am always glad to tell the young writers this: You can't sit in an ivory tower and write because there is nothing to write about. I have been very lucky because periodically I have gone broke and have had to go out in the world and get a job. I have had jobs among all different kinds of people and all different classes of people, which gave me wholly new locales and new character types. I worked in the war agency in Washington, D.C., then I edited the Taos English-Spanish newspaper here for two years. I worked as a consultant in Los Alamos and in Las Vegas during the atomic tests, which meant working with scientists, writing the reports, and gathering information (that was in the fifties, '52 to '55). Then I worked a couple of times on movie scripts in Hollywood. So all those experiences have given me new interests. I was also director of the New Mexico Arts Commission for one year, in '67.

I am not what you call a well-organized writer. My papers have always been in a mess, but now and then I have a young lady come afternoons for several weeks to try and straighten them out, catalog them. But I always still have a lot to do myself.

The idea of a book just comes to you. The prospect of writing one has always frightened me. I would be too afraid to sit down and say, "I'm going to write a book." Instead I say, "Well I think I'll just write a few pages just to see how it goes." Then a few more pages, and so it keeps on going until eventually you have a book.

How do you choose between fiction and nonfiction? I think that choice is already made when you think of an idea. There are some books which can be treated as fiction, others which can't. I have written about eighteen books, and they are about fifty-fifty fiction and nonfiction—nine of each I guess. I don't like research, but a lot of things I tackle take a great deal of research and I do it all myself. I don't know shorthand, so it is a chore. I keep everything together in different folders, and that's about as far as my organization goes.

I have lived alone now for ten or fifteen years. My first wife died; then in the early sixties I got married again. But it only lasted two years, so since then I have been alone. I have no children. I think the main thing is when you "retire," either by going to a home or by staying at your own home but going to the golf course every day, that you soon die. But not if you keep working. Most of the old men that I knew have died, but most of the old artists that I know here are still working hard, and they are happy.

Andrew Dasberg, one of our oldest and finest painters, still paints every day. He had a show of lithographs, I think it was, just recently and he's eighty-eight. As long as you are interested in things you keep on.

I feel just fine. I have about fifteen acres or so that are irrigated back here, but they are no longer planted. I still have the two horses which have been here a long time. This is their home as much as mine, but I don't ride them any more.

I recently spent six months in Mexico studying the pre-Colombian culture and religion of the Toltecs and Aztecs. They conceived the same four-world structure as our Pueblos and Navajos, with one difference. They believed that we have emerged in the *fifth* world which lies at the dead center of the successive four worlds pictured as occupying the quadrants of universal space, like a mandala. The meaning is clear. Further evolution rests in the soul of man. We must, by our own volition and will, reconcile the unconscious and the conscious, the timeless and the evanescent. We must each journey to our own centers, and wake old gods, or perhaps create new ones.

—Excerpt from an interview with Frank Waters by James Petersen, *Psychology Today,* May 1973

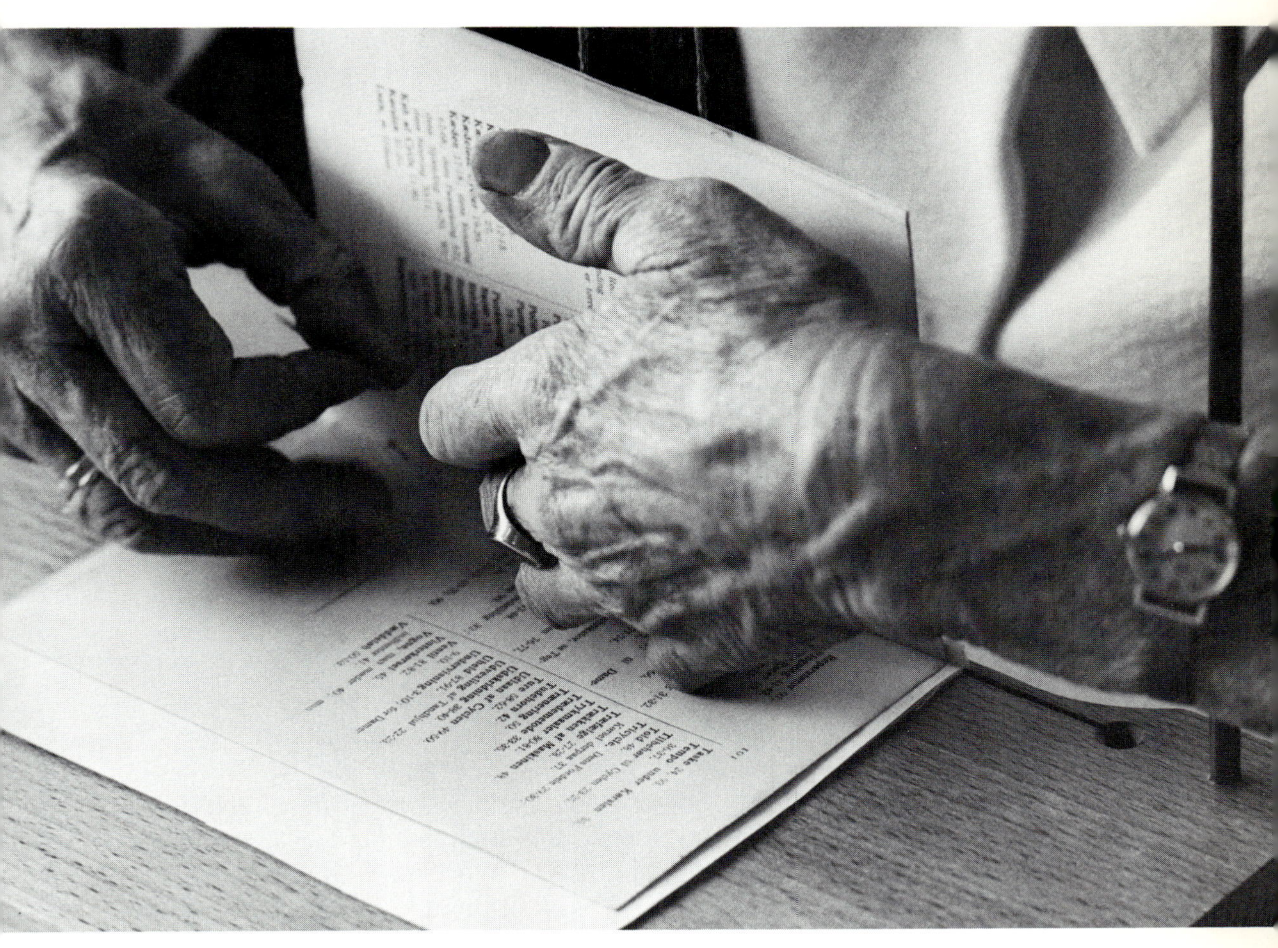

Afterword

MAY SARTON, HERSELF in her sixties and a moving representative for old age, tells us what it means to reach that culminating stage of human existence.

> If the whole of life is a journey toward old age, then I believe it is also a journey toward love. . . . Old age is not a fixed point, any more than sunrise or sunset or the ocean tide. At every instant the psyche is in flux. . . .
>
> On the edge of old age myself I sense that we may be "new-born spirits" at any moment in time if we have the courage. Old age is not an illness; it is a timeless ascent. As power diminishes we grow towards more light.*

Not everyone is a poet like May Sarton, who *can* speak eloquently for the rest of us. But perhaps the words of some of these often little-known people from distant and near parts of the world have also spoken to us with validity.

I think it was Anatole France who said, "Old age is a shipwreck," and most people seem to believe it. But there are many, as I hope I have shown here, who are veterans of the line endowed with fortitude, humor, and respect for the validity of the life process; and they are still growing and changing, which is even more remarkable.

A genuine change seems to be developing and a more positive attitude toward age is emerging. The older masters, philosophers, musicians, painters, writers are spearheading the change. In 1977 an interview with painter Georgia O'Keeffe, ninety-one, was the high-water mark of the television season; the most sought-after concerts were those given by Artur Rubinstein, eighty-nine, and Vladimir Horowitz, seventy-four. We have all been brought up to revere the great works of Rembrandt, Michelangelo, Titian, Tolstoy, Goethe, Victor Hugo, Monet, Renoir, Picasso, Matisse. Leopold Stokowski was ninety-four when he signed a new ten-year contract with his recording company, just before his death last year.

It is pertinent, therefore, that the two lead articles in the Sunday Arts and Leisure Section of *The New York Times* for February 5, 1978 were given over to two artists, both in their seventies. Painter Willem de Kooning, seventy, whose important show was opening at the Guggenheim Museum that week, said:

*"More Light," *The New York Times,* January 30, 1978.

> You get old, you get used to yourself . . . I used to be so nervous I got palpitations. Now I don't have that trouble. I see the canvas, and I begin. But you have to keep on the very edge of something, all the time, or the picture dies.

The other, pianist Claudio Arrau, seventy-four, declared:

> My playing is more intense now, the expression is more concentrated . . . there are new insights . . . what I call . . . spiritual aspects. . . . The older you are, the better the personality is integrated. The message becomes more universal. It still carries the blood of the interpreter, but in a richer, wider and deeper sense.

In an article included in the informative and scholarly catalog to the Cézanne show, *Cézanne, The Late Work* (held at the Museum of Modern Art, New York City, in the fall of 1977), Liliane Brion-Guerry quotes a letter from Cézanne to Emile Bernard, written just a few days before the former's death, which points to Cézanne's never-ending striving to fulfill, to realize his vision: "Will I reach the goal I've sought so long and hard? . . . So I go on with my studies. . . . I'm still studying from nature and it seems to me that I'm making slow progress." Guerry goes on to describe the last portrait painted by the artist:

> Old Vallier, the sublime testament of Cézanne, has also consented to be integrated with the rhythm of the universe, to live and grow old there, but it is by accepting the fact of his aging that he transcends the moment and becomes the very expression of an imperishable "essentiality."*

I mention these masters not in order to imply that they are alone or are exceptional in this ability to use their inner sources to "transcend the moment," that of aging, in order to become "the very expression of an imperishable 'essentiality.' " But because their work is visible, audible to all of us, they can act as guides. In the same way a lesser-known face like that of the old Appalachian woman, Mrs. Hatfield, ninety-seven, or Jim Bell's in Alabama or Rachel Brik's, the Russian babushka, shows us as much as the portrait of Vallier (which struck me, long before I read Guerry, as a self-portrait of Cézanne), what it can mean to be human, that indeed old *is* beautiful. I don't want to idealize old age; it is lonely, often uncomfortable and painful. But there is what you might call a reward. As Robert Neale, author and professor at Union Theological Seminary, says in his introduction to the original publication of a group of these interviews in the Summer 1977 issue of *Journal of Current Social Issues,* "Such faces shine forth an affirmation of destiny and the

* *"The Elusive Goal," Cezanne, The Late Work* (New York: Museum of Modern Art, 1977), p. 80.

reception of ordination.'' Or, as it is said in the Bible (see Ecclesiastes 8:1), wisdom makes the face shine.

What this book—a cross section of faces, of life stories, most of them unknown to us—seems to me to reveal is that the search for the individual and unique meaning of each life is a valid and universal task. It also implies that the old are one step ahead of us along this path. By meeting their gaze unflinchingly we seem to be able to return to them the validating reflection of themselves which they need just as their recognition of us helps us to go forward with confidence toward that old age which sooner or later awaits us all.